Rick Steves®

SNAPSHOT

Scotland

CONTENTS

INTRODUCTION

This Snapshot guide, excerpted from my guidebook *Rick Steves' Great Britain*, introduces you to rugged, feisty, colorful Scotland. The home of kilts, bagpipes, whisky, golf, lochs, and shortbread lives up to its clichéd image—but there's so much more. This book includes a mix of big cities, small towns, and the countryside. Explore the Scottish capital of Edinburgh—with its attractions-studded Royal Mile and stirring hilltop castle—and grittier but quickly gentrifying Glasgow. Golfers and students make a pilgrimage to St. Andrews, with its world-famous links, sandy beaches, and colorful university life. To commune with the traditional Scottish soul, head for the desolate Highlands, with the evocative "Weeping Glen" of Glencoe, handy home-base city of Inverness, historic site of "Bonnie" Prince Charlie's disastrous Battle of Culloden, and mysterious Loch Ness. And hardy souls can set sail for some of Scotland's rugged islands: Iona and Mull (from Oban), or the super-scenic Isle of Skye.

To help you have the best trip possible, I've included the following topics in this book:

• **Planning Your Time,** with advice on how to make the most of your limited time

• **Orientation,** including tourist information (abbreviated as TI), tips on public transportation, local tour options, and helpful hints

• **Sights** with ratings:

▲▲▲—Don't miss

▲▲—Try hard to see

▲—Worthwhile if you can make it

No rating—Worth knowing about

• **Sleeping** and **Eating,** with good-value recommendations in every price range

- **Connections,** with tips on trains, buses, and driving
- **Practicalities**, near the end of this book, has information on money, phoning, hotel reservations, transportation, and more.

To travel smartly, read this little book in its entirety before you go. It's my hope that this guide will make your trip more meaningful and rewarding. Traveling like a temporary local, you'll get the absolute most out of every mile, minute, and dollar.

Happy travels!

Rick Steves

SCOTLAND

SCOTLAND

The country of Scotland makes up about a third of Britain's geographical area (30,400 square miles), but has less than a tenth of its population (just under 5.3 million). This sparsely populated chunk of land stretches to Norwegian latitudes. Its Shetland Islands, at about 60°N (similar to Anchorage, Alaska), are the northernmost point in Britain.

The southern part of Scotland, called the Lowlands, is relatively flat and urbanized. The northern area—the Highlands—fea-

tures a wild, severely undulating terrain, punctuated by lochs (lakes) and fringed by sea lochs (inlets) and islands. The Highland Boundary Fault that divides Scotland geologically also divides it culturally. Historically, there was a big difference between grizzled, kilt-wearing Highlanders in the northern wilderness and the more refined Lowlanders in the southern flatlands and cities. The Highlanders spoke and acted like "true Scots," while the Lowlanders often seemed more "British" than Scottish. Although this division has faded over time, some Scots still cling to it today—city slickers down south think that Highlanders are crude and unrefined, and those who live at higher latitudes grumble about the soft, pampered urbanites in the Lowlands.

The Lowlands are dominated by a pair of rival cities: Edinburgh, the old royal capital, teems with Scottish history and is the country's best tourist attraction. Glasgow, once a gloomy industrial city, is becoming a hip, laid-back city of today, known for its modern architecture. The medieval university town and golf mecca of St. Andrews, the whisky village of Pitlochry, and the historic city of Stirling are my picks as the Lowlands' highlights.

The Highlands provide your best look at traditional Scotland. The sights are subtle, but the warm culture and friendly people are engaging. There are a lot of miles, but they're scenic, the roads are

Scotland

FERRY ROUTES (NOT ALL SHOWN)

ATLANTIC OCEAN

ORKNEY

STROMNESS
KIRKWALL
THURSO
JOHN O'GROATS

50 MILES
30 KM

LEWIS

ULLAPOOL

NORTH UIST

SOUTH UIST

KYLE OF LOCHALSH

MORAY FIRTH

SKYE
PORTREE
KYLEAKIN

CULLODEN
INVERNESS

CALEDONIAN CANAL

HIGHLANDS

LOCH NESS
ABERDEEN

RUM

MALLAIG

FORT AUGUSTUS
BEN NEVIS

COLL

FT. WILLIAM
GLENCOE

PITLOCHRY

NORTH SEA

TIREE

MULL

OBAN

PERTH
DUNDEE

ST. ANDREWS
EAST NEUK

IONA

LOCH LOMOND

STIRLING

JURA

BANNOCK-BURN

FIRTH OF FORTH

ISLAY

GLASGOW
EDINBURGH

CAMPBELTOWN

TROON

ARRAN
AYR

LOWLANDS

BERWICK-UPON-TWEED

ENGLAND

NORTHERN IRELAND
LARNE

CAIRNRYAN
STRANRAER

CARLISLE

NEW-CASTLE

BELFAST

HADRIAN'S WALL

DCH

TO DUBLIN

IRISH SEA

TO LAKE DISTRICT

TO YORK + LONDON

good, and the traffic is light. Generally, the Highlands are hungry for the tourist dollar, and everything overtly Scottish is exploited to the kilt. You'll need more than a quick visit to get away from that. But if you only have two days, you can get a feel for the area with a quick drive to Oban, through Glencoe, then up the Caledonian Canal to Inverness. With more time, the Isles of Iona and Mull (an easy day trip from Oban), the Isle of Skye, and countless brooding countryside castles will flesh out your Highlands experience.

The Highlands are more rocky and harsh than other parts of the British Isles. It's no wonder that many of the exterior scenes of Hogwarts' grounds in the Harry Potter movies were filmed in this moody, sometimes spooky landscape. Though Scotland's "hills" are technically too short to be called "mountains," they do a convincing imitation. Scotland has 282 hills over 3,000 feet. A list of these was first compiled in 1891 by Sir Hugh Munro, and to this day the Scots still call their high hills "Munros." (Hills from 2,500-3,000 feet are

known as "Corbetts," and those from 2,000-2,500 are "Grahams.") According to the Munro Society, more than 5,000 intrepid hikers can brag that they've climbed all of the Munros.

In this northern climate, cold and drizzly weather isn't uncommon—even in midsummer. The blazing sun can quickly be covered over by black clouds and howling wind. Scots warn visitors to prepare for "four seasons in one day." Because Scots feel personally responsible for bad weather, they tend to be overly optimistic about forecasts. Take any Scottish promise of "sun by the afternoon" with a grain of salt—and bring your raincoat.

In the summer, the Highlands swarm with tourists...and midges. These tiny biting insects—like "no-see-ums" in some parts of North America—are bloodthirsty and determined. They can be an annoyance from late May through September, depending on the weather. Hot sun or a stiff breeze blows the tiny buggers away, but they thrive in damp, shady areas. Locals suggest blowing or brushing them off, rather than swatting them—since killing them only seems to attract more (likely because of the smell of fresh blood). Scots say, "If you kill one midge, a million more will come to his funeral." Even if you don't usually travel with bug spray, consider bringing or buying some for a summer visit—or your most vivid memory of your Scottish vacation might be itchy arms and legs.

Keep an eye out for another Scottish animal: shaggy Highland

cattle—those adorable "hairy coos" with their hair falling in their eyes. With a heavy coat to keep them insulated, hairy coos graze on sparse vegetation that other animals ignore. And of course, Scotland's not short on sheep.

The major theme of Scottish history is the drive for independence, especially from England. (Scotland's rabble-rousing national motto is *Nemo me impune lacessit*—"No one provokes me with impunity.") Like Wales, Scotland is a country of ragtag Celts sharing an island with wealthy and powerful Anglo-Saxons. Scotland's Celtic culture is a result of its remoteness—the invading Romans were never able to conquer this rough-and-tumble people, and even built Hadrian's Wall to lock off this distant corner of their empire. The Anglo-Saxons, and their descendants the English, fared little better than the Romans did. Even King Edward I—who so successfully dominated Wales—was unable to hold on to Scotland for long, largely thanks to the relentlessly rebellious William Wallace (a.k.a. "Braveheart").

Failing to conquer Scotland by the blade, England eventually absorbed it politically. In 1603, England's Queen Elizabeth I died without an heir, so Scotland's King James VI took the throne, becoming King James I of England. It took another century or so of battles, both military and diplomatic, but the Act of Union in 1707 definitively (and controversially) unified the Kingdom of Great Britain. In 1745, Bonnie Prince Charlie attempted to reclaim the Scottish throne on behalf of the deposed Stuarts, but his army was slaughtered at the Battle of Culloden (described in the Inverness and the Northern Highlands chapter). This cemented English rule over Scotland, and is seen by many Scots as the last gasp of the traditional Highlands clan system.

Scotland has been joined—however unwillingly—to England ever since, and the Scots have often felt oppressed by their English countrymen. During the Highland Clearances in the 18th and 19th centuries, landowners (mostly English) decided that vast tracks of land were more profitable as grazing land for sheep than as farmland for people. Many Highlanders were forced to abandon their traditional homes and lifestyles and seek employment elsewhere. Large numbers ended up in North America, especially parts of eastern Canada, such as Prince Edward Island and Nova Scotia (literally, "New Scotland").

Today, Americans and Canadians of Scottish descent enjoy coming "home" to Scotland. If you're Scottish, your surname will tell you which clan your ancestors likely belonged to. The prefix "Mac" (or "Mc") means "son of"—so "MacDonald" means the same thing as "Donaldson." Tourist shops everywhere are happy

to help you track down your clan's tartan, or distinctive plaid pattern—many clans have several.

Is Scotland really a country? It's not a sovereign state, but it is a "nation" in that it has its own traditions, ethnic identity, languages (Gaelic and Scots), and football league. To some extent, it even has its own government:

SCOTLAND

Robert Burns
(1759–1796)

Robert Burns, Scotland's national poet, holds a unique place in the heart of Scottish people—a heart that's still beating loud and proud thanks, in large part, to Burns himself.

Born on a farm in southwestern Scotland, Robbie, as he's still affectionately called, was the oldest of seven children. His early years were full of literally backbreaking farm labor, which left him with a lifelong stoop. Though much was later made of his ascendance to literary acclaim from a rural, poverty-stricken upbringing, he was actually quite well-educated (per Scottish tradition), equally as familiar with Latin and French as he was with hard work.

He started writing poetry at 15, but didn't have any published until age 28—to finance a voyage to the West Indies (which promised better farming opportunities). When that first volume, *Poems, Chiefly in the Scottish Dialect*, became a sudden and overwhelming success, he reconsidered his emigration. Instead, he left his farm for Edinburgh, living just off the Royal Mile. He spent a year and a half in the city, schmoozing with literary elites, who celebrated this "heaven taught" farmer from the hinterlands as Scotland's "ploughman poet."

His poetry, written primarily in the Scots dialect, drew on his substantial familiarity with both Scottish tradition and Western literature. By using the language of the common man to create works of beauty and sophistication, he found himself wildly popular among both rural folk and high society. Hearty poems such as "To a Mouse," "To a Louse," and "The Holy Fair" exalted the virtues of physical labor, romantic love, friendship, natural beauty, and drink—all of which he also pursued with vigor in real life. This further endeared him to most Scots, though consider-

Recently, Scotland has enjoyed its greatest measure of political autonomy in centuries—a trend called "devolution." In 1999, the Scottish parliament opened its doors in Edinburgh for the first time in almost 300 years. Though the Scottish parliament's powers are limited (most major decisions are still made in London), the Scots are enjoying the refreshing breeze of increased independence. However, with the power (at the moment) ultimately in Westminster, some locals, especially the younger generation, view the British democracy as two wolves and one sheep deciding what to have for lunch—and Scotland is the sheep.

ably less so to Church fathers, who were particularly displeased with his love life (of Burns' dozen children, nine were by his eventual wife, the others by various servants and barmaids).

After achieving fame and wealth, Burns never lost touch with the concerns of the Scottish people, championing such radical ideas as social equality and economic justice. Burns bravely and loudly supported the French and American revolutions, which inspired one of his most beloved poems, "A Man's a Man for A' That," and even an ode to George Washington—all while other writers were being shipped off to Australia for similar beliefs. While his social causes cost him some aristocratic friends, it cemented his popularity among the masses, and not just within Scotland (he became, and remains, especially beloved in Russia).

Intent on preserving Scotland's rich musical and lyrical traditions, Burns traveled the countryside collecting traditional Scottish ballads. If it weren't for Burns, we'd have to come up with a different song to sing on New Year's Eve—he's the one who found, reworked, and popularized "Auld Lang Syne." His championing of Scottish culture came at a critical time: England had recently and finally crushed Scotland's last hopes of independence, and the Highland clan system was nearing its end. Burns lent the Scots dialect a new prestige, and the scrappy Scottish people a reinvigorated identity.

Burns died at 37 of a heart condition likely exacerbated by so much hard labor (all the carousing probably hadn't helped, either). By that time, his fortune was largely spent, but his celebrity was going strong—around 10,000 people attended his burial. Even the Church eventually overcame its disapproval, installing a window in his honor at St. Giles' Cathedral. In 2009, his nation voted Burns "Greatest Ever Scot" in a TV poll. And every January 25 (the poet's birthday), on Burns' Night, Scots gather to recite his songs and poems, tuck into some haggis ("chieftain o' the puddin' race," according to Burns), and raise their whisky to friendship, and Scotland.

In September 2014, the Scottish people voted on an independence referendum asking the yes-or-no question: "Should Scotland be an independent country?" While some polls predicted a close contest, in the end the Scots favored staying in the United Kingdom by 10 percent. During the campaign, the major British political parties promised Scotland even more political autonomy if it voted "no." While Scottish nationalists want to fast-track these new powers, it's not clear when this may happen. One thing is sure—the vote may be over but the nationalists aren't done fighting yet.

Scotland even has its own currency. While Scots use the same coins as England, Scotland also prints its own bills (with Scottish rather than English people and landmarks). Just to confuse tourists, three different banks print Scottish pound notes, each with a different design. In the Lowlands (around Edinburgh and Glasgow), you'll receive both Scottish and English pounds from ATMs and in change. But in the Highlands, you'll almost never see English pounds. Though most merchants in England accept Scottish pound notes, a few might balk—especially at the rare one-pound note, which their cash registers don't have a slot for. (They are, however, legally required to accept your Scottish currency.)

The Scottish flag—a diagonal, X-shaped white cross on a blue field—represents the cross of Scotland's patron saint, the Apostle Andrew (who was crucified on an X-shaped cross). You may not realize it, but you see the Scottish flag every time you look at the Union Jack: England's flag (the red St. George's cross on a white field) superimposed on Scotland's (a blue field with a white diagonal cross). The diagonal red cross (St. Patrick's cross) over Scotland's white one represents Northern Ireland. (Wales gets no love on the Union Jack.)

Scots are known for their inimitable burr, but they are also proud of their old Celtic language, Scottish Gaelic (pronounced "gallic"; Ireland's closely related Celtic language is spelled the same but pronounced "gaylic"). Gaelic thrives only in the remotest corners of Scotland. In major towns and cities, virtually nobody speaks Gaelic every day, but the language is kept on life-support by a Scottish population keen to remember their heritage. New Gaelic schools are opening all the time, and Scotland has passed a law to replace road signs with new ones listing both English and Gaelic spellings (e.g., *Edinburgh/Dùn Èideann*).

Scotland has another language of its own, called Scots (a.k.a. "Lowland Scots," to distinguish it from Gaelic). Aye, you're likely already a wee bit familiar with a few Scots words, ye lads and lassies. As you travel, you're sure to pick up a bit more (see sidebar) and enjoy the lovely musical lilt as well. Many linguists argue that Scots is technically an ancient dialect of English, rather than a distinct language. These linguists have clearly never heard a Scot read aloud the poetry of Robert Burns, who wrote in unfiltered (and often unintelligible) Scots. (Opening line of "To a Louse": "Ha! Whaur ye gaun, ye crowlin ferlie?") Fortunately, you're unlikely to meet anyone quite that hard to understand; most Scots speak Scottish-accented standard English, peppered with their favorite Scots phrases. If you have a hard time understanding someone, ask them to translate—you may take home some new words as souvenirs.

Scottish Words

Scotch may be the peaty drink the bartender serves you, but the nationality of the bartender is **Scots** or **Scottish**. Here are some other Scottish words that may come in handy during your time here:

aye: yes
auld: old
ben: mountain
blether: talk
bonnie: beautiful
brae: slope, hill
burn: creek or stream
cairn: pile of stones
close: an alley leading to a courtyard or square
craig: rock, cliff
firth: estuary
innis: island
inver: mouth of a river

ken: to know
kirk: church
kyle: strait
loch: lake
nae: no (as in "nae bother"— you're welcome)
neeps: turnips
ree: king, royal ("righ" in Gaelic)
tattie: potato
wee: small
wynd: tight, winding lane connecting major streets

A sharp intake of breath (like a little gasp), sometimes while saying "aye," means "yes."

Scottish cuisine is down-to-earth, often with an emphasis on local produce. Both seafood and "land food" (beef and chicken) are common. One Scottish mainstay—eaten more by tourists than by Scots these days—is the famous haggis (see sidebar in this chapter), tastier than it sounds and worth trying...even before you've tucked into the whisky.

The "Scottish Breakfast" is similar to the English version, but they often add a potato scone (like a flavorless, soggy potato pancake) and haggis (best when served with poached eggs and HP brown sauce).

Breakfast, lunch, or dinner, the Scots love their whisky—and touring one of the country's many distilleries is a sightseeing treat. The Scots are fiercely competitive with the Irish when it comes to this peaty spirit. Scottish "whisky" is distilled twice, whereas Irish "whiskey" adds a third distillation (and an extra *e*). Grain here is roasted over peat fires, giving it a smokier flavor than its Irish cousin. Also note that what we call "scotch"—short for "scotch whisky"—is just "whisky" here. I've listed several of the most convenient and interesting distilleries to visit, but if you're a whisky connoisseur, make a point of tracking down and touring your favorite.

Another unique Scottish flavor to sample is the soft drink called Irn-Bru (pronounced "Iron Brew"). This bright-orange

Haggis: Not Just for Peasants (or Tourists) Anymore

Haggis began as a peasant food: Waste-conscious cooks wrapped sheep's heart, liver, and lungs in stomach lining and boiled these scraps to create a hearty meal that's slightly palatable (thanks to added spices and oats). Traditionally served with "neeps and tatties" (turnips and potatoes), haggis turned a corner and was forever immortalized thanks to Robbie Burns' *Address to a Haggis*, which extolled the dish's virtues.

For generations, haggis was served as a staple in peasant diets; today it's been refined, almost to the point of high cuisine. Cooking methods range from plain deep-fried to "haute and oat" (a term for Scottish fine dining). Instead of using spices to take away the taste, butchers use their own unique mix to complement it. (Good luck getting one to tell you what his secret is.)

You're likely to find haggis on many menus, including at breakfast (often served with blood pudding). You can dress it up with anything from a fine whisky cream sauce to your basic HP brown sauce. The trick to appreciating this iconic Scottish dish is to think of how it tastes, not what it's made of—just like with other favorites such as foie gras, caviar, or hot dogs.

beverage tastes not like orange soda, but like bubblegum with a slightly bitter aftertaste. (The diet version is even more bitter.) While Irn-Bru's appeal eludes non-Scots, it's hugely popular here, even outselling Coke. As the label states, "Bru'd in Scotland to a secret recipe for over 100 years"—they must be doing something right.

Whether toasting with beer, whisky, or Irn-Bru, enjoy meeting the Scottish people. It's easy to fall in love with the irrepressible spirit and beautiful landscape of this faraway corner of Britain.

EDINBURGH

Edinburgh is the historical, cultural, and political capital of Scotland. For nearly a thousand years, Scotland's kings, parliaments, writers, thinkers, and bankers have called Edinburgh home. Today, it remains Scotland's most sophisticated city.

Edinburgh (ED'n-burah—only tourists pronounce it like "Pittsburgh") is Scotland's showpiece and one of Europe's most entertaining cities. It's a place of stunning vistas—nestled among craggy bluffs and studded with a prickly skyline of spires, towers, domes, and steeples. Proud statues of famous Scots dot the urban landscape. The buildings are a harmonious yellow-gray, all built from the same local sandstone.

Culturally, Edinburgh has always been the place where Lowland culture (urban and English) met Highland style (rustic and Gaelic). Tourists will find no end of traditional Scottish clichés: whisky tastings, kilt shops, bagpipe-playing buskers, and gimmicky tours featuring Scotland's bloody history and ghost stories.

Edinburgh is two cities in one. The Old Town stretches along a narrow ridge. Promenade down the Royal Mile through Old Town from the grand castle on top to the palace on the bottom. Along the way, medieval skyscrapers stand shoulder to shoulder, hiding peaceful courtyards. This colorful labyrinth of cobbled streets and narrow lanes is the tourist's Edinburgh.

A few hundred yards north of the Old Town lies the New Town. It's a magnificent planned neighborhood (from the 1700s) laid out in a grid plan. Here, you'll enjoy upscale shops, broad boulevards, straight streets, square squares, circular circuses, and

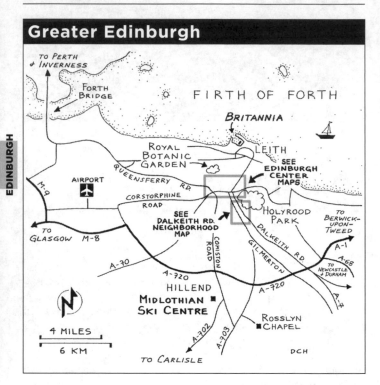

Greater Edinburgh

elegant Georgian mansions decked out in Greek-style columns and statues.

Today's Edinburgh is a thriving city of a half-million. It's big in banking, scientific research, and scholarship at its four universities. Since 1999, when Scotland regained a measure of self-rule, Edinburgh reassumed its place as home of the Scottish Parliament. The city hums with life. Students and professionals pack the pubs and art galleries. It's especially lively in August, when the Edinburgh Festival takes over the town. Historic, monumental, fun, and well organized, Edinburgh is a tourist's delight.

Planning Your Time

While the major sights can be seen in a day, I'd give Edinburgh two days and three nights.

Day 1: Tour the castle (open from 9:30). Then consider catching one of the city bus tours for a one-hour loop (departing from a block below the castle at the Hub/Tolbooth Church; you could munch a sandwich from the top deck if you're into multitasking). Back near the castle, take my self-guided Royal Mile walk or catch the 14:15 Mercat Tours walk (1.5 hours, leaves from Mercat Cross on the Royal Mile). Spend the remainder of your day enjoying the Royal Mile's shops and museums, or touring the Palace of Holyroodhouse (at the bottom of the Mile).

Day 2: Visit the National Museum of Scotland. After lunch, stroll through the Princes Street Gardens and the Scottish National Gallery. Then wander through the New Town, visiting the Georgian House and Scottish National Portrait Gallery, or squeeze in a quick tour of the good ship *Britannia* (last entry at 16:30).

Evenings: Options include various "haunted Edinburgh" walks, literary pub crawls, or live music in pubs. Sadly, traditional folk shows are just about extinct, surviving only in excruciatingly schmaltzy variety shows put on for tour-bus groups. Perhaps the most authentic evening out is just settling down in a pub to sample the whisky and local beers while meeting the locals...and attempting to understand them through their thick Scottish accents.

Orientation to Edinburgh

A Verbal Map

Scotland's Old Town stretches across a ridgeline slung between two bluffs. From west to east, this "Royal Mile" runs from Castle Hill—which is visible from anywhere—to the base of the 822-foot dormant volcano called Arthur's Seat. For most tourists, this east-west axis is the center of the action. North of the Royal Mile ridge is the New Town, a neighborhood of grid-planned streets and elegant Georgian buildings. South of the Royal Mile are the university and the National Museum of Scotland.

In the center of it all, in a drained lake bed between the Old and New Towns, sit the Princes Street Gardens park and Waverley Bridge, where you'll find the Waverley train station, TI, Princes Mall, bus info office (starting point for most city bus tours), Scottish National Gallery, and a covered dance-and-music pavilion.

Tourist Information

The crowded TI is as central as can be atop the Princes Mall and Waverley train station (Mon-Sat 9:00-18:00, Sun 10:00-18:00, July-Aug daily until 19:00, tel. 0131-473-3868, www.edinburgh .org). The staff is knowledgeable and eager to help, but much of their information—including their assessment of museums—is skewed by tourism payola. The TI at the airport is more helpful (on the main concourse, tel. 0131-344-3120).

At either TI, pick up a free map or buy the excellent *Collins Discovering Edinburgh* map (which comes with opinionated commentary and locates almost every major shop and sight). If you're interested in late-night music, ask for the free monthly entertainment *Gig Guide*. (The best monthly entertainment listing, *The List*, sells for a few pounds at newsstands.) The free *Essential Guide to Edinburgh*, while not truly essential, lists additional sights and services (when it's in stock).

The TIs sell the mediocre **Edinburgh Pass,** which provides a ticket for the Airlink airport bus and entry to dozens of B-list sights (£30/1 day, £40/2 days, £50/3 days, doesn't include Edinburgh Castle, Holyroodhouse, or *Britannia*, www.edinburgh .org/pass).

Also at the TI, consider buying a three-day **Explorer Pass**— you'll save money if you visit the castles at both Edinburgh and Stirling, and could save much more if you plan to see many sights (a less-useful 7-day pass is also available, can also buy online or at most participating sites, www.historic-scotland.gov.uk/explorer).

Arrival in Edinburgh

By Train: Arriving by train at Waverley Station puts you in the city center and below the TI. Taxis queue almost trackside; the ramp they come and go on leads to Waverley Bridge. If this taxi lane is closed (due to construction), hike up the ramp and hail one on the street. From the station, *Way Out-1-Princes Street* signs lead up to the TI and the city bus stop (for bus directions from here to my recommended B&Bs, see "Sleeping in Edinburgh," later). For picnic supplies, an **M&S Simply Food** is near platform 2.

By Bus: Scottish Citylink, Megabus, and National Express buses use the bus station (with luggage lockers) in the New Town, two blocks north of the train station on St. Andrew Square.

By Plane: Edinburgh's slingshot of an airport is located eight miles northwest of the center. Airport flight info: Tel. 0844-481-8989, www.edinburghairport.com.

Taxis between the airport and the city center are pricey (£20-25, 20 minutes to downtown or to Dalkeith Road B&Bs). Fortunately, the airport is well connected to central Edinburgh by the convenient, frequent, cheap Lothian **Airlink bus #100** (£3.50, £6 round-trip, 6/hour, 30 minutes, buses run all day and 2/hour through the night, tel. 0131/555-6363, www.flybybus.com). The bus drops you at the center of Waverley Bridge. From here, to reach my recommended B&Bs near Dalkeith Road, you can either take a taxi (about £7), or hop on a city bus (£1.50; for bus directions to recommended B&Bs, see "Sleeping in Edinburgh," later).

If you're headed *to* the airport, you can take this same Airlink bus: To get from the Dalkeith Road B&Bs to the Airlink stop downtown, you can ride a city bus to North Bridge, get off, turn left at the grand Balmoral Hotel and walk a short distance down Princes Street to the next bridge, Waverley, where you'll find the

Airlink bus stop. Or, rather than riding a £25 taxi all the way to the airport, take a £7 taxi to this stop, then hop the bus to the airport.

By Car: If you're arriving from the north, rather than drive through downtown Edinburgh to the recommended B&Bs, circle the city on the A-720 City Bypass road. Approaching Edinburgh on the M-9, take the M-8 (direction: Glasgow) and quickly get onto the A-720 City Bypass (direction: Edinburgh South). After four miles, you'll hit a roundabout. Ignore signs directing you into *Edinburgh North* and stay on the A-720 for 10 more miles to the next and last roundabout, named *Sheriffhall*. Exit the roundabout at the first left (A-7 Edinburgh). From here it's four miles to the B&B neighborhood. After a while, the A-7 becomes Dalkeith Road (you'll pass the Royal Infirmary hospital complex). If you see the huge Royal Commonwealth Pool, you've gone a couple of blocks too far.

If you're driving in on A-68 from the south, take the A-7 Edinburgh exit off the roundabout and follow the directions above.

Helpful Hints

Sunday Activities: Many Royal Mile sights close on Sunday (except during August and the Edinburgh Festival), but other major sights and shops are open. Sunday is a good day to catch a guided walking tour along the Royal Mile or a city bus tour (buses go faster in light traffic). The slopes of Arthur's Seat, an extinct volcano, are lively with hikers and picnickers on weekends.

Festivals: August is a crowded, popular month to visit Edinburgh because of the multiple festivals hosted here, including the official **Edinburgh Festival** (Aug 8-31 in 2014, likely Aug 7-30 in 2015, www.edinburghfestivals.co.uk). Book ahead for hotels, events, and restaurant dinners if you'll be visiting during this month, and expect to pay significantly more for your accommodations.

Internet Access: Many B&Bs and coffee shops, including one at the **Hub,** offer free Wi-Fi. You can also get online at the TI (£1/20 minutes).

Baggage Storage: At the train station, you'll find pricey, high-security luggage storage near platform 2 (£9/24 hours, daily 7:00-23:00). It's cheaper to use the lockers at the bus station on St. Andrew Square, just two blocks north of the train station (£3-10 depending on size and duration—even smallest locker is plenty big, coins only, station open daily 6:00-24:00).

Laundry: The **Ace Cleaning Centre** launderette is located near the recommended B&Bs (£8 self-service, £9 drop-off, Mon-Fri 8:00-20:00, Sat 9:00-17:00, Sun 10:00-16:00, along the

Edinburgh at a Glance

▲▲▲**Royal Mile** Historic road—good for walking—stretching from the castle down to the palace, lined with museums, pubs, and shops. **Hours:** Always open, but best during business hours, with walking tours daily. See page 23.

▲▲▲**Edinburgh Castle** Iconic 11th-century hilltop fort and royal residence complete with crown jewels, Romanesque chapel, memorial, and fine military museum. **Hours:** Daily April-Sept 9:30-18:00, Oct-March 9:30-17:00. See page 35.

▲▲▲**National Museum of Scotland** Intriguing, well-displayed artifacts from prehistoric times to the 20th century. **Hours:** Daily 10:00-17:00. See page 57.

▲▲**Gladstone's Land** Sixteenth-century Royal Mile merchant's residence. **Hours:** Daily July-Aug 10:00-18:30, April-June and Sept-Oct 10:00-17:00, closed Nov-March. See page 45.

▲▲**St. Giles Cathedral** Preaching grounds of Calvinist John Knox, with spectacular organ, Neo-Gothic chapel, and distinctive crown spire. **Hours:** Mon-Sat 9:00-17:00 (until 19:00 Mon-Fri May-Sept), Sun 13:00-17:00. See page 49.

▲▲**Scottish Parliament Building** Striking headquarters for parliament, which returned to Scotland in 1999. **Hours:** If parliament's in session—Mon, Fri-Sat 10:00-17:00, Tue-Thu 9:00-18:30; if parliament's recessed—Mon-Sat 10:00-17:00; closed Sun year-round. See page 55.

▲▲**Georgian New Town** Elegant late 18th-century subdivision spiced with trendy shops, bars, and eateries. **Hours:** Always open. See page 61.

▲▲**Georgian House** Intimate peek at upper-crust life in the late 1700s. **Hours:** Daily April-Oct 10:00-17:00, July-Aug until 18:00, March 11:00-16:00, Nov 11:00-15:00, closed Dec-Feb. See page 64.

▲▲**Scottish National Gallery** Choice sampling of European masters and Scotland's finest. **Hours:** Daily 10:00-17:00, Thu until 19:00, Fri-Wed in Aug until 18:00. See page 66.

▲▲**Scottish National Portrait Gallery** Beautifully displayed *Who's Who* of Scottish history. **Hours:** Daily 10:00-17:00, Thu until 19:00. See page 70.

▲▲*Britannia* The royal yacht with a history of distinguished passengers, a 15-minute trip out of town. **Hours:** Daily July-Sept 9:30-16:30, April-June and Oct 9:30-16:00, Nov-March 10:00-15:30 (these are last entry times). See page 72.

▲**Writers' Museum at Lady Stair's House** Tribute to Scottish literary triumvirate: Robert Burns, Sir Walter Scott, and Robert Louis Stevenson. **Hours:** Mon-Sat 10:00-17:00, closed Sun except during Festival 12:00-17:00. See page 46.

▲**Mary King's Close** Underground street and houses last occupied in the 17th century, viewable by guided tour. **Hours:** April-Oct daily 10:00-21:00, Aug until 23:00; Nov-March daily 10:00-17:00, Fri-Sat until 21:00 (these are last tour times). See page 52.

▲**Museum of Childhood** Five stories of historic fun. **Hours:** Mon-Sat 10:00-17:00, Sun 12:00-17:00. See page 53.

▲**John Knox House** Reputed digs of the great 16th-century reformer. **Hours:** Mon-Sat 10:00-18:00, closed Sun except in July-Aug 12:00-18:00. See page 53.

▲**People's Story Museum** Everyday life from the 18th to 20th centuries. **Hours:** Mon-Sat 10:00-17:00, closed Sun except during Festival 12:00-17:00. See page 54.

▲**Museum of Edinburgh** Historic mementos, from the original National Covenant inscribed on animal skin to early golf balls. **Hours:** Mon-Sat 10:00-17:00, closed Sun except during Festival 12:00-17:00. See page 54.

▲**Palace of Holyroodhouse** The Queen's splendid home away from home, with lavish rooms, 12th-century abbey, and gallery with rotating exhibits. **Hours:** Daily April-Oct 9:30-18:00, Nov-March until 16:30, closed during royal visits. See page 56.

▲**Scott Monument** Climbable tribute to the famed novelist Sir Walter Scott. **Hours:** Daily April-Sept 10:00-19:00, Oct-March 10:00-16:00. See page 65.

bus route to the city center at 13 South Clerk Street, opposite Queens Hall, tel. 0131/667-0549). For a small extra fee, they collect and drop off laundry at the neighborhood B&Bs.

Bike Rental: The laid-back crew at **Cycle Scotland** offers bike tours and happily recommends good bike routes (£15/3 hours, £20/day, daily 10:00-18:00, just off Royal Mile at 29 Blackfriars Street, tel. 0131/556-5560, www.cyclescotland .co.uk).

Dress for the Weather: Weather blows in and out—bring your sweater and be prepared for rain. Locals say the bad weather is one of the disadvantages of living so close to England.

Car Rental: These places have offices both in the town center and at the airport: **Avis** (24 East London Street, tel. 0844-544-6059, airport tel. 0844-544-6004), **Europcar** (Waverley Station, tel. 0871-384-3453, airport tel. 0871-384-3406), **Hertz** (10 Picardy Place, tel. 0843-309-3026, airport tel. 0843-309-3025), and **Budget** (select Waverley Station pick-up; they will meet you at train station and take you to their office at 1 Murrayburn Road, tel. 0131/455-7314, airport tel. 0844-544-4605). Some downtown offices are closed on Sunday, but the airport locations tend to be open daily. If you're going to rent a car, pick it up on your way out of Edinburgh—you won't need it in town.

Blue Badge Local Guides: The following guides charge similar prices and offer half-day and full-day tours: **Jean Blair** (a delightful teacher and guide, £160/day, £380/day with car, tel. 0150/682-5930, mobile 0798-957-0287, www.travelthrough scotland.com, jean@travelthroughscotland.com); **Sergio La Spina** (an Argentinean who adopted Edinburgh as his hometown more than 20 years ago, £175/day, tel. 0131/664-1731, mobile 0797-330-6579, sergiolaspina@aol.com); **Ken Hanley** (who wears his kilt as if pants don't exist, £100/half-day, £150/day, extra charge if he uses his car—seats up to six, tel. 0131/666-1944, mobile 0771-034-2044, www.small-world -tours.co.uk, k.hanley@blueyonder.co.uk); and **Liz Everett** (£100/half-day, £150/day mobile 07821-683-837, liz.everett @live.co.uk).

Updates to this Book: For updates to this book, check www.rick steves.com/update.

Getting Around Edinburgh

Many of Edinburgh's sights are within walking distance of one another, but buses come in handy. Two companies handle the city routes: Lothian (which dominates) and First. Lothian sells a day pass valid only on their buses (£3.50, buy from driver). Buses run from about 6:00 (9:00 on Sun) to 23:00 (£1.50/ride, buy tickets on bus, exact change, Lothian Buses transit office at Old Town end of Waverley Bridge has schedules and route maps, tel. 0131/555-6363, www.lothianbuses.com). Tell the driver where you're going, have change handy (buses require exact change—you lose any extra you put in), take your ticket as you board, and ping the bell as you near your stop. Double-deckers come with fine views upstairs.

The 1,300 **taxis** cruising Edinburgh's streets are easy to flag down (a ride between downtown and the B&B neighborhood costs about £7). They can turn on a dime, so hail them in either direction.

Tours in Edinburgh

Royal Mile Walking Tours

Edinburgh Tour Guides offers your best basic historical walk (without all the ghosts and goblins). The staff of committed guides heads out as long as they have at least two people. Their Royal Mile tour is a gentle two-hour downhill stroll from the castle to the palace (£12; daily at 9:30, 14:00, and 19:00; meet outside Gladstone's Land, near the top of the Royal Mile, must call ahead to reserve, mobile 0785-888-0072, www.edinburghtourguides.com).

Mercat Tours offers 1.5-hour guided walks of the Mile that are more entertaining than intellectual (£11, daily at 14:15, leaves from Mercat Cross on the Royal Mile, tel. 0131/225-5445, www.mercattours.com). The guides, who enjoy making a short story long, ignore the big sights and take you behind the scenes with piles of barely historical gossip, bully-pulpit Scottish pride, and fun but forgettable trivia. These tours can move quickly, scaling the steep hills and steps of Edinburgh—wear good shoes. They also offer several ghost tours, as well as one focused on 18th-century underground vaults on the southern slope of the Royal Mile.

The **Voluntary Guides Association** offers free two-hour walks, but only during the Edinburgh Festival. You don't need a reservation, but it's a good idea to call the TI or drop by there to double-check details, such as departure point and time (daily at about 10:00 and 14:00, generally depart from City Chambers, opposite St. Giles Cathedral, www.edinburghfestivalguides.org).

Edinburgh Bus Tours

Five different one-hour hop-on, hop-off bus tour routes, all run by the same company, circle the town center, stopping at the major sights: **MacTours** (focuses on Old Town, most comprehensive, vintage bus), **Edinburgh Tour** (focuses on the wider city, more panoramic), **World Heritage** (explores historic heritage-listed sites), **City Sightseeing** (Old Town and Edinburgh Castle),

Edinburgh

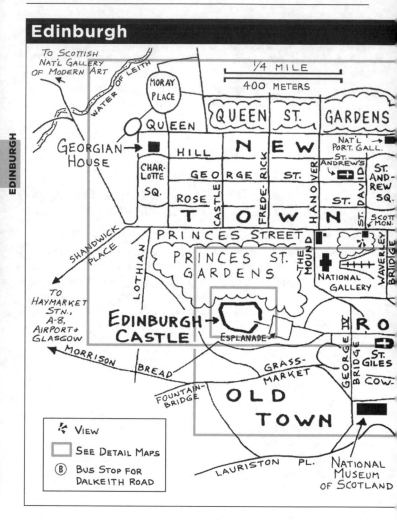

To Scottish Nat'l Gallery of Modern Art

WATER OF LEITH

MORAY PLACE

¼ MILE
400 METERS

QUEEN   QUEEN ST. GARDENS

GEORGIAN HOUSE

HILL   N E W

CHAR-LOTTE SQ.   GE O RGE   FREDE-RICK   ST.   HAN OVER   NAT'L PORT. GALL.
ST. ANDREW'S

ROSE   CASTLE   ST. DAVID   ST. AND-REW SQ.

T O W N   ST.   SCOTT MON.

SHANDWICK PLACE

PRINCES   STREET

LOTHIAN   PRINCES   ST.
GARDENS   THE MOUND   WAVERLEY BRIDGE

NATIONAL GALLERY

To HAYMARKET STN., A-8, AIRPORT & GLASGOW

EDINBURGH CASTLE

ESPLANADE

GEORGE IV   R O

ST. GILES

MORRISON   BREAD   GRASS-MARKET   COW-

FOUNTAIN-BRIDGE   O L D

T O W N

↖ VIEW

☐ SEE DETAIL MAPS

Ⓑ BUS STOP FOR DALKEITH ROAD

LAURISTON   PL.   NATIONAL MUSEUM OF SCOTLAND

Majestic Tour (longer route includes a stop at the *Britannia* and Royal Botanic Garden). The tours all have virtually the same route, cost, and frequency (pick-ups about every 10-15 minutes), but only the first three have live guides—the others use audioguides (£13/tour, £17 for all five tours, £30 family ticket covers two adults and up to three children, tickets give small discounts on most sights along the route, valid 24 hours, buy on bus or at kiosk on Waverley Bridge, tel. 0131/220-

0770, www.edinburghtour.com). Buses run daily year-round (Mac Tours runs only April-Aug); in peak season (April-Oct), they run roughly between 9:30 and 19:00 (last departure from Waverley Bridge at 17:30, later in July-Aug, hours shrink off-season). On sunny days they go topless (the buses), but come with increased traffic noise and exhaust fumes.

Busy sightseers might want to get the **Royal Edinburgh Ticket** (£45, www.edinburghtour.com/ticket-offers), which covers two days of unlimited travel on all five tour buses, as well as admission to Edinburgh Castle (£16), the Palace of Holyroodhouse (£11), and the *Britannia* (£12). If you plan to visit all these sights and to use a tour bus both days, the ticket will save you a few pounds

British, Scottish, and English

Scotland and England have been tied together for 300 years, since the Act of Union in 1707. For a century and a half afterward, Scottish nationalists rioted for independence in Edinburgh's streets and led rebellions in the Highlands. In this controversial union, history is clearly seen through two very different filters.

If you tour a British-oriented sight, such as the National War Museum Scotland, you'll find things told in a "happy union" way, which ignores the long history of Scottish resistance—from the ancient Picts through the time of Robert the Bruce. The official line: In 1706-1707, it was clear to England and some of Scotland (especially landowners from the Lowlands) that it was in their mutual interest to dissolve the Scottish government and fold it into Britain, to be ruled from London.

But talk to a cabbie or your B&B host, and you may get a different spin. Scottish independence is still a hot-button issue today. In 2007, the Scottish National Party (SNP) won a major election, and now has the largest majority in the fledgling Scottish parliament. Alex Salmond, SNP leader and the First Minister of Scotland, is pushing for Scotland to be recognized as an independent nation within the EU, and citizens will vote on this issue in September of 2014. (English leaders are obviously not in favor of breaking up the "united kingdom," though there's a like-minded independence movement in Wales, as well.)

The deep-seated rift shows itself in sports, too. While the English may refer to a British team in international competition as "English," the Scots are careful to call it "British." If a Scottish athlete does well, the English call him "British." If he screws up...he's a clumsy Scot.

(and, in the summer, help you bypass any lines). You can buy these tickets online, from the TI, or from the staff at the tour-bus pick-up point on Waverley Bridge. If your main interest is seeing the *Britannia*, you'll save money by taking a regular bus instead.

Day Trips from Edinburgh

Many companies run a variety of day trips to regional sights. Study the brochures at the TI's rack. (Several of the private guides listed above have cars, too.)

By far the most popular tour is the all-day **Highlands trip.** The standard Highlands tour gives those with limited time a chance to experience the wonders of Scotland's wild and legend-soaked Highlands in a single long day (about £35-45, roughly 8:00-20:30). You'll generally see the vast and brutal Rannoch Moor;

Glencoe, still evocative with memories of the clan massacre; views of Britain's highest mountain, Ben Nevis; Fort Augustus on Loch Ness (some tours have a 1.5-hour stop here with an optional £12 boat ride); and a 45-minute tea or pub break in the fine town of Pitlochry. You learn about the Loch Ness monster, and a bit about Edinburgh to boot as you drive in and out.

Various competing companies run these tours (each offering a slightly different combination of sights), including **Timberbush Highland Tours** (£41, 7- to 36-seat air-con buses, reliable, depart from entrance to Edinburgh Castle, tel. 0131/226-6066, www .timberbushtours.com); **Gray Line** (£41, tel. 0131/555-5558, www .graylinescotland.com); **Rabbie's Trail Burners** (£42-49, maximum 16 per tour, guaranteed departures, depart from their office at 207 High Street, tel. 0131/226-3133, www.rabbies.com); and **Heart of Scotland Tours** (£39-49, 10 percent Rick Steves discount on all-day tours—be sure to mention when booking, daily morning departures beginning at 8:00, leaves from opposite Apex Hotel, bus stop ZE on Waterloo Place near Waverley Station, tel. 0131/228-2888, www.heartofscotlandtours.co.uk, run by Nick Roche). Between November and March a minimum of six people is required for this tour. Be sure to leave a contact number so you can be notified. A final decision is made by 18:00 the night before.

Haggis Adventures runs cheap and youthful tours on 16- to 39-seat buses with a very Scottish driver/guide. Their day trips (£35-45) include a distillery visit and the Highlands, or Loch Lomond and the southern Highlands. Their overnight trips are designed for young backpackers, but they welcome travelers of any age who want a quick look at the countryside and are up for hosteling (2- to 10-day trips, office at 60 High Street, tel. 0131/557-9393, www.haggisadventures.com).

At **Discreet Scotland,** Matthew Wight and his partners specialize in tours of greater Edinburgh and Scotland in spacious SUVs—good for families (£335/9 hours, mobile 0798-941-6990, www.discreetscotland.com). Their 15 day-trips with driver/guides cover the Highlands, St. Andrews, royal castles, and more.

Self-Guided Walk

▲▲▲Royal Mile

The Royal Mile is one of Europe's most interesting historic walks. Start at Edinburgh Castle at the top and amble down to the Palace of Holyroodhouse. Along the way, the street changes names—Castlehill, Lawnmarket, High Street, and Canongate—but it's a straight, downhill shot totaling just over one mile. And nearly every step is packed with shops, cafés, and lanes leading to tiny squares.

The city was born on the easily defended rock at the top where
the castle stands today. Celtic
tribes (and maybe the Romans)
once occupied this site. As the
town grew, it spilled downhill along the sloping ridge that
became the Royal Mile. Because
this strip of land is so narrow,
there was no place to build but up.
So in medieval times, it was densely packed with multistory "ten-
ements"—large edifices under one roof that housed a number of
tenants.

As you walk, you'll be tracing the growth of the city—its birth
atop Castle Hill, its Old Town heyday in the 1600s, its expansion
in the 1700s into the Georgian New Town (leaving the old quarter
an overcrowded, disease-ridden Victorian slum), and on to the 21st
century at the modern Scottish Parliament building (2004).

The way the Royal Mile is developing, it seems it's well on
its way to becoming a touristic mall—all tartans, kilts, and shortbread. But the streets are packed with history, and if you push past
the postcard racks into one of the many side alleys, you can still
find a few surviving rough edges of the old city.

This walk covers the route, but skips the many museums
and indoor attractions along the way. They (and other sights) are
described in walking order after this self-guided walk. You can
stay focused on the walk (which takes about 60 to 90 minutes,
without stops) and return later to visit the various indoor attractions (many of which are free), or you can review the sights beforehand and pop in as you pass them.

• *We'll start at the Castle Esplanade, the big parking lot at the entrance
to...*

Edinburgh Castle

Edinburgh was born on the bluff—a big rock—where the castle
now stands. Since before history, people have lived on this strategic, easily-defended perch.

The **castle** is an imposing symbol of Scottish independence.
Flanking the entryway are statues of the fierce warriors who
battled English invaders, William "Braveheart" Wallace (on the
right) and Robert the Bruce (left). Between them is the Scottish
motto, *Nemo me impune lacessit*—"No one messes with me and gets
away with it." These fighting words are also engraved around the
edge of the Scottish pound coin.

The esplanade—built as a military parade ground (1816)—is
now the site of the annual Military Tattoo. This spectacular mass-

The Kilt

The kilt, Scotland's national dress, is intimately tied in with the country's history. It originated back in the 1500s as a multi-purpose robe, toga, tent, poncho, and ground cloth. A wearer would lay it on the ground to scrunch up pleats, then wrap it around the waist and belt it. Extra fabric was thrown over the shoulder or tucked into the belt, making a rucksack-like pouch.

The kilt was standard dress in the Highlands and came to be a patriotic statement during wars with England. After the tragic-for-Scotland Battle of Culloden in 1746, England wanted to end the Scottish clan system. Wearing the kilt, speaking Gaelic, and playing the bagpipe were all outlawed.

In 1782 kilts were permitted again, but the image of a kilt-dressed man had taken on an unrefined connotation, so most Scots no longer even wanted to wear it. The modern rehabilitation of the kilt really took off when King George IV visited Edinburgh in 1822. He wanted to show he was king of Scotland and needed to dress the part—so he wore a kilt. Scottish aristocrats ended up being charmed by the king's embrace of Scottish pageantry, and suddenly the kilt was in vogue again.

During the king's visit, Sir Walter Scott organized a Highland festival that also helped change the image of traditional Scottish culture, giving it a newfound respectability. A generation later, Queen Victoria raised the image of Scottish culture even higher. She loved Scotland and wallpapered her palace at Balmoral with "tartanry"—as the tartan patterns are called.

The colors and patterns of the original kilts were determined by what dyes were available and who wove them—not by clan patterns, as is commonly thought. The whole tartan thing (a certain pattern, or tartan, that told which clan the wearer was from) started as a scam by fabric salesmen in Victorian times. Since then, tartanry has been embraced as if it were historic.

In modern times the smaller kilt, or philibeg, replaced the big, heavy, and hot traditional kilt. While still heavy, the philibeg has less fabric and is little more than a wraparound skirt. Half the weight of the original old-style kilts, it's the more practical choice.

ing of regimental bands fills the square nightly for most of August. Fans watch from temporary bleacher seats to see kilt-wearing bagpipers marching against the spectacular backdrop of the castle. TV crews broadcast the spectacle to all corners of the globe.

When the bleachers aren't up, there are fine views in both directions from the esplanade. Facing north, you'll see the body of water called the Firth of Forth, and Fife beyond that. (The

Firth of Forth is the estuary where the Forth River flows into the North Sea.) Still facing north, find the lacy spire of the Scott Memorial and two Neoclassical buildings housing art galleries. Beyond them, the stately buildings of Edinburgh's New Town rise. Panning to the right, find the Nelson Monument and some fake Greek ruins atop Calton Hill.

The city's many bluffs, crags, and ridges were built up by volcanoes, then carved down by glaciers—a city formed in "fire and ice," as the locals say. So, during the Ice Age, as a river of glaciers swept in from the west (behind today's castle), it ran into the super-hard volcanic basalt of Castle Hill and flowed around it, cutting valleys on either side and leaving a tail that became the Royal Mile you're about to walk.

At the bottom of the esplanade (where the square hits the road, on the left), a plaque on the wall above the tiny witches' fountain memorializes 300 women who were accused of witchcraft and burned here. Below was the Nor' Loch, the swampy lake where those accused of witchcraft (mostly women) were tested. Bound up, they were dropped into the lake. If they sank and drowned, they were innocent. If they floated, they were guilty, and were burned here in front of the castle, providing the city folk a nice afternoon out. Scotland burned more witches per capita than any other country—17,000 souls between 1479 and 1722. The plaque shows two witches: one good and one bad. Tickle the serpent's snout to sympathize with the witches. (I just made that up.)

• *Start walking down the Royal Mile. The first block is a street called…*

Castlehill

You're immediately in the tourist hubbub. The big tank-like building on your left was the Old Town's reservoir. You'll see the wellheads it served all along this walk. While it once held 1.5 million gallons of water, today it's filled with the touristy Tartan Weaving Mill and Exhibition. If you want to peruse several floors of tartanry and Chinese-produced Scottish kitsch, pop in.

The tower ahead on the left has entertained visitors since the 1850s with its **camera obscura**, a darkened room where a mirror and a series of lenses capture live images of the city surroundings outside. Giggle at the funny mirrors as you walk fatly by. Across the street, filling the old Castle Hill Primary School, is a gimmicky-if-intoxicating whisky-sampling exhibit called the Scotch Whisky Experience (a.k.a. "Malt Disney").

• *Just ahead, in front of the church with the tall, lacy spire, is the old market square known as…*

EDINBURGH

Lawnmarket

During the Royal Mile's heyday, in the 1600s, this intersection was bigger and served as a market for fabric (especially "lawn," a linen-like cloth). The market would fill this space with bustle, hustle, and lots of commerce. The round white hump in the middle of the roundabout is all that remains of the official weighing beam called the Butter Tron—where all goods sold were weighed for honesty and tax purposes.

Towering above Lawnmarket, with the tallest spire in the city, is the former **Tolbooth Church.** This impressive Neo-Gothic structure (1844) is now home to the Hub, Edinburgh's festival ticket and information center. The world-famous Edinburgh Festival fills the month of August with cultural action. The various festivals feature classical music, traditional and fringe theater (especially comedy), art, books, and more. Drop inside the building to get festival info. This is a handy stop for its WC and café (£5-8 lunches, free Wi-Fi).

In the 1600s, this, along with the next stretch, called High Street, was the city's main street. At that time, Edinburgh was bursting with breweries, printing presses, and banks. Tens of thousands of citizens were squeezed into the narrow confines of the Old Town. Here on this ridge, they built tenements (multiple-unit residences) similar to the more recent ones you see today. These tenements, rising up 10 stories and more, were some of the tallest domestic buildings in Europe. The living arrangements shocked class-conscious English visitors to Edinburgh because the tenements were occupied by rich and poor alike—usually the poor in the cellars and attics, and the rich in the middle floors.

Gladstone's Land (at #477b, on the left), a surviving original tenement, was acquired by a wealthy merchant in 1617. Stand in front of the building and look up. That's a centuries-old skyscraper. This design was standard on this street back then: a shop or shops on the ground floor, with columns and an arcade, and residences on the floors above. Because window glass was expensive, the lower halves of window openings were made of cheaper wood, which swung out like shutters for ventilation—and convenient for tossing out garbage.

For a good Royal Mile photo, climb the curved stairway outside Gladstone's Land and look downhill. Notice the snoozing pig outside the front door. Just like every house has a vacuum cleaner today, in the good old days a snorting rubbish collector was a standard feature of any well-equipped house.

Branching off the spine of the Royal Mile are a number of narrow alleyways that go by various local names. A "wynd" (rhymes with "kind") is a narrow, winding lane. A "pend" is an arched gateway. "Gate" is from an old Scandinavian word for street. And a "close" is a tiny alley between two buildings (originally with a door that "close"-ed it at night). A close usually leads to a "court," or courtyard.

To explore one of these alleyways, head into **Lady Stair's Close** (across the street, 10 steps downhill from Gladstone's Land). This alley pops out in a small courtyard, where you'll find the **Writers' Museum.** It's free and well worth a visit for fans of the city's holy trinity of writers (Robert Burns, Sir Walter Scott, and Robert Louis Stevenson), but it's also a glimpse of what a typical home might have looked like in the 1600s. You'll wind up steep staircases through a maze of rooms as you peruse first editions and keepsakes of these great writers. Burns actually lived for a while in this neighborhood, in 1786, when he first arrived in Edinburgh.

Opposite Gladstone's Land (at #322), another close leads to **Riddle's Court.** Wander through here and imagine Edinburgh in the 17th and 18th centuries, when tourists came here to marvel at its skyscrapers. Visualize the labyrinthine maze of the old city, with thousands of people scurrying through these back alleyways, buying and selling, and popping into taverns.

No city in Europe was as densely populated—or perhaps as filthy. Without modern hygiene, it was a living hell of smoke, smell, and noise, with the constant threat of fire, collapse, and disease. The dirt streets were soiled with sewage from bedpans emptied out windows. By the 1700s, the Old Town was rife with poverty and cholera outbreaks. The smoky home fires rising from tenements and the infamous smell (or "reek" in Scottish) that wafted across the city gave it a nickname which sticks today— "Auld Reekie."

• *Return to the Royal Mile and continue down it a few steps to take in some sights at the...*

Bank/High Streets Intersection

A number of sights cluster here, where Bank Street changes its name to High Street and intersects with George IV Bridge.

Begin with **Deacon Brodie's Tavern.** Read the "Doctor Jekyll and Mister Hyde" story of this pub's notorious namesake on the wall facing Bank Street. Then, to see his spooky split personality, check out both sides of the hanging signpost. Brodie—a pillar of the community by day but a burglar by night—epitomizes the divided personality of

1700s Edinburgh. It was a rich, productive city—home to great philosophers and scientists, participants in the Enlightenment of that age. But the Old Town was riddled with crime and squalor. The city was scandalized when a respected surgeon—driven by a passion for medical research and needing corpses—was accused of colluding with two lowlifes to acquire (freshly murdered) corpses for dissection. (In the next century, in the late 1800s, novelist Robert Louis Stevenson would capture the dichotomy of Edinburgh's rich-poor society in his *Strange Case of Dr. Jekyll and Mr. Hyde*.)

In the late 1700s, Edinburgh's upper class moved out of the Old Town into a planned community called the New Town (a quarter-mile north of here). Eventually, most tenements were torn down and replaced with newer **Victorian buildings.** You'll see some at this intersection.

Look left down Bank Street to the green-domed **Bank of Scotland.** This was the headquarters of the bank, which had practiced modern capitalist financing since 1695. The building now houses the Museum on the Mound, a free exhibit on banking history, and it's also the Scottish headquarters for Lloyds Banking Group—which swallowed up the Bank of Scotland after the financial crisis of 2008. The confusing array of mergers here, as in the USA, has led skeptics to see the bank crisis as intentionally created to make big banks "too big to fail."

• *If you **detour** left down the road toward the bank, you'll find the recommended Whiski Rooms Shop. If you head in the other direction down Bank Street (to your right), you'll reach some recommended eateries (The Elephant House and The Outsider), as well as the excellent National Museum of Scotland, the famous Greyfriars Bobby statue, and photogenic Victoria Street, which leads to the fun pub-lined Grassmarket square (all described later in this chapter).*

Otherwise, continue along the Royal Mile.

Across the street from Deacon Brodie's Tavern is a seated green statue of hometown boy **David Hume** (1711-1776)—one of the most influential thinkers not only of Scotland, but in all of Western philosophy. The atheistic Hume was one of the towering figures of the Scottish Enlightenment of the mid-1700s. Thinkers and scientists were using the experimental method to challenge and investigate everything, including religion. Hume questioned cause and effect in thought puzzles such as this: We can see that when one billiard ball strikes another, the second one moves, but how do we know the collision "caused" the movement? Notice his shiny toe: People on their way to trial (in the high court just behind the statue) or students on their way to exams (in the nearby university) rub it for good luck.

Follow David Hume's gaze to the opposite corner, where a

EDINBURGH

brass H in the pavement marks the site of the last public execution in Edinburgh in 1864. Deacon Brodie himself would have been hung about here (in 1788, on a gallows whose design he had helped to improve—smart guy).

• *From the brass H, continue down the Royal Mile, pausing just before the church square at a stone wellhead with the pyramid cap.*

All along the Royal Mile, **wellheads** like this (from 1835) provided townsfolk with water in the days before buildings had plumbing. This neighborhood well was served by the reservoir up at the castle. Imagine long lines of people in need of water standing here, gossiping and sharing the news. Eventually buildings were retrofitted with water pipes—the ones you see running along building exteriors.

• *Ahead of you (past the Victorian statue of some duke, about 10 steps in front of the church), near the street, embedded in the pavement, is a heart. Find it.*

The **Heart of Midlothian** marks the spot of the city's 15th-century municipal building and jail. In times past, in a nearby open space, criminals were hanged, traitors were decapitated, and witches were burned. Citizens hated the rough justice doled out here. Locals still spit on the heart in the pavement. Go ahead... do as the locals do—land one right in the heart of the heart. By the way, Edinburgh has two soccer teams—Heart of Midlothian (known as "Hearts") and Hibernian ("Hibs"). If you're a Hibs fan, spit again.

• *Make your way to the entrance of the church.*

St. Giles Cathedral

This is the flagship of the Church of Scotland (Scotland's largest denomination) and the historic home of Scottish Presbyterianism. These days the interior serves as a kind of Scottish Westminster Abbey, filled with monuments, statues, plaques, and stained-glass windows dedicated to great Scots and moments in history.

A church has stood on this spot since 854, though this structure is an architectural hodgepodge, dating mostly from the 15th through 19th century. In the 16th century, St. Giles was a kind of national stage on which the drama of the Reformation was played out. The reformer John Knox (1514-1572) was the preacher here. His fiery sermons helped turn once-Catholic Edinburgh into a bastion of Protestantism. During the Scottish Reformation, St. Giles was transformed from a Catholic cathedral to a Presbyterian church. The spacious interior is well worth a visit.

• *Walk around the front of the church to the right, into a parking lot.*

Sights Around St. Giles

The grand building next door to St. Giles is the **Old Parliament House.** Since the 13th century, the king had ruled a rubber-stamp parliament of nobles and bishops. But with the Reformation, Protestantism promoted democracy, and the parliament gained real power. From the early 1600s until 1707, this building evolved to become the seat of a true parliament of elected officials. In 1707 Scotland signed an Act of Union, joining what's known today as the United Kingdom and giving up their right to self-rule. (More on that later in the walk.) You can go inside the Old Parliament; it's free, but requires a pass through security.

By the way, the great reformer **John Knox** is buried—with appropriate austerity—under parking lot spot #23. The statue among the cars shows King Charles II riding to a toga party back in 1685.

• *Continue on through the parking lot, around the back end of the church.*

Standard features of any Scottish burgh or town licensed by the king to trade were a "tolbooth" (basically a town hall, with a courthouse, meeting room, and jail); a "tron" (official weighing scale); and a "mercat" (or market) cross. The **market cross** standing just behind St. Giles Cathedral has a slender column decorated with a unicorn holding a flag with the cross of St. Andrew. Royal proclamations have been read at this market cross since the 14th century. In 1952, a town crier heralded the news that Britain had a new queen—three days after the actual event (traditionally the time it took for a horse to speed here from London). Today, Mercat Cross is the meeting point of various walking tours—both historic and ghostly.

• *Circle around to the street side of the church.*

The statue to **Adam Smith** honors the Edinburgh author of the pioneering *Wealth of Nations* (1776), in which he laid out the economics of free market capitalism. Smith theorized that there was an "invisible hand" that wisely guides the unregulated free market. Stand in front of Smith and imagine the intellectual energy of Edinburgh in the mid-1700s when it was Europe's most enlightened city. Adam Smith was right in the center of it. He and David Hume were good friends. James Boswell, the famed biographer of Samuel Johnson, took classes from Smith. James Watt, inventor of the steam engine, was another proud Scotsman of the age. With great intellectuals like these, Edinburgh helped create the modern world. The poet Robert Burns, geologist James Hutton (who's considered the father of modern geology), and the publishers of the first Encyclopedia Britannica all lived in Edinburgh. Steeped in the inquisitive mindset of the Enlightenment, they applied cool rationality and a secular approach to their respective fields.

• *Head on down the Royal Mile.*

More of High Street

A few steps downhill, at #188, is the **Police Information Center.** This place provides a pleasant police presence (say that three times) and a little local law-and-order history to boot. Ask the officer on duty about the impact of modern technology and budget austerity on police work today. Seriously—drop in and discuss whatever law-and-order issue piques your curiosity (free, open daily 10:00-17:30, Aug until 21:30).

Continuing down this stretch of the Royal Mile, which is traffic-free most of the day (notice the bollards that raise and lower for permitted traffic), you'll see the Fringe Festival office (at #180), street musicians, and another wellhead (with horse "sippies," dating from 1675).

Notice those three red boxes. In the 20th century, people used these to make telephonic calls to each other. These cast-iron booths are produced for all of Britain here in Scotland. As phone booths are gradually being decommissioned, they are showing up at British homes as nostalgic garden decorations.

On the left is **Cockburn Street** (pronounced "COE-burn"). This was cut through High Street's dense wall of medieval skyscrapers in the 1860s to give easy access to the Georgian New Town and the train station. Notice how the sliced buildings were thoughtfully capped with facades that fit the aesthetic look of the Royal Mile. In the Middle Ages, only tiny lanes (like Fleshmarket Lane just uphill from Cockburn Street) interrupted the long line of Royal Mile buildings. These days, Cockburn Street has a reputation for its eclectic independent shops and string of trendy bars and eateries.

• *When you reach the **Tron Church** (17th century, currently empty), you're at the intersection of **North and South Bridge streets.** These major streets lead left to Waverley Station and right to the Dalkeith Road B&Bs. Several handy bus lines run along here.*

This is the halfway point of this walk. Stand on the corner diagonally across from the church. Look up to the top of the Royal Mile at the Hub and its 240-foot spire. Notwithstanding its turret and 16th-century charm, the Radisson Blu Hotel just across the street is entirely new construction (1990), built to fit in. The city is protecting its historic look. The Bank Hotel next door was once a fancy bank with a lavish interior. As modern banks are moving away from city centers, sumptuous buildings like these are being converted into ornate pubs and restaurants.

In the next block downhill are three **characteristic pubs**, side by side, that offer free traditional Scottish and folk music in the evenings. Notice the chimneys. Tenement buildings shared stairways and entries, but held individual apartments, each with its own chimney. Take a look back at the spire of St. Giles Cathedral—inspired by the Scottish crown and the thistle, Scotland's national flower.

• *Go down High Street another block, passing near the* **Museum of Childhood** *(worth a stop) and a fragrant* **fudge shop** *where you can sample various flavors as you would gelato (tempting you to buy a slab—£4). Directly across the street, just below another wellhead, is the...*

John Knox House

As mentioned earlier, Knox was a towering figure in Edinburgh's history, converting Scotland to a Calvinist style of Protestantism. His religious bent was "Presbyterianism"—in which parishes are governed by elected officials rather than appointed bishops. As this brand of Christianity was more democratic, it also spurred Scotland toward political democracy. If you're interested in Knox or the Reformation, this sight is worth a visit. Full disclosure: It's not certain that Knox ever actually lived here.

• *A few steps farther down High Street, at the intersection with St. Mary's and Jeffrey streets, you'll reach...*

World's End

For centuries, a wall stood here, marking the end of the burgh of Edinburgh. For residents within the protective walls of the city, this must have felt like the "world's end," indeed. The area beyond was called Canongate, a monastic community associated with Holyrood Abbey. At the intersection, find the brass bricks in the street that trace the gate (demolished in 1764). Look down St. Mary's Street about 200 yards to see a surviving bit of that old wall, known as **Flodden Wall.** In the 1513 Battle of Flodden, the Scottish king James IV made the disastrous decision to invade northern England. James and 10,000 of his Scotsmen were killed. Fearing a brutal English counterattack, Edinburgh scrambled to reinforce its broken-down city wall.

The pub on the corner, No. 1 High Street, is a centrally located venue for live traditional music—pop in and see what's on tonight.

• *Continue down the Royal Mile—leaving old Edinburgh—as High Street changes names to...*

Canongate

About 10 steps down Canongate, look left down Cranston Street (past the train tracks) to a good view of the Calton Cemetery up on Calton Hill. The obelisk, called **Martyrs' Monument,** remembers a group of 18th-century patriots exiled by London to Australia for their reform politics. The round building to the left is the grave of philosopher David Hume. And the big, turreted building to the right was the jail master's house. Today, the main reason to go up Calton Hill is for the fine views.

• *A couple of hundred yards farther along the Royal Mile (on the right at #172) you reach a special shop, Cadenhead's, a serious place to sample and buy whisky. About 30 yards farther along, you'll pass two worthwhile and free museums, the* **People's Story Museum** *(#163) and* **Museum of Edinburgh** *(#142). But our next stop is the church just across from the Museum of Edinburgh.*

The 1688 **Canongate Church**—located not far from the royal residence of Holyroodhouse—is where Queen Elizabeth and her family worship whenever they're in town. (So don't sit in the front pew marked with her crown.) The gilded emblem at the top of the roof, high above the door, has the antlers of a stag from the nearby royal estate of Balmoral. The Queen's granddaughter married here in 2011.

Step inside the lofty blue and red interior, renovated with royal money; the church is filled with light and the flags of various Scottish regiments. In the narthex, peruse the photos of royal family events here, and find the list of priests and ministers of this parish—it goes back to 1143 (with a clear break with the Reformation in 1561).

Outside, in the graveyard, follow the cute little markers to the tomb of **Adam Smith,** the father of capitalism (his monument abuts the back of the People's Story Museum).

Just outside the churchyard, the statue on the sidewalk is of the poet **Robert Fergusson.** One of the first to write verse in Scottish, he so inspired Robert Burns that Burns paid for Fergusson's tombstone in the Canongate churchyard and composed his epitaph.

Now look across the street at the gabled house for shells put there in the 17th century to defend against the evil power of witches yet to be drowned.

• *Walk about 300 yards farther along. In the distance you can see the Palace of Holyroodhouse (the end of this walk) and soon, on the right, you'll come to the modern Scottish parliament building.*

Just opposite the parliament building is **White Horse Close** (in the white arcade). Step into this 17th-century courtyard. It was from here that the Edinburgh stagecoach left for London. Eight days later, the horse-drawn carriage would pull into its destination: Scotland Yard. Note that bus #35 leaves in two directions from here—downhill for the Royal Yacht *Britannia,* and uphill along the Royal Mile (as far as South Bridge) and on to the National Museum of Scotland.

• *Now walk up around the corner to the flagpoles (flying the flags of Europe, Britain, and Scotland) in front of the...*

Scottish Parliament Building

Finally, after centuries of history, we reach the 21st century. And finally, after three centuries of London rule, Scotland has a parliament building...in Scotland. When Scotland united with England in 1707, its parliament was dissolved. But the Scots won it back nearly three centuries years later.

In 1999, the Scottish parliament was re-established, and in 2004, moved into its striking new home. Notice how the eco-friendly building, by the Catalan architect Enric Miralles, mixes wild angles, lots of light, bold windows, oak, and native stone into a startling complex. From the front of the parliament building, look in the distance at the rocky Salisbury Crags, with people hiking the traverse up to the dramatic next summit called Arthur's Seat. Now look at the building in relation to the craggy cliffs. The architect envisioned the building as if were rising right from the base of Arthur's Seat, almost bursting from the rock.

Since it celebrates Scottish democracy, the architecture is not a statement of authority. There are no statues of old heroes. There's not even a grand entry. You feel like you're entering an office park.

• *Across the street is the Queen's Gallery, where she shares part of her amazing personal art collection in excellent revolving exhibits. Finally, walk to the end of the road (Abbey Strand), and step up to the impressive wrought-iron gate of the Queen's palace. Look up at the stag with its holy cross, or "holy rood," on its forehead, and peer into the palace grounds. (The ticket office and palace entryway, a fine café, and a handy public toilet are just through the arch on the right.)*

Palace of Holyroodhouse

Since the 16th century, this palace has marked the end of the Royal Mile. An abbey—part of a 12th-century Augustinian monastery—originally stood in its place. While most of that old building is gone, you can see the surviving nave behind the palace on the left. It was named "holy rood" for a piece of the cross, brought here as a relic by Queen (and later Saint) Margaret. Because Scotland's royalty preferred living at Holyroodhouse to the blustery castle on the rock, the palace evolved over time. If the Queen's not visiting, the palace welcomes visitors.

Your walk—from the castle to the palace, with so much Scottish history packed in between—is complete. And, if your appetite is whetted for more, don't worry; you've just scratched the surface. Enjoy the rest of Edinburgh.

Sights in Edinburgh

▲▲▲Edinburgh Castle

The fortified birthplace of the city 1,300 years ago, this imposing symbol of Edinburgh sits proudly on a rock high above you.

The home of Scotland's kings and queens for centuries, the castle has witnessed royal births, medieval pageantry, and bloody sieges. Today it's a complex of various buildings linked by cobbled roads that survive from its more recent use as a military garrison. The

castle—with expansive views, plenty of history, and the stunning crown jewels of Scotland—is a fascinating and multifaceted sight that deserves several hours of your time.

Cost and Hours: £16, daily April-Sept 9:30-18:00, Oct-March 9:30-17:00, last entry one hour before closing, National War Museum Scotland closes one hour before rest of castle, tel. 0131/225-9846, www.edinburghcastle.gov.uk.

Avoiding Lines: The least crowded times are usually first thing in the morning and after 14:00. To avoid ticket lines (worst in August), book online and print your ticket at home, or pick up your prebooked ticket at the machines by the red phone boxes just inside the entrance.

Getting There: You can walk to the castle, catch a bus (which drops you off a short, uphill walk away), or take a taxi (taxis let you off a block below the esplanade at the Hub/Tolbooth Church).

Tours: Thirty-minute guided introductory tours are free with admission (2-4/hour, depart from Argyle Battery, see clock for next departure; fewer tours off-season). The informative audioguide provides four hours of descriptions, including the National War Museum Scotland (£3.50, slightly cheaper if purchased online with entry ticket).

Services: The clean WC at the entry routinely wins "British Loo of the Year" awards. For lunch, you have two choices. **The Red Coat Café and Jacobite Room**—located within Edinburgh Castle—is a big, bright, efficient cafeteria with great views (£8-

10 quick, healthy meals). Punctuate the two parts of your castle visit (the castle itself and the impressive National War Museum Scotland) with a smart break here. The **Tea Rooms,** in a building at the top of the hill, right across from the crown jewels, serves sit-down meals in its small, tight space (last orders 30 minutes before castle complex closes).

❷ Self-Guided Tour: From the ❶ **entry gate,** start winding your way uphill toward for the main sights—the crown jewels and the Royal Palace—located near

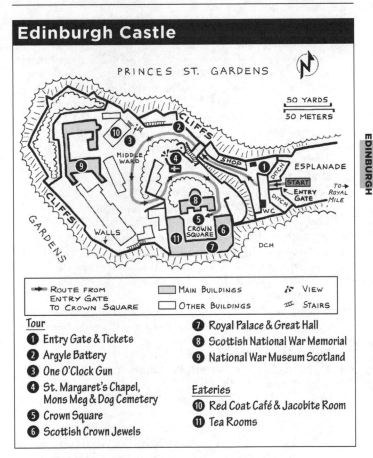

Edinburgh Castle

PRINCES ST. GARDENS

50 YARDS
50 METERS

CLIFFS

MIDDLE
WARD

SHOP

ESPLANADE

DITCH

START

ENTRY
GATE

TO →
ROYAL
MILE

WC

CLIFFS

CROWN
SQUARE

WALLS

DCH

GARDENS

Legend:
- ➡ ROUTE FROM ENTRY GATE TO CROWN SQUARE
- ▨ MAIN BUILDINGS
- ▭ OTHER BUILDINGS
- ↗ VIEW
- ⊞ STAIRS

Tour
1. Entry Gate & Tickets
2. Argyle Battery
3. One O'Clock Gun
4. St. Margaret's Chapel, Mons Meg & Dog Cemetery
5. Crown Square
6. Scottish Crown Jewels
7. Royal Palace & Great Hall
8. Scottish National War Memorial
9. National War Museum Scotland

Eateries
10. Red Coat Café & Jacobite Room
11. Tea Rooms

the summit. Since the castle was protected on three sides by sheer cliffs, the main defense had to be here at the entrance. During the castle's heyday in the 1500s, a 100-foot tower loomed overhead, facing the city.

• *Passing through the portcullis gate, you reach the…*

2 Argyle (Six-Gun) Battery, with View: These front-loading, cast-iron cannons are from the Napoleonic era (c. 1800), when the castle was still a force to be reckoned with.

From here, look north across the valley to the grid blocks of the New Town. The valley sits where the Nor' Loch once was; this lake was drained and filled in when the New Town was built in the late 1700s, its swamps replaced with gardens. Later the land provided sites for the Greek-temple-looking Scottish National Gallery and Waverley Station. Looking farther north, you can make out the port town of Leith with its high-rises and cranes, the Firth of Forth, the island of Inchkeith, and—in the far, far distance (to the east)—the cone-like mountain of North Berwick Law, a former volcano.

Now look down. The sheer north precipice looks impregnable. But on the night of March 14, 1314, 30 armed men silently scaled this rock face. They were loyal to Robert the Bruce and determined to capture the castle, which had fallen into English hands. They caught the English by surprise, took the castle, and—three months later—Bruce defeated the English at the Battle of Bannockburn. This was the last great Scottish military victory.

• *A little farther along, near the café, is the…*

❸ **One O'Clock Gun:** Crowds gather for the 13:00 gun blast, a tradition that gives ships in the bay something to set their navigational devices by. Before the gun, sailors set their clocks with help from the Nelson Monument—that's the tall pillar in the distance on Calton Hill. The monument has a "time ball" affixed to the cross on top, which dropped precisely at the top of the hour. But on foggy days, ships couldn't see the ball, so the cannon shot was instituted instead (1861). The tradition stuck, every day at 13:00—the frugal Scots don't fire it at high noon, as that would cost 11 extra rounds a day.

• *Continue uphill, winding to the left and passing through Foog's Gate. At the very top of the hill is…*

❹ **St. Margaret's Chapel:** This tiny stone chapel is Edinburgh's oldest building (1130) and sits atop its highest point (440 feet). It represents the birth of the city.

In 1057, Malcolm III murdered King Macbeth (of Shakespeare fame) and assumed the Scottish throne. Later, he married Princess Margaret, and the family settled atop this hill. Their marriage united Malcolm's Highland Scots with Margaret's Lowland Anglo-Saxons—the cultural mix that would define Edinburgh.

Step inside the tiny, unadorned church—a testament to Margaret's reputed piety. The style is Romanesque. The nave is wonderfully simple, with classic Norman zigzags decorating the round arch that separates the tiny nave from the sacristy. You'll see a facsimile of St. Margaret's 11th-century gospel book. The small (modern) stained-glass windows feature St. Margaret herself, St. Columba (who brought Christianity to Scotland via Iona), and William Wallace (the brave-hearted defender of Scotland). These days, the place is popular for weddings, and—as it seats only 20—it's particularly popular with brides' parents.

Margaret died at the castle in 1093, and her son King David I built this chapel in her honor (she was sainted in 1250). David expanded the castle and also founded Holyrood Abbey, across town. These two structures were soon linked by a Royal Mile of buildings, and Edinburgh was born.

Mons Meg, in front of the church, is a huge and once-upon-a-time frightening 15th-century siege cannon that fired 330-pound stones nearly two miles. Imagine. It was a gift from the Belgians, who shared a common enemy with the Scots—England—and were eager to arm Scotland. Nearby, belly up to the banister and look down to find the **Dog Cemetery,** a tiny patch of grass with a sweet little line of doggie tombstones, marking the graves of soldiers' faithful canines in arms.

• *Continue on, curving downhill into...*

❺ **Crown Square:** This courtyard is the center of today's Royal Castle complex. Get oriented. You're surrounded by the crown jewels, the Royal Palace (with its Great Hall), and the Scottish National War Memorial.

The castle has evolved over the centuries, and Crown Square is relatively "new." After the time of Malcolm and Margaret, the castle was greatly expanded by David II (1324-1371), complete with tall towers, a Great Hall, dungeon, cellars, and so on. This served as the grand royal residence for two centuries. Then, in 1571-1573, the Protestant citizens of Edinburgh laid siege to the castle and its Catholic/monarchist holdouts, eventually blasting it to smithereens. (You can tour the paltry remains of the medieval castle in nearby **David's Tower.**) The palace was rebuilt nearby—around what is today's Crown Square.

• *We'll tour the buildings around Crown Square. First up, the crown jewels. The main year-round entry to the jewels is on Crown Square. In summer, there's a second option that avoids the line: Head to the left as you face the main entrance and find another entry near the WCs. This route takes you through the Honors of Scotland exhibition—an interesting, if Disney-esque, series of displays (which often moves at a shuffle) telling the story of the crown jewels and how they survived the harrowing centuries.*

❻ **Scottish Crown Jewels:** For centuries, Scotland's monarchs were crowned in elaborate rituals involving three wondrous objects: a jewel-studded crown, scepter, and sword. These objects—along with the ceremonial Stone of Scone (pronounced "skoon")—are known as the "Honors." Scotland's crown jewels may not be as impressive as England's, but they're treasured by locals as a symbol of Scottish nationalism. They're also older than England's; while Oliver Cromwell destroyed England's jewels, the Scots managed to hide theirs.

History of the Jewels: The Honors of Scotland exhibit that leads up to the Crown Room traces the evolution of the jewels, the ceremony, and the often turbulent journey of this precious regalia.

In 1306, Robert the Bruce was crowned with a "circlet of gold" in a ceremony at Scone—a town 40 miles north of Edinburgh, which Scotland's earliest kings had claimed as their capital. Around 1500, King James IV added two new items to the

William Wallace
(c. 1270-1305)

In 1286, Scotland's king died without an heir, plunging the prosperous country into a generation of chaos. As Scottish nobles bickered over naming a successor, the English King Edward I—nicknamed "Longshanks" because of his height—invaded and assumed power (1296). He placed a figurehead on the throne, forced Scottish nobles to sign a pledge of allegiance to England (the "Ragman's Roll"), moved the British parliament north to York, and carried off the highly symbolic 336-pound Stone of Scone to London, where it would remain for the next seven centuries.

A year later, the Scots rose up against Edward, led by William Wallace (nicknamed "Braveheart"). A mix of history and legend portrays Wallace as the son of a poor-but-knightly family that refused to sign the Ragman's Roll. Exceptionally tall and strong, he learned Latin and French from two uncles, who were priests. In his teenage years, his father and older brother were killed by the English. Later, he killed an English sheriff to avenge the death of his wife, Marion. Wallace's rage inspired his fellow Scots to revolt.

In the summer of 1297, Wallace and his guerrillas scored a series of stunning victories over the English. On September 11, a large, well-equipped English army of 10,000 soldiers and 300 horsemen began crossing Stirling Bridge. Half of the army had made it across when Wallace's men attacked. In the chaos, the bridge collapsed, splitting the English ranks in two, and the ragtag Scots drove the confused English into the river. The Battle of Stirling Bridge was a rout, and Wallace was knighted and appointed guardian (a caretaker ruler) of Scotland.

All through the winter, King Edward's men chased Wallace, continually frustrated by the Scots' hit-and-run tactics. Finally, at the Battle of Falkirk (1298), they drew Wallace's men out onto the open battlefield. The English with their horses and archers easily destroyed the spear-carrying Scots. Wallace resigned in disgrace and went on the lam, while his successors negotiated truces with the English, finally surrendering unconditionally in 1304. Wallace alone held out.

In 1305, the English tracked him down and took him to London, where he was convicted of treason and mocked with a crown of oak leaves as the "King of Scotland." On August 23, they stripped him naked and dragged him to the execution site. There he was strangled to near death, castrated, and dismembered. His head was stuck on a stick atop London Bridge, while his body parts were sent on tour around the realm to spook would-be rebels. But Wallace's martyrdom only served to inspire his countrymen, and the torch of independence was picked up by Robert the Bruce (see sidebar on page 43).

coronation ceremony—a scepter (a gift from the pope) and a huge sword (a gift from another pope). In 1540, James V had the original crown augmented by an Edinburgh goldsmith, giving it the imperial-crown shape it has today.

These Honors were used to crown every monarch: nine-month-old Mary, Queen of Scots (she cried); her one-year-old son James VI (future king of England); and Charles I and II. But the days of divine-right rulers were numbered.

In 1649, the Parliament had Charles I (king of both England and Scotland) beheaded. Soon rabid English antiroyalists were marching on Edinburgh. Quick! Legend says two women scooped up the crown and sword, hid them in their skirts and belongings, and buried them in a church far to the northeast until the coast was clear.

When the monarchy was restored, the regalia were used to crown Scotland's last king, Charles II (1660). Then, in 1707, the Treaty of Union with England ended Scotland's independence. The Honors came out for a ceremony to bless the treaty, and were then locked away in a strongbox in the castle. There they lay for a century, until Sir Walter Scott—the writer and great champion of Scottish tradition—forced a detailed search of the castle in 1818. The box was found...and there the Honors were, perfectly preserved. Within a few years, they were put on display, as they have been ever since.

The crown's most recent official appearance was in 1999, when it was taken across town to the grand opening of the reinstated parliament, marking a new chapter in the Scottish nation. As it represents the monarchy, the crown is present whenever a new session of parliament opens. (And if Scotland secedes, you can be sure that crown will be in the front row.)

The Honors: Finally, you enter the Crown Room to see the regalia itself. The four-foot steel sword was made in Italy under orders of Pope Julius II (the man who also commissioned Michelangelo's Sistine Chapel and St. Peter's Basilica). The scepter is made of silver, covered with gold, and topped with a rock crystal and a pearl. The gem- and pearl-encrusted crown has an imperial arch topped with a cross. Legend says the band of gold in the center is the original crown that once adorned the head of Robert the Bruce.

The **Stone of Scone** (a.k.a. the "Stone of Destiny") sits plain and strong next to the jewels. It's a rough-hewn gray slab of sandstone, about 26 by 17 by 10 inches. As far back as the ninth century, Scotland's kings were crowned atop this stone, when it stood at the medieval capital of Scone. But in 1296, the invading army of Edward I of England carried the stone off to Westminster Abbey. For the next seven centuries, English (and subsequently British) kings and queens were crowned sitting on a coronation chair with the Stone of Scone tucked in a compartment underneath.

In 1950, four Scottish students broke into Westminster Abbey on Christmas Day and smuggled the stone back to Scotland in an act of foolhardy patriotism. But what could they do with it? After three months, they abandoned the stone, draped in Scotland's national flag. It was returned to Westminster Abbey, where (in 1953) Queen Elizabeth II was crowned atop it. Then in 1996, in recognition of increased Scottish autonomy, Elizabeth agreed to let the stone go home, on one condition: that it be returned to Westminster Abbey for all British coronations. One day, the next monarch of England—Prince Charles is first in line—will sit atop it, re-enacting a coronation ritual that dates back a thousand years.

• *Exit the crown jewel display and turn left before exiting back into the courtyard through a door that leads into the Royal Palace.*

❼ **Royal Palace and Great Hall:** Scottish royalty lived in the Royal Palace only when safety or protocol required it (they preferred the Palace of Holyroodhouse at the bottom of the Royal Mile). It has several historic but unimpressive rooms. In the smallest one, Mary, Queen of Scots (1542-1587), gave birth to James VI of Scotland, who later became King James I of England. The Presence Chamber leads into Laich Hall (Lower Hall), the dining room of the royal family.

The **Great Hall** (through a separate entrance on Crown Square) was built by James IV to host the castle's official banquets and meetings. It's still used for such purposes today. Most of the interior—its fireplace, carved walls, pikes, and armor—is Victorian. But the well-constructed wood ceiling is original. This hammer-beam roof (constructed like the hull of a ship) is self-supporting. The complex system of braces and arches distributes the weight of the roof outward to the walls, so there's no need for supporting pillars or long cross beams. Before leaving, find the big iron-barred peephole above the fireplace, on the right. This allowed the king to spy on his subjects while they partied.

• *Across the Crown Square courtyard is the...*

❽ **Scottish National War Memorial:** This commemorates the 149,000 Scottish soldiers lost in World War I, the 58,000 who died in World War II, and the nearly 800 (and counting) lost in British battles since. This is a somber spot (put away your camera, phone, etc.). Paid for by public donations, each bay is dedicated to a particular Scottish regiment. The main shrine, featuring a green Italian-marble memorial that contains the original WWI rolls of honor, sits—almost as if it were sacred—on an exposed chunk of the castle rock. Above you, the archangel Michael is busy slaying a dragon. The bronze frieze accurately shows the attire of various wings of Scotland's military. The stained glass starts with Cain

Robert the Bruce
(1274-1329)

In 1314, Robert the Bruce's men attacked Edinburgh's Royal Castle, recapturing it from the English. It was just one of many intense battles between the oppressive English and the plucky Scots during the wars of independence.

In this era, Scotland had to overcome not only its English foes but also its own divisiveness—and no one was more divided than Robert the Bruce. As earl of Carrick, he was born with blood ties to England and a long-standing family claim to the Scottish throne.

When England's King Edward I ("Longshanks") conquered Scotland in 1296, the Bruce family welcomed it, hoping Edward would defeat their rivals and put Bruce's father on the throne. They dutifully signed the "Ragman's Roll" of allegiance—and then Edward chose someone else as king.

Twenty-something Robert the Bruce (the "the" comes from his original family name of "de Bruce") then joined William Wallace's revolt against the English. Legend has it that it was he who knighted Wallace after the victory at Stirling Bridge. When Wallace fell from favor, Bruce became a guardian of Scotland (caretaker ruler in the absence of a king) and continued fighting the English. But when Edward's armies again got the upper hand in 1302, Robert—along with Scotland's other nobles—diplomatically surrendered and again pledged loyalty.

In 1306, Robert the Bruce murdered his chief rival and boldly claimed to be king of Scotland. Few nobles supported him. Edward crushed the revolt and kidnapped Bruce's wife, the church excommunicated him, and Bruce went into hiding on a distant North Sea island. He was now the king of nothing. Legend says he gained inspiration by watching a spider patiently build its web.

The following year, Bruce returned to Scotland and wove alliances with both nobles and the church, slowly gaining acceptance as Scotland's king by a populace chafing under English rule. On June 24, 1314, he decisively defeated the English (now led by Edward's weak son, Edward II) at the Battle of Bannockburn. After a generation of turmoil (1286-1314), England was finally driven from Scotland, and the country was united under Robert I, king of Scotland.

As king, Robert the Bruce's priority was to stabilize the monarchy and establish clear lines of succession. His descendants would rule Scotland for the next 400 years, and even today, Bruce blood runs through the veins of Queen Elizabeth II, Prince Charles, and princes William and Harry.

and Abel on the left, and finishes with a celebration of peace on the right. To appreciate how important this place is, consider that Scottish soldiers died at twice the rate of other British soldiers in World War I.

• *Our final stop is worth the five-minute walk to get there. Backtrack to the café (and One O'Clock Gun), then head downhill to the National War Museum Scotland (closes one hour before rest of castle complex).*

❾ **National War Museum Scotland:** This thoughtful museum covers four centuries of Scottish military history. Instead of the usual musty, dusty displays of endless armor, there's a compelling mix of videos, uniforms, weapons, medals, mementos, and eloquent excerpts from soldiers' letters.

Here you'll learn the story of how the fierce and courageous Scottish warrior changed from being a symbol of resistance against Britain to being a champion of that same empire. Along the way, these military men received many decorations for valor and did more than their share of dying in battle. But even when fighting for—rather than against—England, Scottish regiments still promoted their romantic, kilted-warrior image.

Queen Victoria fueled this ideal throughout the 19th century. She was infatuated with the Scottish Highlands and the culture's untamed, rustic mystique. Highland soldiers, especially officers, went to great personal expense to sport all their elaborate regalia, and the kilted men fought best to the tune of their beloved bagpipes. For centuries the stirring drone of bagpipes accompanied Highland soldiers into battle—inspiring them, raising their spirits, and announcing to the enemy that they were about to meet a fierce and mighty foe.

This museum shows the human side of war as well as the cleverness of government-sponsored ad campaigns that kept the lads enlisting. Two centuries of recruiting posters make the same pitch that still works today: a hefty signing bonus, steady pay, and job security with the promise of a manly and adventurous life—all spiked with a mix of pride and patriotism.

Stepping outside the museum, you're surrounded by cannons that no longer fire, stony walls that tell an amazing story, dramatic views of this grand city, and the clatter of tourists (rather than soldiers) on cobbles. Consider for a moment all the bloody history and valiant struggles, along with British power and Scottish pride, that have shaped the city over which you are perched.

• *There's only one way out—the same way you came in.*

Sights on and near the Royal Mile
Camera Obscura
A big deal when it was built in 1853, this observatory topped with a mirror reflected images onto a disc before the wide eyes of people

who had never seen a photograph or a captured image. Today, you can climb 100 steps for an entertaining 20-minute demonstration (3/hour). At the top, enjoy the best view anywhere of the Royal Mile. Then work your way down through five floors of illusions, holograms, and early photos. This is a big hit with kids, but sadly overpriced. (It's less impressive on cloudy days.)

Cost and Hours: £12, daily July-Aug 9:30-21:00, April-June and Sept-Oct 9:30-18:00, Nov-March 10:00-17:00, last demonstration one hour before closing, tel. 0131/226-3709, www.camera-obscura.co.uk.

Scotch Whisky Experience (a.k.a. "Malt Disney")

This gimmicky ambush is designed only to distill £13 out of your pocket. You kick things off with a slow-moving whisky-barrel train-car ride that goes to great lengths to make whisky production seem thrilling (things get pretty psychedelic when you hit the yeast stage). An informative lecture on whisky regions and production in Scotland includes sampling a wee dram and the chance to stand amid the world's largest Scotch whisky collection (almost 3,500 bottles). At the end, you'll find yourself in the bar, which is worth a quick look for its wall of unusually shaped whisky bottles. People do seem to enjoy this place, but that might have something to do with the sample. If you're visiting Oban, Pitlochry, or the Isle of Skye, you'll find cheaper, less hokey distillery tours there. Serious connoisseurs of the Scottish firewater will want to pop into the Whiski Rooms Shop off North Bank Street or Cadenhead's Whisky Shop at the bottom of the Royal Mile (both described later).

Cost and Hours: £13, daily 10:00-18:30, last tour at 17:30, tel. 0131/220-0441, www.scotchwhiskyexperience.co.uk.

▲▲Gladstone's Land

This is a typical 16th- to 17th-century merchant's "land," or tenement building. These multistory structures—in which merchants ran their shops on the ground floor and lived upstairs—were typi-

cal of the time (the word "tenement" didn't have the slum connotation then that it has today). Gladstone's Land comes complete with an almost-lived-in, furnished interior and guides in each room who love to talk. Keep this place in mind as you stroll the rest of the Mile, imagining other houses as if they still looked like this on the inside. (For a comparison of life in the Old Town versus the New Town, also visit the Georgian House—described later.)

Cost and Hours: £6.50, daily July-Aug 10:00-18:30, April-June and Sept-Oct

Edinburgh's Royal Mile

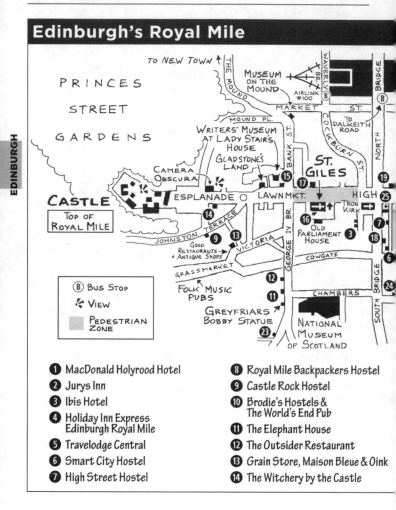

1. MacDonald Holyrood Hotel
2. Jurys Inn
3. Ibis Hotel
4. Holiday Inn Express Edinburgh Royal Mile
5. Travelodge Central
6. Smart City Hostel
7. High Street Hostel
8. Royal Mile Backpackers Hostel
9. Castle Rock Hostel
10. Brodie's Hostels & The World's End Pub
11. The Elephant House
12. The Outsider Restaurant
13. Grain Store, Maison Bleue & Oink
14. The Witchery by the Castle

10:00-17:00, last entry 30 minutes before closing, closed Nov-March, no photos allowed, tel. 0844-493-2100, www.nts.org.uk.

▲Writers' Museum at Lady Stair's House

This aristocrat's house, built in 1622, is filled with well-described manuscripts and knickknacks of Scotland's three greatest literary figures: Robert Burns, Sir Walter Scott, and Robert Louis Stevenson. If you'd like to see Scott's pipe and Burns' snuffboxes, you'll love this little museum. Edinburgh's high society gathered in homes like this in the 1780s to hear the great poet Robbie Burns read his work—it's meant to be read aloud rather than to oneself. In the Burns room, you can hear his poetry—worth a few minutes for anyone, and essential for fans.

Cost and Hours: Free, Mon-Sat 10:00-17:00, closed Sun

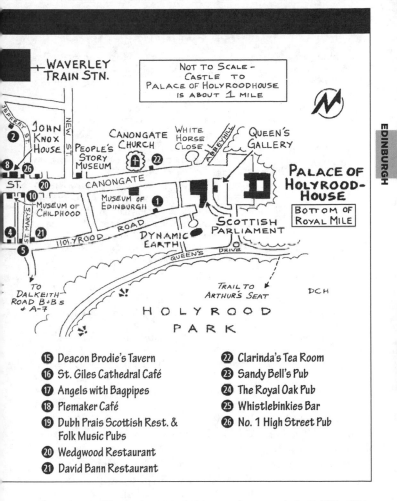

→ WAVERLEY TRAIN STN.

NOT TO SCALE —
CASTLE TO
PALACE OF HOLYROODHOUSE
IS ABOUT 1 MILE

JEFFERY ST.

2 JOHN KNOX HOUSE
NEW ST.
PEOPLE'S STORY MUSEUM
CANONGATE CHURCH
WHITE HORSE CLOSE
ABBEYHILL
QUEEN'S GALLERY

8 26
ST.
20
CANONGATE
22
PALACE OF HOLYROOD-HOUSE

10 MUSEUM OF CHILDHOOD
MUSEUM OF EDINBURGH
1
BOTTOM OF ROYAL MILE

4 ST. MARY'S ST.
21
HOLYROOD ROAD
SCOTTISH PARLIAMENT

5
DYNAMIC EARTH

QUEEN'S DRIVE

TO DALKEITH ROAD B+Bs & A-7

TRAIL TO ARTHUR'S SEAT
DCH

H O L Y R O O D
P A R K

15 Deacon Brodie's Tavern
16 St. Giles Cathedral Café
17 Angels with Bagpipes
18 Piemaker Café
19 Dubh Prais Scottish Rest. & Folk Music Pubs
20 Wedgwood Restaurant
21 David Bann Restaurant

22 Clarinda's Tea Room
23 Sandy Bell's Pub
24 The Royal Oak Pub
25 Whistlebinkies Bar
26 No. 1 High Street Pub

except during Festival 12:00-17:00, no photos, tel. 0131/529-4901, www.edinburghmuseums.org.uk.

Whiski Rooms Shop

The knowledgeable, friendly staff in this shop just off the Royal Mile happily assists novices and experts alike to select the right bottle. Their bar usually has about 200 open bottles—and if you are a serious purchaser, you can get a sample. Even better, try one of their tasting flights, which include four tastes and a £5 voucher toward purchasing a bottle: Intro to Whisky (£17.50); Premium Tasting (£35—the really good stuff); Whisky and Chocolate or Whisky and Cheese (£22.50). Tastings are offered during store hours and last about an hour; call ahead to reserve, especially in peak season.

Scotland's Literary Greats

Edinburgh was home to Scotland's three greatest literary figures: Robert Burns, Robert Louis Stevenson, and Sir Walter Scott.

Robert Burns (1759-1796), quite possibly the most famous and beloved Scot of all time, moved to Edinburgh after achieving overnight celebrity with his first volume of poetry (staying in a house on the spot where Deacon Brodie's Tavern now stands). Even though he wrote in the rough Scots dialect and dared to attack social rank, he was a favorite of Edinburgh's high society, who'd gather in fine homes to hear him recite his works. For more on Burns, see the sidebar on page 6.

One hundred years later, **Robert Louis Stevenson** (1850-1894) also stirred the Scottish soul with his pen. An avid traveler who always packed his notepad, Stevenson created settings that are vivid and filled with wonder. Traveling through Scotland, Europe, and around the world, he distilled his adventures into Romantic classics, including *Kidnapped* and *Treasure Island* (as well as *The Strange Case of Dr. Jekyll and Mr. Hyde*). Stevenson, who was married in San Francisco and spent his last years in the South Pacific, wrote, "Youth is the time to travel—both in mind and in body—to try the manners of different nations." He said, "I travel not to go anywhere...but to simply go." Travel was his inspiration and his success.

Sir Walter Scott (1771-1832) wrote the *Waverley* novels, including *Ivanhoe* and *Rob Roy*. He's considered the father of the Romantic historical novel. Through his writing, he generated

---

Cost and Hours: Daily 10:00-19:00, later in Aug, 4-7 North Bank Street, tel. 0131/225-1532, www.whiskirooms.com.

Museum on the Mound

Located in the basement of the grand Bank of Scotland building (easily spotted from a distance), this exhibit tells the story of the bank, which was founded in 1695 (making it only a year younger than the Bank of England, and the longest operating bank in the world). Featuring displays on cash production, safe technology, and bank robberies, this museum struggles mightily, with some success, to make banking interesting (the case holding £1 million is cool). It's worth popping in if you have some time or find the subject appealing. But no matter how well the information is presented, it's still about...yawn...banking.

Cost and Hours: Free, Tue-Fri 10:00-17:00, Sat-Sun 13:00-17:00, closed Mon, down Bank Street from the Royal Mile—follow the street around to the left and enter through the gate, tel. 0131/243-5464, www.museumonthemound.com.

a worldwide interest in Scotland, and re-awakened his fellow countrymen's pride in their inheritance. His novels helped revive interest in Highland culture—the Gaelic language, kilts, songs, legends, myths, the clan system—and created a national identity. An avid patriot, he wrote, "Every Scottish man has a pedigree. It is a national prerogative, as unalienable as his pride and his poverty." Scott is so revered in Edinburgh that his towering Neo-Gothic monument dominates the city center. With his favorite hound by his side, Sir Walter Scott overlooks the city that he inspired, and that inspired him.

The best way to learn about and experience these literary greats is to visit the Writers' Museum at Lady Stair's House (see page 46) and to take Edinburgh's Literary Pub Tour (see page 77).

While just three writers dominate your Edinburgh sightseeing, consider also the other great writers with Edinburgh connections: J.K. Rowling (who captures the "Gothic" spirit of Edinburgh with her Harry Potter series); current resident Ian Rankin (with his "tartan noir" novels); J.M. Barrie (who attended University of Edinburgh and later created Peter Pan); Sir Arthur Conan Doyle (who was born in Edinburgh, went to medical school here, and is best known for inventing Sherlock Holmes); and James Boswell (who lived 50 yards away from the Writers' Museum, in James Court, and is revered for his biography of Samuel Johnson).

▲▲St. Giles Cathedral

This is Scotland's most important church. Its ornate spire—the Scottish crown steeple from 1495—is a proud part of Edinburgh's skyline. The fascinating interior contains nearly 200 memorials honoring distinguished Scots through the ages.

Cost and Hours: Free but donations encouraged, audioguide-£3, £2 to take photos; Mon-Sat 9:00-17:00 (until 19:00 Mon-Fri May-Sept), Sun 13:00-17:00; tel. 0131/225-9442, www.stgiles cathedral.org.uk.

Concerts: St. Giles' busy concert schedule includes organ recitals and visiting choirs (frequent free events at 12:15, concerts often Wed at 20:00 and Sun at 18:00, see schedule or ask for *Music at St. Giles* pamphlet in gift shop).

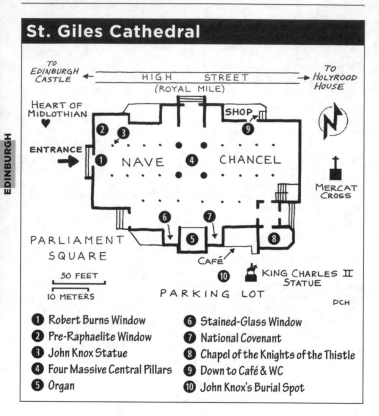

St. Giles Cathedral

1. Robert Burns Window
2. Pre-Raphaelite Window
3. John Knox Statue
4. Four Massive Central Pillars
5. Organ
6. Stained-Glass Window
7. National Covenant
8. Chapel of the Knights of the Thistle
9. Down to Café & WC
10. John Knox's Burial Spot

➔ **Self-Guided Tour:** Today's facade is 19th-century Neo-Gothic, but most of what you'll see inside is from the 14th and 15th centuries. You'll also find cathedral guides trolling around, hoping you'll engage them in conversation. You'll be glad you did.

Just inside the entrance, turn around to see the modern stained-glass **Robert Burns window,** which celebrates Scotland's favorite poet. It was made in 1985 by the Icelandic artist Leifur Breidfjord. The green of the lower level symbolizes the natural world—God's creation. The middle zone with the circle shows the brotherhood of man—Burns was a great internationalist. The top is a rosy red sunburst of creativity, reminding Scots of Burns' famous line, "My love is like a red, red rose"—part of a song near and dear to every Scottish heart.

To the right of the Burns window is a fine **Pre-Raphaelite window.** Like most in the church, it's a memorial to an important patron (in this case, John Marshall). From here stretches a great swath of war memorials.

As you walk along the north wall, find **John Knox's statue** (standing like a six-foot-tall bronze chess piece.) Look into his eyes for 10 seconds from 10 inches away, and think of the Reformation struggles of the 16th century. Knox, the great religious reformer and founder of austere Scottish Presbyterianism, first preached here in 1559. His insistence that every person should be able to personally read the word of God gave Scotland an educational system 300 years ahead of the rest of Europe. Thanks partly to Knox, it was Scottish minds that led the way in math, science, medicine, and engineering. Voltaire called Scotland "the intellectual capital of Europe."

Knox preached Calvinism. Consider that the Dutch and the Scots both embraced this creed of hard work, frugality, and strict ethics. This helps explain why the Scots are so different from the English (and why the Dutch and the Scots—both famous for their thriftiness and industriousness—are so much alike).

The oldest parts of the cathedral—the **four massive central pillars**—are Norman and date from the 12th century. They supported a mostly wooden superstructure that was lost when an invading English force burned in 1385. The Scots rebuilt it bigger and better than ever, and in 1495 its famous crown spire was completed.

During the Reformation—when Knox preached here (1559-1572)—the place was simplified and whitewashed. Before this, when the emphasis was on holy services provided by priests, there were lots of little niches. With the new focus on sermons rather than rituals, the grand pulpit took center stage.

Knox preached against anything that separated you from God, including stained glass (considered the poor man's Bible, as illiterate Christians could learn from its pictures). Knox had the church's fancy medieval glass windows replaced with clear glass, but 19th-century Victorians took them out and installed the brilliantly colored ones you see today.

Cross over to the **organ** (1992, Austrian-built, one of Europe's finest) and take in its sheer might.

Immediately to the right of the organ (as you're facing it) is a tiny chapel for silence and prayer. The dramatic **stained-glass window** above shows the commotion that surrounded Knox when

he preached. Bearded, fiery-eyed Knox had a huge impact on this community. Notice how there were no pews back then. The church was so packed, people even looked through clear windows from across the street. With his hand on the holy book, Knox seems to conduct divine electricity to the Scottish faithful.

To the left of the organ as you face it, in the next alcove, is a copy of the **National Covenant.** It was signed in blood in 1638 by Scottish heroes who refused to compromise their religion for the king's. Most who signed were martyred (their monument is nearby in Grassmarket).

Head toward the east (back) end of the church, and turn right to see the Neo-Gothic **Chapel of the Knights of the Thistle** (£2 donation requested) and its intricate wood carving. Built in two years (1910-1911), entirely with Scottish materials and labor, it is the private chapel of the Knights of the Thistle, the only Scottish chivalric order. It's used about once a year to inaugurate new members. Scotland recognizes its leading citizens by bestowing a membership upon them. The Queen presides over the ritual from her fancy stall, marked by her Scottish coat of arms—a heraldic zoo of symbolism. Are there bagpipes in heaven? Find the tooting angel at the top of a window to the left of the altar.

Downstairs (enter stairs near the chapel entry) is an inviting, recommended café, along with handy public toilets.

Old Parliament House

The building now holds the civil law courts, so you'll need to go through security first. Step in to see the grand hall, with its fine 1639 hammer-beam ceiling and stained glass. This space housed the Scottish parliament until the Act of Union in 1707. Find the big stained-glass depiction of the initiation of the first Scottish High Court in 1532. The building now holds the civil law courts and is busy with wigged and robed lawyers hard at work in the old library (peek through the door) or pacing the hall deep in discussion. The cleverly named Writz Café, in the basement, is literally their supreme court's restaurant (cheap, Mon-Fri 9:00-14:00, closed Sat-Sun).

Cost and Hours: Free, public welcome Mon-Fri 9:00-16:30, closed Sat-Sun, no photos, borrow info sheet at security for more information, enter behind St. Giles Cathedral; open-to-the-public trials are just across the street at the High Court—the doorman has the day's docket.

▲Mary King's Close

For an unusual peek at Edinburgh's gritty, plague-ridden past, join a costumed performer on an hour-long trip through an excavated underground street and buildings on the northern slope of the Royal Mile. Tours cover the standard goofy, crowd-pleasing ghost stories, but also provide authentic and historical insight into a part of town entombed by later construction. It's best to book (and pay) ahead by phone or on their website (or drop by in person for a same-day booking)—even though tours leave every 20 minutes, groups are small and the sight is popular.

Cost and Hours: £13; April-Oct daily 10:00-21:00, Aug until

23:00; Nov-March daily 10:00-17:00, Fri-Sat until 21:00; these are last tour times, no kids under 5, across from St. Giles at 2 Warriston's Close, tel. 0845-070-6244, www.realmarykingsclose .com.

▲Museum of Childhood

This five-story playground of historical toys and games is rich in nostalgia and history. Each well-signed gallery is as jovial as a Norman Rockwell painting, highlighting the delights and simplicity of childhood. The museum does a fair job of representing culturally relevant oddities, such as ancient Egyptian, Peruvian, and voodoo dolls, and displays early versions of toys it's probably best didn't make the final cut (a grim snake-centered precursor to the popular board game Chutes and Ladders is one example).

Cost and Hours: Free, Mon-Sat 10:00-17:00, Sun 12:00-17:00, last entry 15 minutes before closing.

▲John Knox House

Intriguing for Reformation buffs, this fine medieval house dates back to 1470 and offers a well-explained look at the life of the great

16th-century reformer. Although most contend he never actually lived here, preservationists called it "Knox's house" to save it from the wrecking ball in the 1840s.

Regardless, the place has good information on Knox and his intellectual sparring partner, Mary, Queen of Scots. Imagine—even though it likely never happened—the Protestant firebrand John Knox and the devout Catholic Mary sitting face to face in these old rooms, discussing the most intimate matters of their spiritual lives as they decided the course of Scotland's religious future.

The house contains some period furniture, and on the top floor there's a fun photo op with a dress-up cape, hat, and feather pen.

Cost and Hours: £5, Mon-Sat 10:00-18:00, closed Sun except in July-Aug 12:00-18:00, 43 High Street, tel. 0131/556-9579, www .tracscotland.org.

Lickety Splits Gallery

This quirky shop is part art, part candy, and completely full of character. Naomi, who claims to specialize in all things sweet, stocks her shelves with traditional candies and local crafts, and shares fascinating historical tidbits on the origins of your favorite childhood treats—such as the scandal over how Chelsea Whoppers became Tootsie Rolls. Candy lovers can mix and match a little bag of goodies to go.

Cost and Hours: Free entry, Mon-Sat 11:00-17:30, Sun 12:00-16:00, mobile 0753-575-4299, 6 Jeffrey Street, www.licketysplits gallery.co.uk.

▲Cadenhead's Whisky Shop

The shop is not a tourist sight. Founded in 1842, this firm prides itself on bottling good whisky straight from casks at the distilleries, without all the compromises that come with profitable mass production (coloring with sugar to fit the expected look, watering down to lessen the alcohol tax, and so on). Those drinking from Cadenhead-bottled whiskies will enjoy the pure product as the distilleries' owners themselves do, not as the sorry public does.

Mark, Neil, and Alan happily explain the sometimes-complex whisky storyboard and talk you through flavor profiles. Mark is amazing with analogies (for example, "A single cask whisky is like a football team where all the players come from the same town."). Buy the right bottle to enjoy in your hotel room night after night (prices start around £13 for about 7 ounces). Unlike wine, whisky has a long shelf life after it's opened. The bottles are extremely durable—just ask the staff to demonstrate (but get a second cap and twist off carefully, as they can break). They host whisky tastings a couple of times a month (posted in the shop)—a hit with aficionados.

Cost and Hours: Free entry, Mon-Sat 10:30-17:30, closed Sun, 172 Canongate, tel. 0131/556-5864, www.wmcadenhead.com.

▲People's Story Museum

This interesting exhibition traces the working and social lives of ordinary people through the 18th, 19th, and 20th centuries. You'll see objects related to important Edinburgh trades (printing, brewing), tools and the finished products made with them, a wartime kitchen, and even a former jail, an original part of the historic building (the Canongate Tolbooth, built in 1591).

Cost and Hours: Free, Mon-Sat 10:00-17:00, closed Sun except during Festival 12:00-17:00, last entry 15 minutes before closing, 163 Canongate, tel. 0131/529-4057, www.edinburghmuseums .org.uk.

▲Museum of Edinburgh

Another old house full of old stuff, this one is worth a look for its early Edinburgh history and handy ground-floor WC. Be sure to see the original copy of the National Covenant (written in 1638 on an animal skin), sketches of pre-Georgian Edinburgh (which show a lake, later filled in to become Princes Street Gardens when the New Town was built), and early golf balls. A favorite Scottish say-it-aloud joke: "Balls," said the queen. "If I had two, I'd be king." The king laughed—he had to.

Cost and Hours: Free, same hours as People's Story Museum—listed above, 142 Canongate, tel. 0131/529-4143, www

.edinburghmuseums.org.uk.

▲▲Scottish Parliament Building

Scotland's parliament originated in 1293 and was dissolved when

Scotland united with England in 1707. But after the Scottish electorate and the British parliament gave their consent, in 1998 it was decided that there would be "a Scottish parliament guided by justice, wisdom, integrity, and compassion." Formally reconvened by Queen Elizabeth after elections in 1999, the Scottish parliament now enjoys self-rule (except for matters of defense, foreign policy, immigration, and taxation). The current government, run by the Scottish Nationalist Party, is pushing for more independence.

The innovative building, opened in 2004, brought together all the functions of the fledgling parliament in one complex. It's a people-oriented structure (conceived by Catalan architect Enric Miralles). Signs are written in both English and Gaelic (the Scots' Celtic tongue).

For a peek at the building and a lesson in how the Scottish

parliament works, drop in, pass through security, and find the visitors' desk. You're welcome into the public parts of the building, including a viewing gallery overlooking the impressive Debating Chambers, and anyone can attend committee meetings.

Cost and Hours: Free; in-session hours: Mon, Fri-Sat 10:00-17:00, Tue-Thu 9:00-18:30, recess hours (including July-Aug and other holidays): Mon-Sat 10:00-17:00, closed Sun year-round; last entry 30 minutes before closing, www.scottish.parliament.uk. For a complete list of recess dates or to book tickets for debates, check their website or call their visitors services line at tel. 0131/348-5200.

Tours: Worthwhile hour-long tours by proud locals are offered (free, 2/hour, usually when parliament is recessed). While you can just drop in, it's best to call or check online for times and reserve a spot.

Seeing Parliament in Session: You can call or sign up online to witness the Scottish parliament's hugely popular debates (usually Tue-Thu 14:00-18:00). On Thursdays from 12:00-12:30 the First Minister is on the hot seat and has to field questions from members across all parties.

▲Palace of Holyroodhouse

Founded as a monastery in 1128, this palace was the true home, birthplace, and coronation spot of Scottish kings in their heyday (James IV, Mary, Queen of Scots, and Charles I). It's particularly memorable as the site of some dramatic moments from the short reign of Mary, Queen of Scots—including the murder of her personal secretary, David Rizzio, by agents of her jealous husband. Today, it's one of the Queen's official residences. She generally stops here on the way to vacationing at Balmoral Palace.

Consider touring the interior. The building, rich in history and decor, is filled with elegantly furnished Victorian rooms and a few darker, older rooms with glass cases of historic bits and Scottish pieces that locals find fascinating.

Bring the palace to life with the included one-hour audioguide. You'll learn which of the kings featured in the 110 portraits lining the Great Gallery are real and which are fictional, what touches were added to the bedchambers to flatter King Charles II, and why the exiled Comte d'Artois took refuge in the palace. You'll also hear a goofy reenactment of the moment when conspirators stormed into the chambers of Mary, Queen of Scots, and stabbed her male secretary 56 times.

Cost and Hours: £11 includes a quality audioguide, £15.50 combo-ticket includes Queen's Gallery—listed below, tickets sold in Queen's Gallery (see below), daily April-Oct 9:30-18:00, Nov-March until 16:30, last entry an hour and a half before closing, tel. 0131/556-5100, www.royalcollection.org.uk. It's still a working palace, so it's closed when the Queen or other VIPs are in residence.

Palace Gardens: After exiting the palace, you're free to stroll through the ruined abbey (destroyed by the English during the time of Mary, Queen of Scots, in the 16th century) and the palace gardens (closed in winter). The Queen hosts a magnificent tea party here every July, with honored ladies sporting fancy hats. For a 30-minute guided tour of the garden, check at the ticket office on entry to the palace (£3.75, daily May-Sept 10:00-17:00).

Nearby: Hikers—note that the wonderful trail up Arthur's Seat starts just across the street from the gardens.

Queen's Gallery

This small museum features rotating exhibits of artwork from the royal collection. For more than five centuries, the royal family has amassed a wealth of art treasures. While the Queen keeps most in her many private palaces, she shares an impressive load of it here, with exhibits changing about every six months. Though the

gallery occupies just a few rooms, its displays can be exquisite. The entry fee includes an excellent audioguide, written and read by the curator.

Cost and Hours: £6.25, £15.50 combo-ticket includes Palace of Holyroodhouse, daily April-Oct 9:30-18:00, Nov-March until 16:30, café, last entry one hour before closing, on the palace grounds, to the right of the palace entrance, www.royalcollection .org.uk. Buses #35 and #36 stop outside, and can save you a walk to or from Princes Street/North Bridge.

Sights South of the Royal Mile
▲▲▲ National Museum of Scotland

This huge museum has amassed more historic artifacts than every other place I've seen in Scotland combined. It's all wonderfully

displayed, with fine descriptions offering a best-anywhere hike through the history of Scotland.

The place gives you two museums in one. One wing houses a popular natural history collection, with everything from kid-friendly T-Rex skeletons to Egyptian mummies. But we'll focus on the other wing, which sweeps you through Scottish history from prehistory until today, covering Roman and Viking times, Edinburgh's witch-burning craze and clan massacres, the struggle for Scottish independence, the Industrial Revolution, and right up to Scotland in the 21st century.

Cost and Hours: Free, daily 10:00-17:00; free one-hour "Highlights" tours daily at 11:00 and 15:00, themed tours at 13:00—confirm tour schedule at info desk or on TV screens; two long blocks south of St. Giles Cathedral and the Royal Mile, on Chambers Street off George IV Bridge, tel. 0131/247-4422, www .nms.ac.uk.

Eating: On the museum's top floor, the dressy and upscale **Tower restaurant** serves good food with a castle view (£16 two-course lunch special served 12:00-18:30, £16 afternoon tea 14:30-17:30, £33 three-course dinner special, fancy £18-25 meals, open daily 12:00-23:00—later than the museum itself, tel. 0131/225-3003).

○ Self-Guided Tour: Get oriented on level 1, in the impressive glass-roofed Grand Gallery. This part of the building houses the natural history collection. To reach the Scottish history wing, exit the Grand Gallery at the far right end, under the clock. Pause in the "Connect" hall long enough to find Dolly the sheep—the world's first cloned mammal—born in Edinburgh and now stuffed and on display.

Continue into Hawthornden Court (level 1), where our tour begins. (It's possible to detour downstairs from here to level -1 for Scotland's prehistoric origins—geologic formation, Celts, Romans, Vikings.)

Kingdom of the Scots (c.1300-1700): From its very start, Scotland was determined to be free. You're greeted with proud quotes from what's been called the Scottish Declaration of Independence—the Declaration of Arboath, a defiant letter written to the pope in 1320. As early as the ninth century, Scotland's patron saint, Andrew (see the small statue), had—according to legend—miraculously intervened to help the Picts of Scotland remain free by defeating the Angles of England. Andrew's X-shaped cross still decorates the Scottish flag today.

Turning right, enter the first room on your right, with swords, battle-axes, and objects related to Scotland's most famous patriots—William ("Braveheart") Wallace and Robert the Bruce. Bruce's family, the Stuarts (or "Stewarts"), went on to rule Scotland for the next 300 years. Eventually, James I (see his baby cradle) came to rule England as well.

In the next room, a big guillotine recalls the harsh justice meted out to criminals, witches, and "Covenanters" (politically active Protestants who didn't want to conform with the Church of England). Also check out the tomb (a copy) of Mary, Queen of Scots, the Stuart monarch who opposed those Protestants. Educated and raised in Renaissance France, Mary brought refinement to the Scottish throne. After she was imprisoned and then executed by the English in 1587, her countrymen rallied each other by  invoking her memory. Pendants and coins with her portrait stoked the irrepressible Scottish spirit. Near the replica of Mary's tomb are tiny cameos, pieces of jewelry, and coins with her image.

Browse the rest of level 1 to see everyday medieval objects—carved panels, cookware, and clothes.

• *Backtrack to Hawthornden Court and take the elevator to level 3.*

Scotland Transformed (1700s): You'll see artifacts related to Bonnie Prince Charlie and the Jacobite Rebellion as well as the ornate Act of Union document, signed in 1707 by the Scottish parliament. This act voluntarily united Scotland with England under the single parliament of Great Britain. For some Scots, this move was an inevitable step in connecting to the wider world, but for others it symbolized the end of Scotland's existence.

Union with England brought stability and investment to Scotland. In this same era, the advances of the Industrial Revolution were making a big impact on Scottish life. Mechanized textile looms (on display) replaced hand craftsmanship. The huge Newcomen steam-engine water pump helped the mining industry to develop sites with tricky drainage. (The museum puts the device in motion twice a day, around 11:15 and 14:15.) Nearby is a model of a coal mine (or "colliery"); coal-rich Scotland exploited this natural resource to fuel its textile factories.

How the parsimonious Scots financed these new, large-scale enterprises is explained in an exhibit on the Bank of Scotland. Powered by the Scottish work ethic and the new opportunities that came from the Industrial Revolution, the country came into relative prosperity. Education and medicine thrived. With the dawn of the modern age came leisure time, the concept of "healthful sports," and golf—a Scottish invention. The first golf balls, which date from about 1820, were leather stuffed with feathers.

• *Return to the elevator and journey up to level 5.*

Industry and Empire (1800s): Circle around to survey Scottish life in the 19th century. Industry had transformed the country. Highland farmers left their land to find work in Lowland factories and foundries. Modern inventions—the phonograph, the steam-powered train—revolutionized everyday life. Scotland was at the forefront of literature (Robert Burns, Sir Walter Scott, Robert Louis Stevenson, the first printing of the Encyclopedia Britannica) and world exploration (David Livingstone in Africa, Sir Alexander Mackenzie in Canada).

• *Climb the stairs to level 6.*

Scotland: A Changing Nation (1900s): The two world wars did a number on Scotland, decimating the population of this already wee nation. In addition, hundreds of thousands emigrated, especially to Canada (where one in eight Canadians has Scottish origins). The small country has made a big mark on the world: In the Sports Hall of Fame you'll see the pioneers of modern golf (Tom Morris, from St. Andrews), auto racing (Jackie Stewart and Jim Clark), and a signed baseball by Glasgow-born Bobby (1951 home run) Thomson. Finally, you'll learn how Scots have gone global in the world of entertainment, from early boy band Bay City Rollers to funk masters Average White Band to the Proclaimers ("I Would Walk 500 Miles") to actor-comedians Billy Connolly and Craig Ferguson.

• *Finish your visit on level 7, the rooftop.*

Garden Terrace: Don't miss the great views of Edinburgh from this well-described roof garden, growing grasses and heathers from every corner of Scotland.

EDINBURGH

Greyfriars Bobby

This famous statue of Edinburgh's favorite dog is across the street from the National Museum of Scotland. Every business nearby, it seems, is named for this Victorian Skye terrier, who is reputed to have stood by his master's grave in Greyfriars Cemetery for 14 years. The story was immortalized in a 1960s Disney flick, but recent research suggests that 19th-century businessmen bribed a stray to hang out in the cemetery to attract sightseers. If it was a ruse, it still works.

Grassmarket

Once Edinburgh's site for hangings (residents rented out their windows—above the rudely named "Last Drop" pub—for the view), today Grassmarket is being renovated into a people-friendly piazza. It was originally the city's garage, a depot for horses and cows (hence the name). It's rowdy here at night—a popular place for "hen" and "stag" parties. In the early evening, the literary pub tour departs from here. Budget shoppers might want to look at W. Armstrong & Son, a fun vintage-clothing store. Victoria Street, built in the Victorian Age, is lined with colorful little shops and eateries.

Hiding in the blur of traffic is a monument to the "Covenanters." These strict 17th-century Scottish Protestants were killed for refusing to accept the king's Episcopalian prayer book. To this day, Scots celebrate their emphatically democratic church government. Rather than big-shot bishops (as in the Anglican or Roman Catholic churches), they have a low-key "moderator" who's elected each year.

Dynamic Earth

Located about a five-minute walk from the Palace of Holyroodhouse, this immense exhibit tells the story of our planet, filling

several underground floors under a vast, white Gore-Tex tent. It's pitched, appropriately, at the base of the Salisbury Crags. The exhibit is designed for younger kids and does the same thing an American science exhibit would do—but with a charming Scottish accent. Standing in a time tunnel, you watch the years rewind from Churchill to dinosaurs to the Big Bang. After viewing several short films on stars, tectonic plates, ice caps, and worldwide weather (in a "4-D" exhibit), you're free to wander past salty pools, a re-created rain forest, and various TV screens.

Cost and Hours: £11.50, daily 10:00-17:30, July-Aug until 18:00, Nov-March closed Mon-Tue, last admission at 16:00, on Holyrood Road, between the palace and mountain, tel. 0131/550-7800, www.dynamicearth.co.uk. Dynamic Earth is a stop on the hop-on, hop-off bus route.

Bonnie Wee Sights in the New Town

The New Town itself is worth a wander. Here's an overview, along with some of the sights you'll see as you stroll. Save energy for the two major museums—the Scottish National Gallery and the Scottish National Portrait Gallery—which are covered in the next section.

▲▲Georgian New Town

The grid-planned new town, laid out in 1776 when George III was king, was a model of urban planning in its day. And it came with a clear message: to celebrate the union of Scotland with England into the United Kingdom. St. Andrew Square (patron saint of Scotland) and Charlotte Square (George III's queen) bookend the New Town with its three main streets named for the royal family of the time (George, Queen, and Princes). Thistle and Rose streets are named for the national flowers of Scotland and England.

The plan for the New Town was the masterstroke of the 23-year-old urban designer James Craig. George Street—20 feet wider than the others (so a four-horse carriage could make a U-turn)—was the main drag. Running down the high spine of the area, it afforded grand, unobstructed views (thanks to the parks on either side) of the River Forth in one direction and the Old Town in the other.

While Princes Street—busy with buses and taxis—has gone down-market, George Street still maintains its old grace. Mostly pedestrianized Rose Street is famous for its rowdy pubs. Sprinkled with popular restaurants and bars, the stately New Town is turning trendy.

Jenners Department Store

As you're standing outside the venerable Jenners (on Rose Street, near St. Andrew Square and across from Sainsbury's supermarket), notice how statues of women support the building—just as real women support the business. The arrival of new fashions here was such a big deal in the old days that they'd announce it by flying flags on the Nelson Monument atop Calton Hill. Step inside. The central space—filled with a towering tree at Christmas—is classic Industrial Age architecture. The Queen's coat of arms high on the wall indicates she shops here.

Edinburgh's New Town

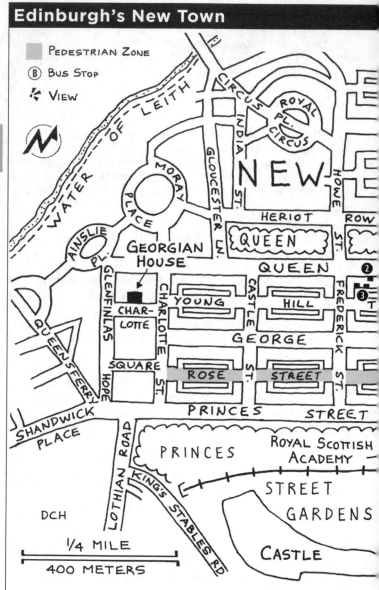

EDINBURGH

TO ROYAL BOTANIC GARDEN & BRITANNIA

DRUMMOND PLACE

GREAT KING ST.

DUNDAS ST.

TOWN

ABERCROMBY PL.

GARDENS

SCOTTISH NATIONAL PORTRAIT GALLERY

ST.

STREET

HANOVER ST.

STREET

HISTLE

STREET

DAVID ST.

ST. AND.

SQUARE

ROSE STREET

JENNERS DEP'T STORE

YORK PL.

TO ①

BUS STATION

LEITH ST.

PRINCES MALL

WATERLOO PL.

HALF-PRICE HUT

THE MOUND

SCOTT MON.

AIRLINK #100 Ⓑ

MARKET

WAVERLEY BR.

TATTOO TICKETS

ST.

COCKBURN

NORTH BRIDGE

BALMORAL HOTEL

CALTON RD.

Ⓑ ←TO DALKEITH ROAD

WAVERLEY TRAIN STN.

SCOTTISH NATIONAL GALLERY

N. BANK

ROYAL

JEFFREY

MILE

① To Holiday Inn Express Edinburgh City Centre & Central Youth Hostel

② Travelodges (4)

③ The Bon Vivant Rest. & Le Café St. Honoré

④ Café Royal

⑤ The Dome Restaurant

⑥ St. Andrew's & St. George's Church Undercroft Café

⑦ Henderson's Salad Table

⑧ Hanover St. Ethnic Eateries

⑨ M&S Food Hall

⑩ Sainsbury's Supermarket

St. Andrew Square

This green space is dedicated to the patron saint of Scotland. In the early 19th century, there were no shops around here—just fine residences; this was a private garden for the fancy people living here. Now open to the public, the square is a popular lunch hangout for workers. The Melville Monument honors a power-monger member of parliament who, for four decades (around 1800), was nicknamed the "uncrowned king of Scotland."

St. Andrew's and St. George's Church

Designed as part of the New Town in the 1780s, the church is a product of the Scottish Enlightenment. It has an elliptical plan (the first in Britain) so that all can focus on the pulpit. A fine leaflet tells the story of the church, and a handy cafeteria downstairs serves cheap and cheery lunches.

Cost and Hours: Free entry, Mon-Fri 10:00-15:00, 13 George Street, tel. 0131/225-3847.

Charlotte Square

The building of New Town started cheap with St. Andrew Square, but finished well with this stately square. In 1791 the Edinburgh town council asked the prestigious Scottish architect Robert Adam to pump up the design for Charlotte Square. The council hoped that Adam's plan would answer criticism that the New Town buildings lacked innovation or ambition, and they got what they wanted. Adam's design, which raised the standard of New Town architecture to "international class," created Edinburgh's finest Georgian square.

▲▲Georgian House

This refurbished Neoclassical house, set on Charlotte Square, is a trip back to 1796. It recounts the era when a newly gentrified and well-educated Edinburgh was nicknamed the "Athens of the North." A volunteer guide in each of the five rooms shares stories and trivia—from the kitchen in the basement to the fully stocked medicine cabinet in the bedroom. Start your visit in the basement and view the interesting 16-minute video, which shows the life of the first family who owned this property and touches on the architecture of the Georgian period. A walk down George Street after your visit here can be fun for the imagination.

Cost and Hours: £6.50, daily April-Oct 10:00-17:00, July-Aug until 18:00, March 11:00-16:00, Nov 11:00-15:00, last entry 30 minutes before closing, closed Dec-Feb, 7 Charlotte Square, tel. 0844-493-2117, www.nts.org.uk.

Princes Street Gardens

The grassy park, a former lakebed, separates Edinburgh's New and Old Towns and offers a wonderful escape from the bustle of the city. Once the private domain of the wealthy, it was opened to the public around 1870—not as a democratic gesture, but because it was thought that allowing the public into the park would increase sales for the Princes Street department stores. Join the office workers for a picnic lunch break, and don't miss the oldest floral clock in the world.

In summer, you can watch or join in **Scottish country dancing** in the park (£4, May-July Mon 19:30-21:30, at Ross Bandstand, also ask about summer dances held Tue at St. Peter's Church on Lutton Place—near recommended Dalkeith Road B&Bs, tel. 0131/228-8616, www.princesstreetgardensdancing.org.uk).

The big lake, **Nor' Loch,** was drained around 1800 as part of the Georgian expansion of Edinburgh. Before that, the lake was the town's sewer, water reservoir, and a handy place for drowning witches. Much was written about the town's infamous stink (a.k.a. the "flowers of Edinburgh"). The town's nickname, "Auld Reekie," referred to both the smoke of its industry and the stench of its squalor. Although the loch is now long gone, memories of the countless women drowned as witches remain. With their thumbs tied to their ankles, they'd be lashed to dunking stools. Those who survived the ordeal were considered "aided by the devil" and burned as witches. If they died, they were innocent and given a good Christian burial. Until 1720, Edinburgh was Europe's witch-burning mecca—any perceived "sign," including a small birthmark, could condemn you.

The Mound
The Scottish National Gallery sits upon what's known as "the Mound." When the Georgian New Town was built, tons of rubble from the excavations were piled into the Mound (1781-1830), forming a dirt bridge that would connect the new development with the Old Town and allay merchant concerns about being disconnected from the future heart of the city. The two fine Neoclassical buildings here (which house museums) date from the 1840s. From the Mound, you can enjoy fine views of medieval Edinburgh, with its 10-story-plus "skyscrapers."

▲Scott Monument
Built in 1840, this elaborate Neo-Gothic monument honors the great author Sir Walter Scott, one of Edinburgh's many illustrious sons. When Scott died in 1832, it was said that "Scotland never owed so much to one man." Scott almost singlehandedly created the "Scotland" we know. Just as the country was in danger of being assimilated into England, Scott celebrated its songs, legends, myths, and kilts, thereby reviving the Highland culture and cementing a national identity. And, as the father of the Romantic historical novel, he contributed to Western literature in general.

The 200-foot monument shelters a marble statue of Scott and his favorite pet, Maida, a deerhound who was one of 30 canines this dog lover owned during his lifetime. They're surrounded by busts of 16 great Scottish poets and 64 characters from his books. Climbing the tight, stony spiral staircase of 287 steps earns you a peek at a tiny museum midway, a fine city view at the top, and intimate encounters going up and down.

Cost and Hours: £4; daily April-Sept 10:00-19:00, Oct-March 10:00-16:00, last entry 30 minutes before closing, tel. 0131/529-4068, www.edinburghmuseums.org.uk.

Museums in the New Town
▲▲ Scottish National Gallery

This delightfully small museum has Scotland's best collection of paintings. In a short visit, you can admire works by Old Masters (Raphael, Rembrandt, Rubens), Impressionists (Monet, Degas, Gauguin), and underrated Scottish painters. Although there are no iconic masterpieces, it's a surprisingly enjoyable collection that's truly world class. There's no audioguide, but each painting is well described. If you can't find what you're looking for, ask one of the friendly tartan-sporting guards, or visit the info desk downstairs near the WCs and gallery shop.

Cost and Hours: Free, daily 10:00-17:00, Thu until 19:00, Fri-Wed in Aug until 18:00, photos OK unless noted, the Mound (between Princes and Market streets), tel. 0131/624-6200, www .nationalgalleries.org.

Next Door: The skippable **Royal Scottish Academy** hosts temporary art exhibits and is connected to the Scottish National Gallery at the garden level (underneath the gallery) by the Weston Link building (same hours as the gallery, fine café and restaurant).

◉ Self-Guided Tour: Start at the gallery entrance (at the north end of the building). Climb the stairs to the upper level (north end), and take a left. Ask the attendant to point out these three stars:

Van der Goes—*Trinity Altarpiece Panels* (c. 1478-1479): For more than five centuries, these panels have stood on this spot in Edinburgh—first in a church, then (when the church was leveled to build Waverley train station) in this museum. The panels likely flanked a central scene of the Virgin Mary that was destroyed by Protestant vandals during the Reformation.

In the left panel is the Trinity: God the Father, in a rich red robe, cradles a spindly, just-crucified Christ, while the dove of the Holy Spirit hovers between them. On the right, the church's director (the man who commissioned the painting from the well-known Flemish painter) kneels and looks on while an angel plays a hymn on the church organ. In typically medieval fashion, the details are meticulous—expressive faces, intricate folds in the robes, Christ's pallid skin, observant angels. The donor's face is a remarkable portrait, with realistic skin tone and a five-o'clock shadow. But the painting lacks true 3-D realism—God's gold throne is overly exaggerated, and Christ's cardboard-cutout body hovers weightlessly.

The flip side of the panels depicts Scotland's king and queen, who are best known to history as the parents of the boy kneeling alongside them. (You can ask the guard to open the panels.) He grew up to become James IV, the Renaissance king who made Edinburgh a cultural capital.

Botticelli—*The Virgin Adoring the Sleeping Christ Child* (c. 1490): Mary looks down at her baby, peacefully sleeping in a flower-filled garden. It's easy to appreciate Botticelli's masterful style: the precisely drawn outlines, the Virgin's pristine skin, the translucent glow. Botticelli creates a serene world in which no shadows are cast. The scene is painted on canvas—unusual at a time when wood panels were the norm. For the Virgin's rich cloak, Botticelli used ground-up lapis lazuli (a very pricey semiprecious stone), and her hem is decorated with gold leaf.

Renaissance-era art lovers would instantly catch the symbolism. Mary wears a wispy halo and blue cloak that recalls the sky blue of heaven. The roses without thorns and enclosed garden are both symbols of virginity, while the violet flowers (at bottom) represent humility. Darker symbolism hints at what's to come. The strawberries (lower right) signify Christ's blood, soon to be shed, while the roses—though thornless now—will become the Crown of Thorns. For now, Mary can adore her sleeping, blissful baby in a peaceful garden. But in a few decades she'll be kneeling again to weep over the dead, crucified Messiah.

Raphael—*Holy Family with a Palm Tree* (1506-1507): Mary, Joseph, and the Christ Child fit snugly within a round frame (a tondo), their pose symbolizing geometric perfection and the perfect family unit. Joseph kneels to offer Jesus flowers. Mary curves toward him. Baby Jesus dangles in between, linking the family together. Raphael also connects the figures through eye contact: Mary eyes Joseph, who locks onto Jesus, who gazes precociously back. Like in a cameo, we see the faces incised in profile, while their bodies bulge out toward us.

• *Back downstairs at ground level is the main gallery space. Again, ask the attendant to locate these three highlights:*

Rubens—*Feast of Herod* (c.1635-1638): All eyes turn to watch the dramatic culmination of the story of John the Baptist. Salome (standing in center) presents John's severed head on a platter to a horrified King Herod. Meanwhile, Herod's wife—who cooked up the nasty plot—pokes spitefully at John's head with a fork. A dog tugs at Herod's foot like a nasty conscience. The canvas—big, colorful, full of motion and drama—is totally Baroque. Some have suggested that the features of Herod's wife and Salome are those of Rubens' wife and ex-wives, and the head is Rubens himself.

Rembrandt—*Self-Portrait, Aged 51* (c. 1657): It's 1657, and 51-year-old Rembrandt has just declared bankruptcy. Besides financial hardship and the auctioning-off of his personal belongings, he's also facing social stigma and behind-the-back ridicule. Once Holland's most renowned painter, he's begun a slow decline into poverty and obscurity.

His face says it all. Holding a steady gaze, he stares with matter-of-fact acceptance, with his lips pursed. He's dressed in dark clothes against a dark background, with the only spot of light shining on the worry lines of his forehead. Get close enough to the canvas to see the thick paste of paint he used for the wrinkles around his eyes—a study in aging.

Gainsborough—*The Honorable Mrs. Graham* (1775-1777): The slender, elegant, lavishly dressed woman was the teenage bride of a wealthy Scottish landowner. She leans on a column, ostrich feather in hand, staring off to the side (thoughtfully? Determinedly? Haughtily?). Her faultless face and smooth neck stand out from the elaborately ruffled dress and background foliage. This 18th-century woman wears a silvery dress that echoes 17th-century style—Gainsborough's way of showing how, though she was young, she was classy. Thomas ("Blue Boy") Gainsborough—the product of a clothes-making father and a flower-painting mother—uses aspects of both in this lush portrait. The ruby brooch on her bodice marks the center of this harmonious composition.

• *Elsewhere on the ground floor, you'll find nice works by Bellini, Titian, Velázquez, and El Greco. Then climb the stairs to the upper level (south end) and turn right for the Impressionists and Post-Impressionists.*

Impressionist Collection: The gallery has a smattering of (mostly smaller-scale) works from all the main artists of the Impressionist and Post-Impressionist eras. You'll see Degas' ballet scenes, Renoir's pastel-colored family scenes, Van Gogh's peasants, and Seurat's pointillism.

Monet's *Poplars on the Epte* (1891) was part of the artist's famous "series" paintings. He set up several canvases in a floating studio near his home in Giverny. He'd start on one canvas in the morning (to catch the morning light), then move to the next as the light changed. This particular canvas captures a perfect summer day, showing both the poplars on the riverbank and their mirror image in the still water. The subject matter begins to dissolve into a pure pattern of color, anticipating abstract art.

Gauguin's *Vision of the Sermon* (1888) shows French peas-ant women imagining the miraculous event they've just heard preached about in church—when Jacob wrestles with an angel. The painting is a watershed in art history, as Gauguin throws out the rules of "realism" that had reigned since the Renaissance. The colors are surreal, there are no shadows, the figures are arranged almost randomly, and there's no attempt to make the wrestlers appear distant. The diagonal tree branch is the only thing separat-ing the everyday world from the miraculous. Later, when Gauguin moved to Tahiti (see his *Three Tahitians* nearby), he painted a simi-lar world, where the everyday and magical coexist, with symbolic power.

Sargent's *Lady Agnew of Lochnaw* (1892) is the work that launched the career of this American-born portrait artist. Lady Agnew—the young wife of a wealthy old Scotsman—lounges back languidly and gazes out self-assuredly. The Impressionistic smudges of paint on her dress and the chair contrast with her clear skin and luminous eyeballs. Her relaxed pose (one arm hanging down the side) contrasts with her intensity: head tilted slightly down while she gazes up, a corner of her mouth askew, and an eyebrow cocked seductively.

• *End your visit downstairs on the lower level, home to the...*

Scottish Collection: Though Scotland has produced few "name" painters, this small wing lets you sample some of the best. It's all in one room, designed to be toured chronologically (clockwise).

Allan Ramsay (son of the well-known poet Allan Ramsay) painted portraits of curly-wigged men of the Enlightenment era (the philosopher David Hume, King George III) as well as like-nesses of his two wives. Ramsay's portrait of the duke of Argyll (founder of the Royal Bank of Scotland) appears on the Scottish 5-pound note.

Sir Henry Raeburn chronicled the next generation: Sir Walter Scott, the proud kilt-wearing Alastair Macdonell, and the ice-skating Reverend Robert Walker, minister of the Canongate Church.

Sir David Wilkie's forte was small-scale scenes of everyday life. *The Letter of Introduction* (1813) captures Wilkie's own experi-ence of trying to impress skeptical art patrons in London; even the dog is sniffing the Scotsman out. *Distraining for Rent* (1815) shows the plight of a poor farmer about to lose his farm—a com-mon occurrence during 19th-century industrialization.

Pause and swoon before **William Dyce's** *Francesca da Rimini* (1837). The star-crossed lovers—a young wife and her husband's kid brother—can't help but indulge their passion. The husband later finds out and kills her; at the far left, you see his ominous hand.

Finally, take in **William McTaggart's** impressionistic landscape scenes from the late 1800s for a glimpse of the unique light, powerful clouds, and natural wonder of the Highlands.

▲▲Scottish National Portrait Gallery

Put a face on Scotland's history by enjoying these portraits of famous Scots from the earliest times until today. From its Neo-Gothic facade to a grand entry hall featuring a *Who's Who* of Scotland, to galleries highlighting the great Scots of each age, this impressive museum will fascinate anyone interested in Scottish culture. The gallery also hosts temporary exhibits highlighting the work of more contemporary Scots.

Cost and Hours: Free, daily 10:00-17:00, Thu until 19:00—when occasionally there is live music at 18:00; good cafeteria serving £5-7 soups, sandwiches, and heartier fare, café closes 30 minutes before museum; 1 Queen Street, tel. 0131/624-6490, www.nationalgalleries.org.

Visiting the Gallery: In the **entrance hall** you'll see a frieze showing a parade of great Scots and murals depicting important events in Scottish history. (These are better viewed from the first floor and its mezzanine—described later). We'll start on the **second floor**, right into the thick of the struggle between Scotland and England over who should rule this land.

Reformation to Revolution (gallery 1): The collection starts with a portrait of **Mary, Queen of Scots** (1542-1587), her cross and rosary prominent. This controversial ruler set off two centuries of strife. Mary was born with Stuart blood (the ruling family of Scotland) and the Tudor blood of England's monarchs (Queen Elizabeth I was her cousin). Catholic and French-educated, Mary was unpopular in her own increasingly Protestant homeland. Then came a series of scandals: She married unpopular Lord Darnley, then (possibly) cheated on him, causing Darnley to (possibly) murder her lover, causing Mary to (possibly) murder Darnley, then run off with another man, and (possibly) plot against Queen Elizabeth.

Amid all that drama, Mary was forced by her own people to abdicate in favor of her infant son, **James VI.** Find his portraits as a child and as a grown-up. James grew up to rule Scotland, and when Queen Elizabeth (the Virgin Queen) died without an heir, he also became king of England (James I). But James' son, **Charles I,** after a bitter civil war, was arrested and executed in 1649 (see the large *Execution of Charles I* painting high on the far wall), his blood-dripping head displayed to the crowd. Charles II (see portrait as 12-year-old boy) briefly restored the Stuarts to power before they were sent into exile in France. There the Stuarts stewed, planning a return to power, waiting for someone to lead them in what would come to be known as the Jacobite Rebellion.

The Jacobite Cause (gallery 4): The biggest painting in the room is *The Baptism of Prince Charles Edward Stuart*. Born in 1720, this heir to the thrones of Great Britain and Ireland is better known to history as "Bonnie Prince Charlie." (See his bonnie features in various portraits nearby, as a child, young man, and grown man.) Charismatic Charles convinced France to invade Scotland and put him back on the throne there. In 1745, he entered Edinburgh in triumph. But he was defeated at the tide-turning Battle of Culloden (1746). The Stuart cause died forever, and Bonnie Prince Charlie went into exile, eventually dying drunk and wasted in Rome, far from the land he nearly ruled.

Citizens of the World (galleries 5-6): The two biggest paintings here are of King George III and Queen Charlotte (namesakes of the New Town's main street and square). In the late 18th century, Scotland was doing just fine being ruled from England. Paintings here show the confidence of this age, when the New Town of Edinburgh was designed and built. In the 1760s, Edinburgh was the center of Europe's Enlightenment, powered by philosophers such as David Hume and his economist friend Adam Smith. Before moving on, find the portrait of Hume (by Allan Ramsay, who also painted the likeness of George III) and a cameo medallion of Smith.

The Age of Improvement (gallery 7): The faces portrayed here belonged to a new society whose hard work and public spirit achieved progress with a Scottish accent. Social equality and the Industrial Revolution "transformed" Scotland—you'll see portraits of the great poet Robert Burns, the son of a farmer (Burns was heralded as a "heaven-taught ploughman" when his poems were first published) and the inventor of the steam engine, James Watt.

Sports (gallery 10): Lighten things up with a swing through old-time sports in Scotland, including early golf, curling, Highland Games (including "putting the stone"—similar to shot put), fox hunting, and croquet.

Central Atrium (first floor): Great Scots! The atrium is decorated in a parade of late 19th-century Romantic Historicism. The **frieze** (working counterclockwise) is a visual encyclopedia, from an ax-wielding Stone Age man and a druid, to the early mythical monarchs (Macbeth), to warriors William Wallace and Robert the Bruce, to many kings (James I, II, III, and so on), to great thinkers, inventors, and artists (Allan Ramsay, Flora MacDonald, David Hume, Adam Smith, James Boswell, James Watt), the three greatest Scottish writers (Robert Burns, Sir Walter Scott,

Robert Louis Stevenson), and culminating with the poet Thomas Carlyle, who was the driving spirit (powered by the fortune of a local newspaper baron) behind creating this portrait gallery.

Best viewed from the first-floor mezzanine are the large-scale **murals** depicting great events in Scottish history, including the landing of St. Margaret at Queensferry in 1068, the Battle of Stirling Bridge in 1297, the Battle of Bannockburn in 1314, and the marriage procession of James IV and Margaret Tudor through the streets of Edinburgh in 1509.

The Modern Scot (gallery 11): Paintings on the first floor make it clear that Scotland continues to contribute. You'll see distinguished Scottish scientists such as physicist Peter Higgs, theorizer of the Higgs boson, the so-called God particle. He was researching at the University of Edinburgh in the 1960s when he speculated on the existence of a subatomic particle that might tie together many other theories on the structure of the universe. Nearby is the stirring *Three Oncologists*, a ghostly painting depicting the anxiety and terror of cancer and the dedication of those working so hard to conquer it.

Sights near Edinburgh
▲▲*Britannia*

This much-revered vessel, which transported Britain's royal family for more than 40 years on 900 voyages before being retired in 1997, is permanently moored at the Ocean Terminal Shopping Mall in Edinburgh's port of Leith. It's open to the public and worth the half-hour bus or taxi ride from the center; figure on spending about 2.5 hours total on the outing.

Cost and Hours: £12, daily July-Sept 9:30-16:30, April-June and Oct 9:30-16:00, Nov-March 10:00-15:30, these are last-entry times, tearoom, on Ocean Drive in Leith, tel. 0131/555-5566, www.royalyachtbritannia.co.uk.

Getting There: From central Edinburgh, catch Lothian bus #11, #22, or #35 at Waverley Bridge to Ocean Terminal. If you're doing a city bus tour, consider the Majestic Tour, which includes transportation to the *Britannia*. Entrance to the museum is on the second floor at the north (right) end of the shopping center.

Visiting the Ship: Explore the museum, filled with engrossing royal-family-afloat history. Then, armed with your included 90-minute audioguide, you're welcome aboard.

This was the last in a line of royal yachts that stretches back to 1660. With all its royal functions, the ship required a crew of more than 200. The captain's bridge feels like it's been preserved from the day it was launched in 1953. Queen Elizabeth II, who enjoyed the ship for 40 years, said, "This is the only place I can truly relax." The Sunny Lounge, just off the back Veranda Deck, was the Queen's favorite, with Burmese teak and the same phone system she was used to in Buckingham Palace.

The back deck was the favorite place for outdoor entertainment. Ronald Reagan, Boris Yeltsin, Bill Clinton, and Nelson Mandela all sipped champagne here with the Queen. When she wasn't entertaining, the Queen liked it quiet. The crew wore sneakers, communicated in hand signals, and (at least near the Queen's quarters) had to be finished with all their work by 8:00 in the morning.

The state dining room, decorated with gifts given by the ship's many noteworthy guests, enabled the Queen to entertain a good-size crowd. The silver pantry was just down the hall. The drawing room, while rather simple, was perfect for casual relaxing among royals. Princess Diana played the piano, which is bolted to the deck. Royal family photos evoke the fine times the Windsors enjoyed on the *Britannia*. Visitors can also see the crew's quarters and engine room.

Rosslyn Chapel
Founded in 1446 by the Sinclair family, this church is a fascinating riot of carved iconography. The patterned ceiling and walls have left scholars guessing about its symbolism for centuries, particularly questioning if there's a link to the Knights Templar and the Masons. But much of the speculation, especially the *Da Vinci Code* connections, has been debunked.

Cost and Hours: £9, Mon-Sat 9:30-18:00, until 17:00 Oct-March, Sun 12:00-16:45 year-round, last entry 30 minutes before closing, no photos, located in Roslin Village, www.rosslynchapel .org.uk.

Getting There: Ride Lothian **bus** #15 from the station at St. Andrew Square (1-2/hour, 45 minutes). By **car,** take the A-701 to Penicuik/Peebles, and follow signs for *Roslin;* once you're in the village, you'll see signs for the chapel.

Royal Botanic Garden
Britain's second-oldest botanical garden (after Oxford) was established in 1670 for medicinal herbs, and this 70-acre refuge is now one of Europe's best.

Cost and Hours: Gardens free, greenhouse admission-£4.50, daily March-Sept 10:00-18:00, until 16:00 Nov-Jan, until 17:00 Feb and Oct, 1-hour tours April-Oct daily at 11:00 and 14:00 for £5, maps-£1, café, a mile north of the city center at Inverleith Row; tel. 0131/552-7171, www.rbge.org.uk.

Getting There: It's a 10-minute bus ride from the city center: Take Lothian bus #8 from North Bridge, #23 from the Mound, or #27 from George IV Bridge; Majestic Tour also stops here.

EDINBURGH

Scottish National Gallery of Modern Art

This museum, set in a beautiful parkland, houses Scottish and international paintings and sculpture from 1900 to the present, including works by Matisse, Duchamp, Picasso, and Warhol. The grounds include a pleasant outdoor sculpture park and a café.

Cost and Hours: Free, daily 10:00-17:00, Aug until 18:00, 75 Belford Road, tel. 0131/624-6336, www.nationalgalleries.org.

Getting There: It's about a 20-minute walk west from the city center. Public transportation options aren't good, but a free shuttle bus runs about every half-hour between this museum and the Scottish National Gallery (daily 11:00-18:00, confirm times on website).

Activities in Edinburgh

▲▲Arthur's Seat Hike

A 45-minute hike up the 822-foot remains of an extinct volcano (surrounded by a fine park overlooking Edinburgh) starts from the parking lot below the Palace of Holyroodhouse.

You can run up like they did in *Chariots of Fire,* or just stroll—at the summit, you'll be rewarded with commanding views of the town and surroundings. On May Day, be on the summit at dawn and wash your face in the morning dew to commemorate the Celtic holiday of Beltaine, the celebration of spring. (Morning dew is supposedly very good for your complexion.)

From the parking lot below the Palace of Holyroodhouse, there are two trailheads. Take the wide path on the left (easier grade, through the abbey ruins and "Hunter's Bog"). After making the summit, you can return along the other path (to the right, with the steps), which skirts the base of the cliffs.

Those staying at my recommended B&Bs can enjoy a pre-breakfast or late-evening hike starting from the other side (in June, the sun comes up early, and it stays light until nearly midnight). From the Commonwealth Pool, take Holyrood Park Road, turn right on Queen's Drive, and continue to a small parking lot. From here it's a 20-minute hike.

If you have a car, you can drive up most of the way from behind (follow the one-way street from the palace, park safely and for free by the little lake, and hike up).

More Hikes

You can hike along the river (called Water of Leith) through Edinburgh. Locals favor the stretch between Roseburn and Dean Village, but the 1.5-mile walk from Dean Village to the Royal

Botanic Garden is also good. For more information on these and other hikes, ask at the TI for the free *Walks In and Around Edinburgh* one-page flier (if it's unavailable, consider their £3 guide to walks).

Brush Skiing

If you like skiing, but not all that pesky snow, head a little south of town to Hillend, where the Midlothian Snowsports Centre has a hill with a chairlift, two slopes, a jump slope, and rentable skis, boots, and poles. It feels like snow-skiing on a slushy day, even though you're schussing over what seems like a million toothbrushes. Beware: Doctors are used to treating an ailment called "Hillend Thumb"—thumbs dislocated when people fall here and get tangled in the brush. Locals say that skiing here is like falling on a carrot grater.

Cost and Hours: £12/first hour, then £5.30/hour, includes gear, beginners must take a lesson, generally Mon-Tue 18:30-22:00, Wed 13:00-20:00, Thu-Fri 18:00-21:00, Sat-Sun 14:00-19:00—but call to confirm before showing up, probably closes if it snows, 40 minutes away on Lothian bus #4 or #15 from Princes Street—garden side, tel. 0131/445-4433, www.midlothian.gov.uk.

Royal Commonwealth Pool

This indoor fitness and activity complex on Dalkeith Road—in the shadow of Arthur's Seat—includes a 50-meter pool (bring a suit and towel), gym/fitness studio, café, and kids' soft play zone.

Cost and Hours: Pool day pass-£5.80 for individual or £13.70 for families, gym pass-£7, £21 for family swim and soft play package; Mon-Fri 5:30-22:00, Sat 5:30-20:00, Sun 7:30-20:00; open swim nearly all the time but not Sat-Sun after 13:00; lockers available; tel. 0131/667-7211, www.edinburghleisure.co.uk.

Prestonfield Golf Club

The club has golfers feeling like they're in a country estate. A dress code is enforced—no jeans, shorts, T-shirts, sweats, or tennis shoes. It's at the foot of Arthur's Seat, a mile and a half from town (and easy walking distance from my recommended Dalkeith Road B&Bs).

Cost and Hours: £32-38/person plus £15-20 for clubs, cart-£3 (pull) or £22 (power); 6 Priestfield Road North, tel. 0131/667-9665, www.prestonfieldgolf.com.

Shopping

The streets to browse are Princes Street (the elegant old Jenners department store is close by on Rose Street, near St. Andrew Square), Victoria Street (antiques galore), Nicolson Street (south of the Royal Mile, line of secondhand stores), and the Royal Mile (touristy but competitively priced). Shops are usually open 10:00-18:00 (later on Thu). If you want to be sure you are taking home local merchandise, check if the labels read: "Made in Scotland." "Designed in Scotland" actually means "Made in China."

Experiences in Edinburgh

Edinburgh Festival

One of Europe's great cultural events, Edinburgh's annual festival turns the city into a carnival of the arts. There are enough music, dance, drama, and multicultural events to make even the most jaded traveler giddy with excitement. Every day is jammed with formal and spontaneous fun. A riot of festivals—official, fringe, book, and jazz and blues—rages simultaneously for about three weeks each August, with the Military Tattoo starting (and ending) a week earlier. The best overall website is www.edinburgh festivals.co.uk.

Many city sights run on extended hours, and those along the Royal Mile that normally close on Sunday are open in the afternoon. It's a glorious time to be in Edinburgh—if you have (and can afford) a room.

The official **Edinburgh International Festival** (Aug 8-31 in 2014, likely Aug 7-30 in 2015) is the original—it's more formal, and the most likely to get booked up. Major events sell out well in advance. The ticket office is at the Hub, located in the former Tolbooth Church, near the top of the Royal Mile (tickets-£5-75, booking from late March, office open Mon-Sat 10:00-17:00 or longer, in Aug 9:00-19:30 plus Sun 10:00-19:30, tel. 0131/473-2000, www.hubtickets.co.uk or www.eif.co.uk).

Pick up your ticket at the Hub office on the day of the show or at the venue before noon. Several publications—including the festival's official schedule, the *Edinburgh Festivals Guide Daily, The List, Fringe Program,* and *Daily Diary*—list and evaluate festival events.

The less formal **Fringe Festival,** featuring "on the edge" comedy and theater, is huge—with 2,000 shows (Aug 1-25 in 2014, ticket/info office just below St. Giles Cathedral on the Royal Mile, 180 High Street, bookings tel. 0131/226-0000, can book online from mid-May on, www.edfringe.com). Tickets may be available at the door, and half-price tickets for some events are sold on the day of the show at the Half-Price Hut, located at the Mound, near the Scottish National Gallery (daily 10:00-21:00).

The **Military Tattoo** is a massing of bands, drums, and bagpipes, with groups from all over the former British Empire. Displaying military finesse with a stirring lone-piper finale, this grand spectacle fills the Castle Esplanade nightly except Sunday, normally from a week before the festival starts until a week before it finishes (Aug 1-23 in 2014, Mon-Fri at 21:00, Sat at 19:30 and 22:30, £25-60, booking starts in Dec, Fri-Sat shows sell out first, all seats generally sold out by early summer, some scattered same-day tickets may be available; office open Mon-Fri 10:00-16:30, closed Sat-Sun, during Tattoo open until show time and Sat 10:00-22:30, closed Sun; 32 Market Street, behind Waverley Station, tel. 0131/225-1188, www.edintattoo.co.uk). The last day is filmed by the BBC and later broadcast as a big national television special.

The **Festival of Politics,** adding yet another dimension to Edinburgh's festival action, is held in August in the Scottish parliament building. It's a busy four days of discussions and lectures on environmentalism, globalization, terrorism, gender, and other issues (www.festivalofpolitics.org.uk).

Other summer festivals cover jazz and blues (early August, tel. 0131/467-5200, www.edinburghjazzfestival.co.uk), film (mid-June, tel. 0131/228-4051, www.edfilmfest.org.uk), and books (mid-late August, tel. 0131/718-5666, www.edbookfest.co.uk).

If you do plan to hit Edinburgh during a festival, book a room far in advance and extend your stay by a day or two. Once you know your dates, reserve tickets to any show you really want to see.

Nightlife in Edinburgh

▲▲Literary Pub Tour

This two-hour walk is interesting even if you think Sir Walter Scott was an Antarctic explorer. You'll follow the witty dialogue of two actors as they debate whether the great literature of Scotland was high art or the creative re-creation of fun-loving louts fueled by a love of whisky. You'll wander from the Grassmarket over the Old Town and New Town, with stops in three pubs as your guides share their takes on Scotland's literary greats. The tour meets at the Beehive pub on Grassmarket (£14, book online and save £2, May-Sept nightly at 19:30, March-April and Oct Thu-Sun, Nov-Feb Fri only, www.edinburghliterarypubtour.co.uk).

▲Ghost Walks

These walks are an entertaining and cheap night out (offered nightly, most around 19:00 and 21:00, easy socializing for solo travelers). The theatrical and creatively staged **Witchery Tours,** the most established outfit, offers two different walks: "Ghosts and Gore" (1.5 hours, April-Aug only) and "Murder and Mystery" (1.25 hours, year-round). The former is better suited for kids than the latter (either tour £8.50, includes book of stories, leaves from top of Royal Mile, outside the Witchery Restaurant, near Castle Esplanade, reservations required, tel. 0131/225-6745, www.witchery tours.com).

Auld Reekie Tours offers a scary array of walks daily and nightly (£9-12, 50-90 minutes, leaves from front steps of the Tron Church building on Cockburn Street, tel. 0131/557-4700, pick up brochure or visit www.auldreekietours.com). Auld Reekie focuses on the paranormal, witch covens, and pagan temples, taking groups into the "haunted vaults" under the old bridges "where it was so dark, so crowded, and so squalid that the people there knew each other not by how they looked, but by how they sounded, felt, and smelt." If you want more, there's plenty of it (complete with screaming Gothic "jumpers").

Scottish Folk Evenings

These £35-40 dinner shows, generally for tour groups intent on photographing old cultural clichés, are held in the huge halls of expensive hotels. (Prices are bloated to include 20 percent commissions.) Your "traditional" meal is followed by a full slate of swirling kilts, blaring bagpipes, and Scottish folk dancing with an old-time music hall emcee. If you like Lawrence Welk, you're in for a treat. But for most travelers, these are painfully cheesy variety shows. You can sometimes see the show without dinner for about two-thirds the price. The TI has fliers on all the latest venues.

Prestonfield House offers its kitschy "Taste of Scotland" folk evening—a plaid fantasy of smiling performers accompanied by electric keyboards—with or without dinner Sunday to Friday. For £45, you get the show with two drinks and a wad of haggis; £58 buys you the same, plus a three-course meal and a half-bottle of wine (be there at 18:45, dinner at 19:00, show runs 20:00-22:00, May-Oct only). It's in the stables of "the handsomest house in Edinburgh," which is now home to the recommended Rhubarb Restaurant (Priestfield Road, a 10-minute walk from Dalkeith Road B&Bs, tel. 0131/225-7800, www.scottishshow.co.uk).

Theater

Even outside festival time, Edinburgh is a fine place for lively and affordable theater. Pick up *The List* for a complete rundown of what's on (sold at newsstands for a few pounds; also online at www.list.co.uk).

▲▲Live Music in Pubs

Edinburgh used to be a better place for traditional folk music, but in the last few years, pub owners—out of economic necessity—are catering to college-age customers more interested in beer drinking. And several pubs that were famous for folk music have gone pop. But, if you know where to look, you'll still find pubs that can deliver a traditional folk-music fix. The monthly *Gig Guide* (free at TI, accommodations, and various pubs, www.gigguide.co.uk) lists 8 or 10 places each night that have live music, divided by genre (pop, rock, world, and folk).

South of High Street: **Sandy Bell's** is a tight little pub with live folk music nightly from 21:30 (just outside the tourist zone, a few minutes' walk from the Greyfriars Bobby statue and the National Museum of Scotland at 25 Forrest Road, tel. 0131/225-2751). Food is very simple (toasted sandwiches and soup), drinks are cheap, tables are small, and the vibe is local. They also have weekend

Sampling Whisky

While pub-hopping tourists generally think in terms of beer, many pubs are just as enthusiastic about serving whisky. If you are unfamiliar with whisky (what Americans call "Scotch"), it's a great conversation starter. Many pubs (including Leslie's, described on next page) have lists of dozens of whiskies available. Lists include descriptions of their personalities (peaty, heavy iodine finish, and so on), which are much easier to discern than most wine flavors. A glass generally costs around £2.50. Let a local teach you how to drink it "neat," then add a little water. Learn how to swish it around and let your gums taste it, too. Keep experimenting until you discover "the nurse's knickers."

In Edinburgh you can peruse the selection at the Whiski Rooms Shop or Cadenhead's, join a whisky tasting, or stop in at the Scotch Whisky Experience (for details on each of these, see "Sights in Edinburgh," earlier). Outside Edinburgh, Luvians Bottle Shop in St. Andrews and the Pot Still in Glasgow are fine places to sample a wee dram. Authentic distillery tours abound in Oban or Pitlochry and on the Isle of Skye. (For more on these options, see their respective chapters in this book.)

But don't neglect the easiest and perhaps best option for sampling Scotland's national drink: Find a local pub with a passion for whisky that's filled with locals who share that passion. Make a friend, buy a few shots, and learn by drinking.

afternoon sessions (Sat-Sun at 14:00).

The Royal Oak is another good place for a dose of Celtic music (just off South Bridge opposite Chambers Road at 1 Infirmary Street, tel. 0131/557-2976).

The **Grassmarket** neighborhood (below the castle) bustles with live music and rowdy people spilling out of the pubs and into what was (once upon a time) a busy market square. While it used to be a mecca for Scottish folk music, today it's more youthful with a heavy-drinking, rockin' feel. It's fun to just wander through this area late at night and check out the scene. Thanks to the music and crowds, you'll know where to go...and where not to. Have a beer and follow your ear to places like **Biddy Mulligans** or **White Hart Inn** (both on Grassmarket). **Finnegans Wake** on Victoria Street (which leads down to Grassmarket) also has live folk and rock each night.

On High Street: Three characteristic pubs within a few steps of each other on High Street (opposite Radisson Hotel) offer a fun setting, classic pub architecture and ambience, and live music for the cost of a beer: **Whiski Bar** (trad and folk nightly at 22:00), **Royal Mile** (pop and folk, nightly at 22:00), and **Mitre Bar** (nightly at 21:00 or 21:30, trad on Tue and Thu). Just a block away (on South Bridge) is **Whistlebinkies Live Music Bar.** While they rarely do folk or Scottish trad, this is the most serious of the music pubs, with an actual stage and several acts nightly (schedule posted outside the door makes the genre clear: rock, pop, jazz or blues, music starts at 19:00 or earlier, young crowd, fun energy, no cover, tel. 0131/557-5114). **No. 1 High Street** is an accessible little pub with a love of folk and traditional music and free performances many nights from 21:00 (Scottish trad on Tue-Wed, bluegrass on Thu). Drop by during your sightseeing as you walk the lower part of the Royal Mile, and ask what's on tonight (across from World's End, 1 High Street, tel. 0131/556-5758).

In the New Town: All the beer drinkers seem to head for the pedestrianized Rose Street, famous for having the most pubs per square inch anywhere in Scotland—and plenty of live music.

Near Dalkeith Road B&Bs: The first three listed below are classic pubs (without a lot of noisy machines and rowdy twenty-somethings). They cluster within 100 yards of each other around the intersection of Duncan Street and Causewayside.

Leslie's Pub, sitting between a working-class and an upper-class neighborhood, has two sides. Originally, the gang would go in on the right to gather around the great hardwood bar, glittering with a century of *Cheers* ambience. Meanwhile, the more delicate folks would slip in on the left, with its discreet doors, plush snugs (cozy private booths), and ornate ordering windows. Since 1896, this Victorian classic has been appreciated for both its real ales and its huge selection of fine whiskies (listed on a lengthy menu). Dive into the whisky mosh pit on the right, and let them show you how whisky can become "a very good friend." (Leslie's is a block downhill from the next two pubs, at 49 Ratcliffe Terrace, daily 11:00-24:00, tel. 0131/667-7205.)

The Old Bell Inn, with a nostalgic sports-bar vibe, serves only drinks after 19:00.

Swanny's Pub is not quite as welcoming, but it's a quintessential hangout for the working-class boys of the neighborhood, with some fun characters to get to know (Mon-Sat 11:00-24:00, Sun 12:30-late).

The Salisbury Arms Pub is an inviting place to mingle with locals, enjoy a three-ale sampler for around £3.50, or simply unwind over a few drinks after a long day of sightseeing.

EDINBURGH

Sleeping in Edinburgh

The advent of big, inexpensive hotels has made life more of a struggle for B&Bs, which are tending to go plush to compete. Still, book ahead, especially in August, when the annual Festival fills Edinburgh. Conventions, rugby matches, school holidays, and weekends can make finding a room tough at almost any time of year. For the best prices, skip middleman websites or the for-profit TI (which charges a higher room fee and levies a £4 booking fee) and book direct. "Standard" rooms, with toilets and showers a tissue-toss away, are cheaper than "en suite" rooms (with a private bathroom). At B&Bs, you can usually save some money by paying cash; although most B&Bs take credit cards, many add the card service fee to your bill (about three percent of the price).

B&Bs off Dalkeith Road

South of town near the Royal Commonwealth Pool, these B&Bs—just off Dalkeith Road—are nearly all top-end, sporting three or four stars. While pricey, they come with uniformly friendly hosts and great cooked breakfasts, and are a good value for people with enough money. At these not-quite-interchangeable places, character is provided by the personality quirks of the hosts.

Most listings are on quiet streets and within a two-minute walk of a bus stop. Though you won't find phones in the rooms, most have Wi-Fi and several offer guest computers. Most can provide triples or even quads for families.

Prices listed are for most of peak season; if there's a range, prices slide up with summer demand. During the Festival in

---

Sleep Code

(£1 = about $1.60, country code: 44, area code: 0131)
S = Single, **D** = Double/Twin, **T** = Triple, **Q** = Quad, **b** = bathroom, **s** = shower only. Unless otherwise noted, credit cards are accepted and prices include breakfast.

To help you sort easily through these listings, I've divided the accommodations into three categories based on the price for a standard double room with bath (during high season):

$$$ Higher Priced—Most rooms £80 or more.
$$ Moderately Priced—Most rooms between £60-80.
$ Lower Priced—Most rooms £60 or less.

Prices can change without notice; verify the hotel's current rates online or by email. For the best prices, always book direct.

EDINBURGH

Edinburgh's Dalkeith Road Neighborhood

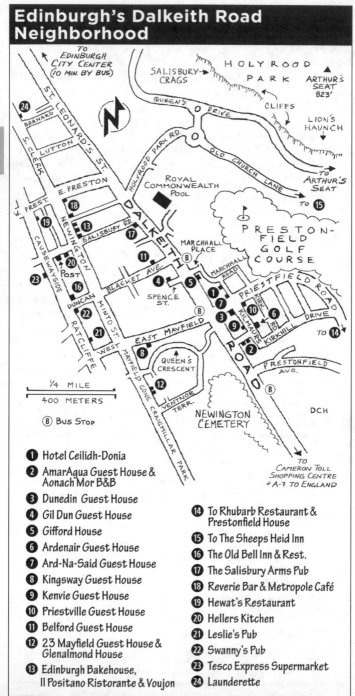

TO EDINBURGH CITY CENTER (10 MIN. BY BUS)

HOLYROOD PARK

SALISBURY CRAGS →

ARTHUR'S SEAT 823'

QUEEN'S DRIVE

CLIFFS

LION'S HAUNCH

ST. LEONARD'S ST.

BERNARD ST.

LUTTON

S. CLERK

OLD CHURCH LANE

TO ARTHUR'S SEAT

TO ㉕

HOLYROOD PARK RD.

E. PRESTON

W. PREST.

NEWINGTON

SALISBURY RD.

DALKEITH

ROYAL COMMONWEALTH POOL

MARCHHALL PLACE

PRESTON-FIELD GOLF COURSE

CAUSEWAYSIDE

POST

BLACKET AVE.

SPENCE ST.

MARCHHALL ROAD

PRIESTFIELD ROAD

KIRKHILL

KILMAURS RD.

DRIVE

TO ⑭

DUNCAN

MINTO ST.

EAST MAYFIELD

RATCLIFFE

WEST

MAYFIELD GDNS.

QUEEN'S CRESCENT

PRESTONFIELD AVE.

¼ MILE

400 METERS

CRAIGMILLAR PARK

VENTNOR TERR.

NEWINGTON CEMETERY

DCH

Ⓑ BUS STOP

TO CAMERON TOLL SHOPPING CENTRE + A-7 TO ENGLAND

① Hotel Ceilidh-Donia

② AmarAgua Guest House & Aonach Mor B&B

③ Dunedin Guest House

④ Gil Dun Guest House

⑤ Gifford House

⑥ Ardenair Guest House

⑦ Ard-Na-Said Guest House

⑧ Kingsway Guest House

⑨ Kenvie Guest House

⑩ Priestville Guest House

⑪ Belford Guest House

⑫ 23 Mayfield Guest House & Glenalmond House

⑬ Edinburgh Bakehouse, Il Positano Ristorante & Voujon

⑭ To Rhubarb Restaurant & Prestonfield House

⑮ To The Sheeps Heid Inn

⑯ The Old Bell Inn & Rest.

⑰ The Salisbury Arms Pub

⑱ Reverie Bar & Metropole Café

⑲ Hewat's Restaurant

⑳ Hellers Kitchen

㉑ Leslie's Pub

㉒ Swanny's Pub

㉓ Tesco Express Supermarket

㉔ Launderette

August, prices are higher; B&Bs also do not accept bookings for one-night stays during this time. Conversely, in winter, when demand is light, prices get really soft (less than what's listed here). These prices are for cash; expect a 3-5 percent fee for using your credit card.

Near the B&Bs, you'll find plenty of great eateries (see "Eating in Edinburgh," later) and several good, classic pubs (see "Nightlife in Edinburgh," earlier). A few places have their own private parking spots; others offer access to easy, free street parking (ask about it when booking—or better yet, don't rent a car for your time in Edinburgh).

If you bring in take-out food, your host would probably prefer you eat it in the breakfast area rather than muck up your room—ask. The nearest launderette is Ace Cleaning Centre (which picks up and drops off).

Getting There: This comfortable, safe neighborhood is a 10-minute bus ride from the Royal Mile. From the train station, the nearest place to catch the bus (at least while tram construction is under way) is around the corner on North Bridge (exit the station onto Princes Street, turn right, cross the street, and walk up the bridge). If you're here after the Princes Street construction is finished, use the bus stop in front of the Marks & Spencer department store (£1.50, use exact change; catch Lothian bus #14, #30, or #33 or First bus #86). Tell the driver your destination is Dalkeith Road; about 10 minutes into the ride, after following South Clerk Street for a while, the bus makes a left turn, then a right—depending on where you're staying, you'll get off at the first or second stop after the turn (confirm specifics with your B&B). These buses also stop at the corner of North Bridge and High Street on the Royal Mile. Buses run from 6:00 (9:00 on Sun) to 23:00. Taxi fare between the train station or Royal Mile and the B&Bs is about £7. Taxis are easy to hail on Dalkeith Road if it isn't raining.

$$$ Hotel Ceilidh-Donia rents 17 contemporary rooms with a pleasant back deck, a quiet bar, a free DVD lending library, and your choice of full Scottish, English, American, or vegetarian breakfast (Sb-£50-66, Db-£70-120, more in Aug and for special events, less off-season, guest computer, free Wi-Fi, 14-16 Marchhall Crescent, tel. 0131/667-2743, www.hotelceilidh-donia .co.uk, reservations@hotelceilidh-donia.co.uk, Max and Annette).

$$$ AmarAgua Guest House is an inviting Victorian home away from home, with five welcoming rooms and a Japanese garden. It's given a little extra sparkle by its energetic proprietors, former entertainers Dawn-Ann and Tony Costa (Db-£70-85, Tb-£90-110, more for fancy four-poster rooms, 2-night minimum, guest computer and iPads, free Wi-Fi, 10 Kilmaurs Terrace, tel. 0131/667-6775, www.amaragua.co.uk, reservations@amaragua.co.uk).

$$$ Dunedin Guest House (dun-EE-din) is a fine value: bright, plush, and elegantly Scottish, with seven nice, airy rooms and a spacious breakfast room (S with private b on hall-£52-67, Db-£79-124, family rooms for up to 5, less off-season, free Wi-Fi, 8 Priestfield Road, tel. 0131/668-1949, www.dunedinguesthouse .co.uk, reservations@dunedinguesthouse.co.uk, David and Irene Wright).

$$$ Gil Dun Guest House, with eight rooms on a quiet cul-de-sac just off Dalkeith Road, is comfortable, pleasant, and managed with care by Gerry and Bill (Sb-£40-50, Db-£85-90, or £130 in Aug, great bathrooms, family deals, free Wi-Fi, pleasant garden, 9 Spence Street, tel. 0131/667-1368, www.gildun.co.uk, gildun.edin@btinternet.com).

$$$ Gifford House, on busy Dalkeith Road, is a bright, flowery, creaky-floor retreat with six surprisingly peaceful rooms, some with ornate cornices, super-king-size beds, and views of Arthur's Seat (Sb-£70-80, Db-£80-90, Tb-£114-120, Qb-£130-140, free Wi-Fi, street parking, 103 Dalkeith Road, tel. 0131/667-4688, www.giffordhouseedinburgh.com, giffordhouse@btinternet .com, David and Margaret).

$$ Airdenair Guest House, offering views and a friendly welcome, has five attractive rooms on the second floor with a lofty above-it-all feeling. Homemade scones and Jill's pulse on the latest neighborhood information are staples here (Sb-£40-45, Db-£70-80, Tb-£85-95, less off-season, free Wi-Fi, 29 Kilmaurs Road, tel. 0131/668-2336, www.airdenair.com, jill@airdenair.com, Jill and Doug McLennan).

$$ Ard-Na-Said B&B is an elegant 1875 Victorian house with a comfy lounge. It offers seven bright, spacious rooms with modern bathrooms—including one ground-floor room with a pleasant patio (Sb-£35-50, Db-£65-95, huge four-poster Db-£70-105, Tb-£90-120, prices depend on size of room as well as season, guest computer, free Wi-Fi, DVD players, free parking, 5 Priestfield Road, tel. 0131/667-8754, www.ardnasaid.co.uk, enquiries @ardnasaid.co.uk, Jim and Olive Lyons—or Olive and Jim Lyons, depending on whom you ask).

$$ Kingsway Guest House has seven high-quality, stylish, Scottish-modern rooms. Delightful owners Gary and Lizzie have thought of all the little touches, like take-away breakfast for early departures and bike and golf club rental (Sb-£45-65, Db-£60-85, Tb-£80-115, Qb-£90-125, 5 percent off these prices with cash and this book—mention Rick Steves when booking, free Wi-Fi, free parking, 5 East Mayfield, tel. 0131/667-5029, www.edinburgh -guesthouse.com, room@edinburgh-guesthouse.com).

$$ Aonach Mor B&B's eight plush rooms have views of either nearby Arthur's Seat or walled gardens (Db-£45-85, more in July-Aug, online specials, free Wi-Fi, 14 Kilmaurs Terrace, tel. 0131/667-8694, www.aonachmor.com, info@aonachmor.com, Tom and Fiona).

$$ Kenvie Guest House, expertly run by Dorothy Vidler, comes with five pleasant rooms (D-£64-68, Db-£72-78, these prices with cash and this book—but must claim when you reserve, family deals, guest computer, free Wi-Fi, 16 Kilmaurs Road, tel. 0131/668-1964, www.kenvie.co.uk, dorothy@kenvie.co.uk).

$$ Priestville Guest House is homey, with a dramatic skylight above the stairs, a sunny breakfast room, and cozy charm— not fancy, but more than workable, and great for families. The six rooms have Wi-Fi, VCRs, and a free video library (D-£50-64, Db-£56-80, Tb-£100, Q-£120, these prices when booked via email and paid in cash, discount for 2 or more nights, guest computer, free Wi-Fi, family rooms, 10 Priestfield Road, tel. 0131/667-2435, www.priestville.com, bookings@priestville.com, Trina and Colin Warwick).

$$ Belford Guest House is a tidy, homey place offering three basic rooms all with renovated en suite bathrooms (Sb-£45, Db-£70-75, family room, cheaper for longer stays, cash only, free parking, 13 Blacket Avenue—no sign out front, tel. 0131/667-2422, www.belfordguesthouse.com, tom@belfordguesthouse.com, Tom Borthwick).

Guesthouses on Mayfield Gardens

These two very well-run B&Bs come with a little street noise, but are bigger buildings with more spacious rooms, finer public lounges, and nice comforts (such as iPod-compatible bedside radios).

$$$ At 23 Mayfield Guest House, Ross (and Grandma Mary) rent nine splurge-worthy, thoughtfully appointed rooms complete with high-tech bathrooms and a hot tub in the garden. Little extras—such as locally sourced gourmet breakfasts, an inviting guest lounge outfitted with Sir Arthur Conan Doyle books, an "honesty bar," and classic black-and-white movie screenings—make you feel like royalty (Sb-£65-95, Db-£80-110, bigger Db-£90-140, four-poster Db-£120-170, family room for up to 4, 7 percent Rick Steves discount if you pay with cash, guest computer, free Wi-Fi, swap library, free parking, 23 Mayfield Gardens, tel. 0131/667-5806, www.23mayfield.co.uk, info@23mayfield.co.uk). If you can't wait until tomorrow for another taste of Ross' delicious cuisine (or aren't lucky enough to book a room), stop by his Copper Coffee stand for a goat cheese and roasted red pepper *panini* (22a St. Patrick Square, just off the route to/from downtown Edinburgh).

$$$ Glenalmond House, run by Jimmy and Fiona Mackie, has 10 beautiful rooms with fancy modern bathrooms (Db-£80-100, bigger four-poster Db-up to £125, Tb-£80-120, Qb-£120-150, 5 percent Rick Steves discount off these prices if you book direct and pay cash, less off-season, discount for longer stays, guest computer, free Wi-Fi, free parking, 25 Mayfield Gardens, tel. 0131/668-2392, www.glenalmondhouse.com, enquiries@glenalmondhouse.com).

Big, Modern Hotels

The first listing's a splurge. The rest are cheaper than most of the city's other chain hotels, and offer more comfort than character. In each case, I'd skip the institutional breakfast and eat out. You'll generally pay £10 a day to park near these hotels.

$$$ Macdonald Holyrood Hotel, my only fancy listing, is a four-star splurge, with 156 rooms up the street from the new Parliament building. With its classy marble-and-wood decor, fitness center, and pool, it's hard to leave. On a gray winter day in Edinburgh, this could be worth it, but some parts may be undergoing renovation in 2014. Prices can vary wildly (Db-£110-170, breakfast extra, check for specials online, family deals, near bottom of Royal Mile, across from Dynamic Earth, 81 Holyrood Road, tel. 0131/528-8000, www.macdonaldhotels.co.uk).

$$$ Jurys Inn offers a more enjoyable feeling than the Ibis and Travelodge (listed below). A cookie-cutter place with 186 dependably comfortable and bright rooms, it is capably run and well-situated a short walk from the station (Sb/Db/Tb-£99, less on weekdays, can be much cheaper off-season and for online bookings, much more in Aug, breakfast-£9-11, some views, pay Wi-Fi, laundry service, pub/restaurant, on quiet street just off Royal Mile, 43 Jeffrey Street, tel. 0131/200-3300, www.jurysinns.com).

$$$ Ibis Hotel, at the middle of the Royal Mile, is well-run and perfectly located. It has 99 soulless but clean and comfy rooms drenched in prefab American "charm." Room rates vary widely—book online to get their best offers (Db in June-Sept-£80-149, more during Festival, less off-season, breakfast-£8, pay guest computer and Wi-Fi, 6 Hunter Square, tel. 0131/240-7000, www.ibishotels.com, h2039@accor.com).

$$$ Holiday Inn Express Edinburgh Royal Mile rents 78 rooms with stark modern efficiency in a fine location, a five-minute walk from the train station (Db-£95-135 depending on day, generally most expensive on Fri-Sat, much more during Festival, cheaper off-season, for best rates book online, free Wi-Fi, just off the Royal Mile down St. Mary's Street, 300 Cowgate, tel. 0131/524-8400, www.hiexpressedinburgh.co.uk). Another Holiday Inn Express is on Picardy Place (Db-£95-135, 16 Picardy Place, tel. 0131/558-

2300, www.hieedinburgh.co.uk).

$$ Travelodge Central has 193 well-located, no-nonsense rooms, all decorated in sky blue. All rooms are the same and suitable for two adults with two kids, or three adults. While sleepable, it has a cheap feel with a quickly revolving staff (Sb/Db/Tb-£60-70, weekend Db-£70-85, Aug Db-£150, cheaper off-season and when booked online in advance, breakfast-£8, 33 St. Mary's Street, a block off Royal Mile, tel. 0871-984-6137, www.travelodge.co.uk). They have four other locations in the New Town: at 37-43 Rose Street; on Meuse Lane off Princes Street; at 30-31 Queen Street; and at 3 Waterloo Place, on the east end of Princes Street. Book online for any location.

Hostels

Edinburgh has two five-star hostels with dorm beds for about £20, slick modern efficiency, and careful management. They offer the best cheap beds in town. These places welcome families—travelers of any age feel comfortable here. Anyone on a tight budget wanting a twin room should think of these as simple hotels. The alternative is one of Edinburgh's scruffy bohemian hostels, each of which offers a youthful, mellow ambience and beds for around £15.

$ Edinburgh Central Youth Hostel rents 300 beds in rooms with one to eight beds (all with private bathrooms and lockers). Guests can eat cheaply in the cafeteria, or cook for the cost of groceries in the members' kitchen. Prices include sheets; towel rental costs £2 extra (£18-29/person in 4- to 8-bed rooms, Sb-£43-57, Db-£71-88, Tb-£73-127, Qb-£100-158, depends on season, non-members pay £2 extra per night, single-sex dorms, cooked breakfast-£6, continental breakfast-£4.50, open 24/7, pay guest computer and Wi-Fi, laundry facilities, 15-minute downhill walk from Waverley Station—head down Leith Walk, pass through two roundabouts, hostel is on your left—or take Lothian bus #22 or #25 to Elm Rowe, 9 Haddington Place off Leith Walk, tel. 0131/524-2090, www.syha.org.uk).

$ Smart City Hostel is a godsend for backpackers and anyone looking for simple, efficient rooms in the old center for cheap. You'll pay £10-20 (depends on season) for a bed in an austere, industrial-strength 4- to 12-bed dorm—each with its own private bathroom. But it can get crazy with raucous weekend stag and hen parties. Bar 50 in the basement has an inviting lounge with cheap meals. Half of the rooms function as a university dorm during the school year, becoming available just in time for the tourists (620 beds, Db-£50-120, bunky Qb-£60-165, includes linens and towels, cooked breakfast-£5, usually some female-only rooms but can't guarantee in summer, lockers, kitchen, lots of modern and efficient extras, pay Wi-Fi, coin-op laundry, 50 Blackfriars Street, tel. 0131/524-1989, www.smartcityhostels.com, info@smartcity hostels.com).

Cheap and Scruffy Bohemian Hostels in the Center: These first three sister hostels—popular crash pads for young, hip back-packers—are beautifully located in the noisy center (£13.50-20 depending on time of year, twin D-£40-55, www.scotlandstop hostels.com): **High Street Hostel** (130 beds, 8 Blackfriars Street, just off High Street/Royal Mile, tel. 0131/557-3984); **Royal Mile Backpackers** (40 beds, dorms only—no private rooms, 105 High Street, tel. 0131/557-6120); and **Castle Rock Hostel** (300 beds, just below the castle and above the pubs, 15 Johnston Terrace, tel. 0131/225-9666). **Brodie's Hostels,** somewhere between spar-tan and dumpy in the middle of the Royal Mile, rents 130 cheap beds in 4- to 16-bed dorms (£10-13 beds, D-£55-65, Db-£65-75, includes linens, lockers-£1/day, kitchen, pay guest computer and Wi-Fi, laundry, 93 High Street, tel. 0131/556-2223, www.brodies hostels.co.uk).

Eating in Edinburgh

Reservations for restaurants are essential in August and on week-ends, and a good idea anytime. Children aren't allowed in many of the pubs. All restaurants in Scotland are smoke-free.

Along the Royal Mile

Historic pubs and doily cafés with reasonable, unremarkable meals abound. Though the eateries along this most-crowded stretch of the city are invariably touristy, the scene is fun, and competition makes a well-chosen place a good value. Here are some handy, affordable options for a good bite to eat (listed roughly in downhill order). Sprinkled in this list are some places a block or two off the main drag offering better values—and correspondingly filled with more locals than tourists.

The first two restaurants are in a clus-ter of pleasant eateries happily removed from the Royal Mile melee. Consider stop-ping at one of these on your way to the National Museum of Scotland, which is a half-block away.

The Elephant House, two blocks out of the touristy zone, is a comfy neighbor-hood coffee shop where relaxed patrons browse newspapers in the stay-awhile back room, listen to soft rock, enjoy the castle and cemetery vistas, and sip coffee or munch a light meal. During the day, you'll pick up food at the counter and grab your own seat; after 17:00, the café switches to table service. It's easy to imagine J. K. Rowling annoying waiters with her baby pram while spending long afternoons here writing the first Harry Potter book (£8 dinner plates, traditional meat pies, great desserts, daily 8:00-22:00, vegetarian options, 2 blocks south of Royal Mile near National Museum of Scotland at 21 George IV Bridge, tel. 0131/220-5355).

The Outsider, also without a hint of Royal Mile tourism, is a sleek spot serving creative and trendy cuisine (good fish and grilled meats and vegetables) in a minimalist, stylish, hardwood, candlelit castle-view setting. It's noisy with enthusiasm, and the service is crisp and youthful. As you'll be competing with yuppies, reserve for dinner (£7 lunch plates 12:00-19:00, £13-16 main dishes, always a vegetarian course, good wines by the glass, daily 12:00-23:00, 30 yards up from The Elephant House at 15 George IV Bridge, tel. 0131/226-3131).

Grain Store Restaurant, a dressy world of wood, stone, and candles tucked away above busy Victoria Street, has served Scottish produce with a French twist for more than two decades. While they have inexpensive £12.50 two-course lunch specials, dinner is à la carte (£10-14 starters, £18-28 main dishes, daily, reservations smart, 30 Victoria Street, tel. 0131/225-7635, www .grainstore-restaurant.co.uk).

Maison Bleue Restaurant is popular for their à la carte French/Scottish/North African menu and £15 dinner special from 17:00-19:00 (£7-9 starters, £15-27 main dishes, daily, 36 Victoria Street, tel. 0131/226-1900).

Oink, a short detour off the Royal Mile from the George IV Bridge, carves from a freshly roasted pig each afternoon for mouthwatering sandwiches that come in "oink" (160 grams-£3.60) or "grunter" (250 grams-£4.60) portions. Watch the pig shrink in the front window throughout the day (daily 11:00-18:00 or whenever they run out of meat, cash only, 34 Victoria Street, tel. 01890/761-355).

The Witchery by the Castle is set in a lushly decorated 16th-century building just below the castle on the Royal Mile, with wood paneling, antique candlesticks, tapestries, and opulent red leather upholstery. Frequented by celebrities, tourists, and locals out for a splurge, the restaurant's emphasis is on fresh— and pricey—Scottish meats and seafood (£16 two-course lunch specials 12:00-16:00, specials also good 17:30-18:30 & 22:30-23:30, £33 three-course dinner menu, £23-28 main dishes, daily 12:00-16:00 & 17:30-23:30, dress smart, reservations critical, tel. 0131/225-5613, www.thewitchery.com).

Deacon Brodie's Tavern, at a dead-center location on the

EDINBURGH

Royal Mile Accommodations & Eateries

TO NEW TOWN ↑

PRINCES STREET GARDENS

THE MOUND

MUSEUM ON THE MOUND

AIRLINK #100

WAVERLY BR.

MARKET ST.

TO DALKEITH ROAD

COCKBURN ST.

NORTH BRIDGE

MOUND PL.

WRITERS' MUSEUM AT LADY STAIRS HOUSE

GLADSTONE'S LAND

BANK ST.

ST. GILES

CAMERA OBSCURA

CASTLE

TOP OF ROYAL MILE

ESPLANADE

LAWN MKT.

HIGH

TRON KIRK

15

17

19

25

JOHNSTON TERRACE

14

9

13

VICTORIA

GEORGE IV BR.

16

OLD PARLIAMENT HOUSE

3

18

7

6

SOUTH BRIDGE

GOOD RESTAURANTS + ANTIQUE SHOPS

GRASSMARKET

COWGATE

FOLK MUSIC PUBS

12

11

CHAMBERS

24

GREYFRIARS BOBBY STATUE

23

NATIONAL MUSEUM OF SCOTLAND

B BUS STOP

View

PEDESTRIAN ZONE

1 MacDonald Holyrood Hotel

2 Jurys Inn

3 Ibis Hotel

4 Holiday Inn Express Edinburgh Royal Mile

5 Travelodge Central

6 Smart City Hostel

7 High Street Hostel

8 Royal Mile Backpackers Hostel

9 Castle Rock Hostel

10 Brodie's Hostels & The World's End Pub

11 The Elephant House

12 The Outsider Restaurant

13 Grain Store, Maison Bleue & Oink

14 The Witchery by the Castle

Royal Mile, is a sloppy pub on the ground floor with a sloppy restaurant upstairs serving basic £8-11 pub meals. While painfully touristy, it comes with a fun history and decent food (daily 10:00-22:00, hearty salads, kids' menu, kids welcome upstairs—but they're not allowed to enter after 20:00, tel. 0131/220-0317).

St. Giles Cathedral Café, hiding under the landmark church, is *the* place for paupers to munch prayerfully. Stairs on the back side of the church lead into the basement, where you'll find simple, light lunches from 11:30 and coffee with cakes all day (Mon-Sat 9:00-17:00, Sun 11:00-17:00, tel. 0131/225-5147).

Angels with Bagpipes, in the shadow of St. Giles Cathedral, serves sophisticated Scottish staples in the plush interior (daily

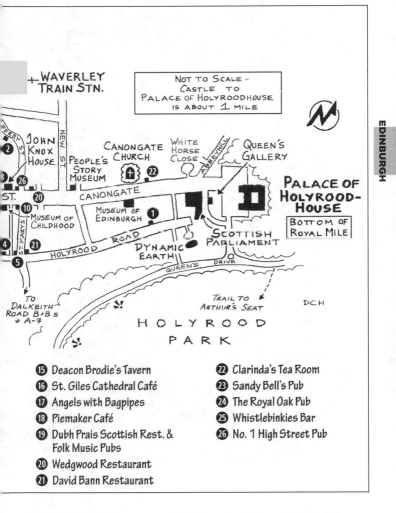

EDINBURGH

Map labels:

WAVERLEY TRAIN STN.

NOT TO SCALE – CASTLE TO PALACE OF HOLYROODHOUSE IS ABOUT 1 MILE

JOHN KNOX HOUSE

PEOPLE'S STORY MUSEUM

CANONGATE CHURCH

WHITE HORSE CLOSE

QUEEN'S GALLERY

ST.

CANONGATE

MUSEUM OF EDINBURGH

MUSEUM OF CHILDHOOD

HOLYROOD ROAD

DYNAMIC EARTH

SCOTTISH PARLIAMENT

QUEEN'S DRIVE

PALACE OF HOLYROOD-HOUSE

BOTTOM OF ROYAL MILE

TO DALKEITH ROAD B+Bs + A-7

TRAIL TO ARTHUR'S SEAT

DCH

HOLYROOD PARK

15 Deacon Brodie's Tavern
16 St. Giles Cathedral Café
17 Angels with Bagpipes
18 Piemaker Café
19 Dubh Prais Scottish Rest. & Folk Music Pubs
20 Wedgwood Restaurant
21 David Bann Restaurant

22 Clarinda's Tea Room
23 Sandy Bell's Pub
24 The Royal Oak Pub
25 Whistlebinkies Bar
26 No. 1 High Street Pub

12:00-22:00, £6-9 starters, £14-18 main dishes, 343 High Street, tel. 0131/220-1111).

Piemaker is a great place to grab a cheap and tasty meal, especially if you're in a hurry. Their meat pies and pastries—try the cherry—are "so fresh they'll pinch your bum and call you darlin'" (most everything under £3, daily 10:00-19:00, until 23:00 on Tue, Fri, and Sat, about 100 yards off the Royal Mile at 38 South Bridge, tel. 0131/556-8566).

Dubh Prais Scottish Restaurant (pronounced "DOO-prash") is a dressy nine-table place filling a cellar 10 steps and a world away from the High Street bustle. The owner-chef, James McWilliams, proudly serves Scottish "fayre" at its very best (including gourmet haggis). The daily specials are not printed, to guard against "zombie waiters." They like to get to know you a bit by explaining things (£16-24 main dishes, open Tue-Sat 17:00-22:30, closed Sun-Mon, reservations wise, opposite Radisson Blu Hotel at 123b High Street, tel. 0131/557-5732, www.dubhprais restaurant.com).

Wedgwood Restaurant is romantic, contemporary, chic, and as gourmet as possible with no pretense. Paul Wedgwood cooks while his wife Lisa serves with appetizing charm. The cuisine: creative, modern Scottish with an international twist and a whiff of Asia. The pigeon and haggis starter is scrumptious. Paul and Lisa believe in making the meal the event of the evening—don't come here to eat and run. I like the ground level with the Royal Mile view, but the busy kitchen ambience in the basement is also fine (£7-9 starters, £18-24 main courses, fine wine by the glass, daily 12:00-15:00 & 18:00-22:00, Sun open at 12:30, reservations advised, 267 Canongate on Royal Mile, tel. 0131/558-8737, www .wedgwoodtherestaurant.co.uk).

The World's End Pub, a colorful old place, dishes up hearty £9-11 meals from a creative menu in a fun, dark, and noisy space (daily 12:00-22:00, 4 High Street, tel. 0131/556-3628).

David Bann, just a three-minute walk off the Royal Mile, is a worthwhile stop for well-heeled vegetarians in need of a break from the morning fry. While vegetarian as can be, there's not a hint of hippie here. It's upscale (it has a cocktail bar), sleek, minimalist, and stylish (gorgeously presented dishes), serious about quality, and organic—they serve polenta, tartlets, soups, and light meals (£6 starters, £11-13 main dishes, decadent desserts, Mon-Fri 12:00-22:00, Sat-Sun 11:00-22:00, vegan options, 56-58 St. Mary's Street, tel. 0131/556-5888).

Clarinda's Tea Room, near the bottom of the Royal Mile, is charming and girlish—a fine and tasty place to relax after touring the Mile or the Palace of Holyroodhouse. Stop in for a £5 quiche, salad, or soup lunch. It's also great for sandwiches and tea and cake anytime (Mon-Sat 8:30-16:45, Sun 9:30-16:45, 69 Canongate, tel. 0131/557-1888).

In the New Town

While most of your sightseeing will be along the Royal Mile, it's important that your Edinburgh experience stretches beyond this happy tourist gauntlet. Just a few minutes away, in the Georgian town, you'll find a bustling world of office workers, students, and pensioners doing their thing. And at midday, that includes eating. Simply hiking over to one of these places will give you a good helping of modern Edinburgh. All these places are within a few minutes' walk of the TI and main Waverley Bridge tour-bus depot.

The Bon Vivant is woody, youthful, and candlelit, with a rotating menu of eclectic Mediterranean/Asian dishes and a companion wine shop serving 50 wines by the glass. They have fun £1.50 tapas plates and heartier dishes (daily 12:00-22:00, 55 Thistle Street, tel. 0131/225-3275, www.bonvivantedinburgh.co.uk).

Le Café St. Honoré, tucked away like a secret bit of old Paris, is a charming place with friendly service and walls lined by tempting wine bottles. It serves French-Scottish cuisine in tight, Old World, cut-glass elegance to a dressy crowd (daily £18 two-course and £23 three-course lunch and dinner specials, open daily 12:00-14:00 & Mon-Fri 17:15-22:00, Sat-Sun 18:00-22:00, reservations smart—ask to sit upstairs, down Thistle Street from Hanover Street, 34 Northwest Thistle Street Lane, tel. 0131/226-2211, www.cafesthonore.com).

Café Royal is a movie producer's dream pub—the perfect fin de siècle setting for a coffee, beer, or light meal. (In fact, parts of *Chariots of Fire* were filmed here.) Drop in, if only to admire the 1880 tiles featuring famous inventors (daily 12:00-14:30 & 17:00-21:30, bar food available during the afternoon, two blocks from Princes Mall on 19 West Register Street, tel. 0131/556-1884). There are two cateries here: the noisy pub (£10-13 main dishes, Mon-Sat 11:00-21:30, Sun open at 12:30) and the dressier restaurant, specializing in oysters, fish, and game (£14-20 plates, daily 12:00-14:30 & 17:00-21:30, reserve for dinner—it's quite small and understandably popular).

The Dome Restaurant, in what was a fancy bank, serves decent, modern international cuisine around a classy bar and under the elegant 19th-century skylight dome. With soft jazz and chic, white-tablecloth ambience, it feels a world apart (£12-16 plates until 17:00, £14-20 dinners until 21:45, daily 12:00-23:00, reserve for dinner, open for a drink any time under the dome; the adjacent, more intimate Club Room serves food Mon-Sat 10:00-17:00, Thu-Sat until late, closed Sun; 14 George Street, tel. 0131/624-8634). As you leave, look up to take in the facade of this former bank building—the pediment is filled with figures demonstrating various ways to make money, which they do with all the nobility of classical gods.

St. Andrew's and St. George's Church Undercroft Café, in the basement of a fine old church, is the cheapest place in town for lunch—under £5 for a sandwich and soup. Your tiny bill helps support the Church of Scotland (Mon-Fri 10:00-14:00, closed Sat-Sun, at 13 George Street, just off St. Andrew Square, tel. 0131/225-3847).

Henderson's Salad Table and Wine Bar has fed a generation of New Town vegetarians hearty cuisine and salads. Even carnivores love this place for its delectable salads and desserts (two-course lunch for £10, Mon-Sat 8:00-22:00, Thu-Sat until 23:00, closed Sun except in Aug 11:00-19:00, strictly vegetarian, take-away available, pleasant live music nightly in wine bar—generally guitar or jazz; between Queen and George streets at 94 Hanover Street, tel. 0131/225-2131). Henderson's two different seating areas use the same self-serve cafeteria line. For the identical healthy food with more elegant seating and table service, eat at the attached **Henderson's Bistro** (daily 12:00-20:30, Thu-Sat until 21:30).

Fun Ethnic Eateries on Hanover Street: Hanover Street is lined with Thai, Greek, Turkish, Italian, and other restaurants. Stroll the block to eye your options.

Supermarkets: **Marks & Spencer Food Hall** offers an assortment of tasty hot foods, prepared sandwiches, fresh bakery items, a wide selection of wines and beverages, and plastic utensils at the checkout queue. It's just a block from the Scott Monument and the picnic-perfect Princes Street Gardens (Mon-Sat 8:00-19:00, Thu until 20:00, Sun 11:00-18:00, 4 Waverley Bridge—on Princes Street, separate stairway next to main M&S entrance leads directly to food hall, tel. 0131/225-2301). **Sainsbury's** supermarket, a block off Princes Street, also offers grab-and-go items for a quick lunch (Mon-Sat 7:00-22:00, Sun 9:00-20:00, on corner of Rose Street on St. Andrew Square, across the street from Jenners, the classy department store).

The Dalkeith Road Area, near B&Bs

Nearly all of these places (except for The Sheeps Heid Inn) are within a 10-minute walk of my recommended B&Bs. Most are on or near the intersection of Newington Road and East Preston Street. Reserve on weekends and during the Festival. The nearest grocery store is **Tesco Express** (daily 6:00-23:00, 158 Causewayside). Cameron Toll Shopping Centre, about a half-mile south, houses a **Sainsbury's** superstore for more substantial supplies (and gasoline), handy on your way out of town (Mon-Sat 7:30-22:00, Sun 8:00-20:00, 6 Lady Road, tel. 0131/666-5200). For a cozy drink after dinner, visit the recommended pubs in the area (see "Nightlife in Edinburgh," earlier).

Scottish/French Restaurants

At **Edinburgh Bakehouse**, award-winning baker James Lynch makes fresh breads, sweets, and meat pies from scratch in this laid-back, nondescript shop. Locals line up for his morning rolls—which earned him the title "baker of the year." Stop by to see the friendly staff and open kitchen in action and judge for yourself (£2-5, cash only, daily 7:00-18:00, 101 Newington Road).

Rhubarb Restaurant specializes in Old World elegance. It's in "Edinburgh's most handsome house"—a riot of antiques, velvet, tassels, and fringes. The plush dark-rhubarb color theme reminds visitors that this was the place where rhubarb was first grown in Britain. It's a 10-minute walk past the other recommended eateries behind Arthur's Seat, in a huge estate with big, shaggy Highland cattle enjoying their salads al fresco. At night, it's a candlelit wonder. While most spend a wad here (£20-34 plates), they have an £18 two-course lunch and a £33 three-course dinner (Sun-Thu 12:00-14:00 & 18:30-23:00, Fri-Sat 12:00-14:00 & 18:00-22:00, afternoon tea served daily 14:00-19:00, reserve in advance and dress up if you can, in Prestonfield House, Priestfield Road, tel. 0131/225-1333, www.prestonfield.com). For details on their schmaltzy Scottish folk evening, see "Nightlife in Edinburgh," earlier.

The Sheeps Heid Inn, Edinburgh's oldest public house, is equally notable for its history, date-night appeal, and hearty portions of affordable, classy dishes. Though it requires a cab ride, it is worth the fare to dine in this dreamy setting in the presence of past queens and kings (£7-9 starters, £11-17 main dishes; open Mon-Sat 12:00-22:00, Sun 12:30-21:30, 43-45 The Causeway, tel. 0131/661-7974, www.thesheepheidedinburgh.co.uk).

Scottish Grub and Pubs

The Old Bell Inn, with an old-time sports-bar ambience—fishing, golf, horses—serves simple £8 pub meals. This is a classic "snug pub"—all dark woods and brass beer taps, littered with evocative knickknacks. It comes with sidewalk seating and a mixed-age crowd (open daily until 24:00; food served Sun-Thu 12:00-21:00, Fri-Sat 12:00-19:30, 233 Causewayside, tel. 0131/668-1573). The fancier restaurant upstairs serves good Italian food in a wonderful ambience.

The Salisbury Arms Pub, with a nice garden terrace, serves upscale, pleasing traditional classics with yuppie flair in a space that exudes more Martha Stewart and Pottery Barn than traditional public house (£4-7 starters, £12-17 main dishes, evening specials, daily 12:00-22:00, pub open until 23:00, 58 Dalkeith Road, tel. 0131/667-4518).

Reverie Bar is just your basic, fun traditional pub with a focus on food rather than drinking, and free live music most nights from 21:30 (every other Sun-jazz, Mon-quiz night, Tue-traditional/folk, Thu-blues; £9-12 main dishes, food served daily 12:00-15:00 & 17:00-21:00, real ales, 1-5 Newington Road, tel. 0131/667-8870, http://thereverie.co.uk).

Hewat's Restaurant is the neighborhood hit. Sample Scottish cuisine or their popular steak dishes in this elegantly whimsical dining space (£10.25 dinner deals Mon-Thu until 19:30; pre-the-ater menu £15 for two courses, £18 for three courses until 18:45; midweek dinner menu £18.50 for two courses, £22.50 for three courses; open Mon-Sat 18:00-21:30, Fri-Sat 18:00-22:00, Wed-Sat also open for lunch 12:00-14:00, closed Sun, 19-21b Causeway, tel. 0131/466-6660, www.hewatsrestaurant.co.uk).

Hellers Kitchen is a casual blond-wood space specializing in dishes using local produce and fresh-baked breads. Check the big chalkboard to see what's on (£5-6 light bites and sandwiches, £7-10 main dishes, daily 12:00-15:00 & 17:00-22:00, next to post office at 15 Salisbury Place, tel. 0131/667-4654).

Metropole Café is a fresh, healthy eatery with a Starbucks ambience, serving light bites for £3-4, or 3/£8.50, and simple meals for £8 (Mon-Sat 8:00-20:00, Sun 9:00-18:00, always a good veg-etarian dish, free Wi-Fi, 33 Newington Road, tel. 0131/668-4999).

Ethnic Options

Il Positano Ristorante has a spirited Italian ambience, as man-ager Donato injects a love of life and food into his little restau-rant. The moment you step through the door, you know you're in for good, classic Italian cuisine (£7-10 pizzas and pastas, £11-15 plates, daily 12:00-14:00 & 17:00-23:00, 85-87 Newington Road, tel. 0131/662-9977).

Voujon Restaurant serves a fusion menu flaunting high-lights of Bengali and Indian cuisines. Vegetarians delight at the expansive yet inexpensive offerings starting at £8 (lunch specials, dinner main dishes £11-17, daily 12:00-14:00 & 17:30-23:30, 107 Newington Road, tel. 0131/667-5046, www.voujonedinburgh.co.uk).

Edinburgh Connections

By Train or Bus

From Edinburgh by Train to: Glasgow (4/hour, 50 minutes), **St. Andrews** (train to Leuchars, 1-2/hour, 1 hour, then 10-minute bus into St. Andrews), **Stirling** (roughly 2/hour, 1 hour), **Pitlochry** (6/day direct, 2 hours), **Inverness** (every 1-2 hours, 3.5-4 hours, some with change in Perth), **Oban** (2/day, 4.25 hours, change in Glasgow), **York** (2/hour, 2.5 hours), **London** (1-2/hour, 4.5 hours), **Durham** (hourly direct, 2 hours, more with changes, less frequent in winter), **Newcastle** (2/hour, 1.5 hours), **Keswick/Lake District** (8-10/day to Penrith—some via Carlisle, 1.75 hours, then 40-min-ute bus ride to Keswick), **Birmingham** (at least hourly, 4-5 hours, some with change in Newcastle or York), **Crewe** (every 2 hours, 3 hours), **Bristol,** near Bath (hourly, 6-6.5 hours), **Blackpool** (roughly hourly, 3-3.5 hours, transfer in Preston). **Train info**: Tel.

0845-748-4950, www.nationalrail.co.uk.

By Bus to: Glasgow (4/hour, 1.25-1.5 hours), **Oban** (7/day Mon-Sat, 4-5 hours; 1 direct, rest with transfer in Glasgow), **Fort William** (7/day, 4-5 hours, 1 direct, rest with change in Glasgow or Tyndrum), **Portree** on the Isle of Skye (4/day, 7.5-8 hours, transfer in Inverness or Glasgow), **Inverness** (nearly hourly, 3.5-4.5 hours). For bus info, call Scottish Citylink (tel. 0871-266-3333, www.city link.co.uk) or National Express (expensive toll tel. 0871-781-8181, £1/minute; booking online is smarter—and free). Megabus also operates some long-distance routes (www.megabus.com). You can get info and tickets at the bus desk inside the Princes Mall TI or at the bus station.

Route Tips for Drivers

It's 100 miles south from Edinburgh to Hadrian's Wall; to Durham, it's another 50 miles.

To Hadrian's Wall: From Edinburgh, Dalkeith Road leads south and eventually becomes the A-68 (handy Cameron Toll supermarket with cheap gas is on the left as you leave Edinburgh Town, 10 minutes south of Edinburgh; gas and parking behind store). The A-68 road takes you to Hadrian's Wall in 2.5 hours. You'll pass Jedburgh and its abbey after one hour. (For one last shot of Scotland shopping, there's a coach tour's delight just before Jedburgh, with kilt makers, woolens, and a sheepskin shop.) Across from Jedburgh's lovely abbey is a free parking lot, a good visitors center, and public toilets (£0.20 to pee). The England/Scotland border is a fun, quick stop (great view, ice cream, and tea caravan). Just after the turn for Colwell, turn right onto the A-6079, and roller-coaster four miles down to Low Brunton. Then turn right onto the B-6318, and stay on it by turning left at Chollerford, following the Roman wall westward.

To Durham: If you're heading straight to Durham, you can take the scenic coastal route on the A-1 (a few more miles than the A-68, but similar time), which takes you near Holy Island and Bamburgh Castle.

ST. ANDREWS

St. Andrews • The East Neuk

For many, St. Andrews is synonymous with golf. But there's more to this charming town than its famous links. Dramatically situated at the edge of a sandy bay, St. Andrews is the home of Scotland's most important university—think of it as the Scottish Cambridge. And centuries ago, the town was the religious capital of the country.

In its long history, St. Andrews has seen two boom periods. First, in the early Middle Ages, the relics of St. Andrew made the town cathedral one of the most important pilgrimage sites in Christendom. The faithful flocked here from all over Europe, leaving the town with a medieval all-roads-lead-to-the-cathedral street plan that survives today. But after the Scottish Reformation, the cathedral rotted away and the town became a forgotten backwater. A new wave of visitors arrived in the mid-19th century, when a visionary mayor named (appropriately enough) Provost Playfair began to promote the town's connection with the newly in-vogue game of golf. Most buildings in town date from this time (similar to Edinburgh's New Town).

Today St. Andrews remains a popular spot for students, golf devotees (including professional golfers and celebrities such as Scotsman Sean Connery, often seen out on the links), and occasionally Britain's royal couple, Will and Kate. With vast sandy beaches, golfing opportunities for pros and novices alike, playgrounds of ruins, a fun-loving student vibe, and a string of relaxing fishing villages nearby (the East Neuk), St. Andrews is an appealing place to take a vacation from your busy vacation.

Planning Your Time

St. Andrews, hugging the east coast of Scotland, is a bit off the main tourist track. But it's well-connected by train to Edinburgh (via bus from nearby Leuchars), making it a worthwhile day trip from the capital. Better yet, spend a night (or more, if you're a golfer) to enjoy this university town after dark.

If you're not here to golf, this is a good way to spend a day: Follow my self-guided walk, which connects the golf course, the university quad, the castle, and the cathedral. Dip into the Golf Museum, watch the golfers on the Old Course, and play a round at "the Himalayas" putting green. With more time, walk along the West Sands beach or take a spin by car or bus to the nearby East Neuk.

Orientation to St. Andrews

St. Andrews (pop. 16,000), situated at the tip of a peninsula next to a broad bay, retains its old medieval street plan: Three main streets (North, Market, and South) converge at the cathedral, which overlooks the sea at the tip of town. The middle street—Market Street—has the TI and many handy shops and eateries. North of North Street, the seafront street called The Scores connects the cathedral with the golf scene, which huddles along the West Sands beach at the base of the old town. St. Andrews is enjoyably compact: You can stroll across town—from the cathedral to the historic golf course—in about 15 minutes.

Tourist Information

St. Andrews' helpful TI is on Market Street, about two blocks in front of the cathedral (July-Aug Mon-Sat 9:15-18:00, Sun 10:00-17:00; April-June and Sept-mid-Oct Mon-Sat 9:15-17:00, Sun 11:00-16:00; mid-Oct-March Mon-Sat 9:15-17:00, Sun 10:00-17:00; 70 Market Street, tel. 01334/472-021, www.visitfife.com or www.visitscotland.com). Pick up their stack of brochures on the town and region, and ask about other tours (such as ghost walks or witches walks). They also have Internet access (£1/20 minutes) and can find you a room for a £4 fee.

Arrival in St. Andrews

By Train and Bus: The nearest train station is in the village of Leuchars, five miles away. From there, a 10-minute bus ride takes you right into St. Andrews (£2.75, buy ticket from driver, round-trip day tickets are cheaper; buses meet most trains, see schedule at bus shelter for next bus to St. Andrews; while waiting, read the historical info under the nearby flagpole). St. Andrews' bus station is near the base of Market Street—a short walk from most

ST. ANDREWS

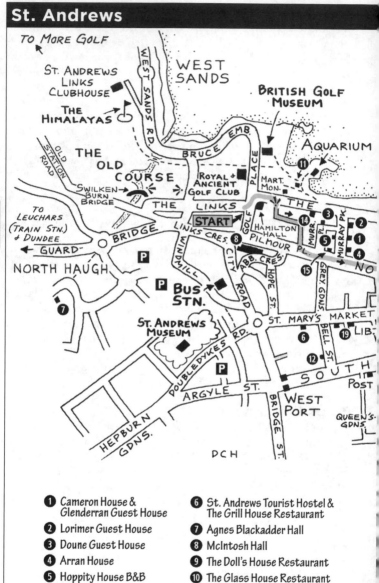

St. Andrews

TO MORE GOLF

ST. ANDREWS LINKS CLUBHOUSE

THE HIMALAYAS

WEST SANDS RD.

WEST SANDS

BRITISH GOLF MUSEUM

AQUARIUM

OLD STATION ROAD

THE OLD COURSE

BRUCE EMB.

Swilken Burn Bridge

ROYAL & ANCIENT GOLF CLUB

GOLF PLACE

MART. MON.

THE LINKS

START

THE

TO LEUCHARS (TRAIN STN.) & DUNDEE

GUARD-

BRIDGE

LINKS CRES.

HAMILTON HALL

PILMOUR PL.

MURR. PL.

MURRAY PK.

NO

WINDMILL

CITY ROAD

HOPE ST.

ABB. CRES.

GREY GDNS.

NORTH HAUGH

P

P

BUS STN.

ST. ANDREWS MUSEUM

DOUBLEDYKES RD.

ST. MARY'S

BELL ST.

MARKET

LIB.

SOUTH

Post

P

ARGYLE ST.

WEST PORT

BRIDGE ST.

QUEEN'S GDNS.

HEPBURN GDNS.

DCH

ST. ANDREWS *(side tab)*

1. Cameron House & Glenderran Guest House
2. Lorimer Guest House
3. Doune Guest House
4. Arran House
5. Hoppity House B&B
6. St. Andrews Tourist Hostel & The Grill House Restaurant
7. Agnes Blackadder Hall
8. McIntosh Hall
9. The Doll's House Restaurant
10. The Glass House Restaurant

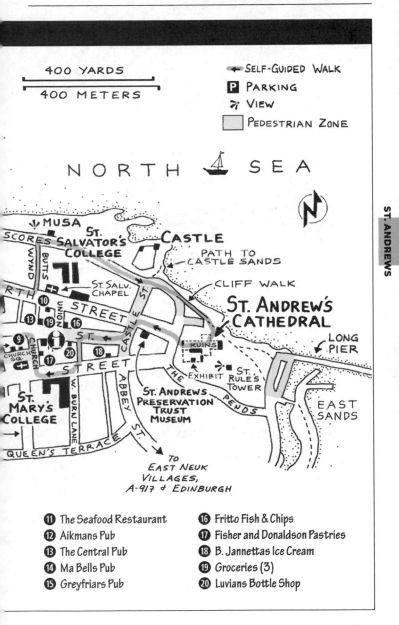

400 YARDS

400 METERS

← SELF-GUIDED WALK
P PARKING
↗ VIEW
▢ PEDESTRIAN ZONE

N O R T H ⛵ S E A

↯ MUSA
SCORES WYND
ST. SALVATOR'S COLLEGE
BUTTS
CASTLE
PATH TO CASTLE SANDS
CLIFF WALK
ST. ANDREW'S CATHEDRAL
ST. SALV. CHAPEL
STREET
NORTH
UNION
LONG PIER
RUINS
EXHIBIT
ST. RULE'S TOWER
CHURCH SQ.
W. BURN LANE
CASTLE ST.
THE PENDS
EAST SANDS
ST. ANDREWS PRESERVATION TRUST MUSEUM
ST. MARY'S COLLEGE
ABBEY ST.
QUEEN'S TERRACE

TO EAST NEUK VILLAGES, A-917 & EDINBURGH

⓫ The Seafood Restaurant
⓬ Aikmans Pub
⓭ The Central Pub
⓮ Ma Bells Pub
⓯ Greyfriars Pub

⓰ Fritto Fish & Chips
⓱ Fisher and Donaldson Pastries
⓲ B. Jannettas Ice Cream
⓳ Groceries (3)
⓴ Luvians Bottle Shop

B&Bs and the TI (follow the map). A taxi from Leuchars into St. Andrews costs about £12.

By Car: For a short stay, drivers can simply head into the town center and park anywhere along the street. Easy-to-use meters dispense stickers (£1/hour, coins only, 2-hour limit, monitored Mon-Sat 9:00-17:00). For longer stays, you can park for free along certain streets near the center (such as along The Scores), or use one of the long-stay lots near the entrance to town.

Helpful Hints

Golf Events: Every five years, St. Andrews is swamped with about 100,000 visitors when it hosts the British Open (called simply "The Open" around here; the next one is in 2015). The town also fills up every year in early October for the Alfred Dunhill Links Championship. Unless you're a golf pilgrim, avoid the town at these times (as room rates skyrocket).

School Term: The University of St. Andrews has two terms: spring semester ("Candlemas"), from mid-February through May; and fall semester ("Martinmas"), from mid-September until December. St. Andrews feels downright sleepy in summer, when most students leave and golfers take over the town.

Internet Access: You can get online for free at the **public library,** behind the church on South Street (photo ID required, Mon and Fri-Sat 9:30-17:00, Tue-Thu 9:30-19:00, closed Sun, tel. 01334/659-378). The TI also has two pay terminals (£1/20 minutes).

Self-Guided Walk

Welcome to St. Andrews

This walk links all of St. Andrews' must-see sights and takes you down hidden medieval streets. Allow a couple of hours or more if you detour for the sights along the way.

• *Start at the base of the seaside street called The Scores, overlooking the famous golf course. (There are benches with nice views by the Links Golf Shop for those with a sandwich to munch.)*

▲The Old Course

You're looking at the mecca of golf. The 18th hole of the world's first golf course is a few yards away, on your left (for info on playing the course, see "Golfing in St. Andrews," later).

The gray Neoclassical building to the right of the 18th hole is the **Royal and Ancient Golf Club** (or "R&A" for short), which is the world's governing body for golf (like the British version of the PGA). The R&A is a private club with membership by invitation only, and only men can be members. (In Scotland, men-only clubs lose tax benefits, which is quite costly, but they generally don't care about expenses because their membership is wealthy.) Women can enter the R&A building only during the Women's British Open on St. Andrew's Day (Nov 30). Anyone can enter the shop nearby, which is a great spot to buy a souvenir for the golf lover back home. Even if you're not golfing, watch the action for a while. (Serious fans can walk around to the low-profile stone bridge across the creek called Swilken Burn, with golf's single most iconic view: back over the 18th hole and the R&A.)

Overlooking the course is the big, red-sandstone **Hamilton Hall,** an old hotel long used as a university dormitory and now under renovation to become swanky apartments. According to town legend, the grand building was built to upstage the R&A by an American upset over being declined membership to the exclusive club.

Between Hamilton Hall and the beach is the low-profile **British Golf Museum.**

• *Now, turn your back to the golf course and walk through the park (along the street called The Scores) a few steps to the obelisk.*

Martyrs' Monument

This obelisk commemorates all those who died for their Protestant beliefs during the Scottish Reformation. Walk to the benches on the bluff for a good look at the cliffs on your right. For a time, the sea below was called "Witches' Lake" because of all the women and men pushed off the cliff on suspicion of witchcraft. The Victorian bandstand gazebo recalls the town's genteel heyday as a seaside resort, when the train line ran all the way to town.

The broad, two-mile-long sandy beach that stretches below the golf course is the West Sands (a.k.a. "Chariots of Fire beach"). It's a wonderful place for a relaxing and/or invigorating walk. Or do a slo-mo jog, humming the theme to *Chariots of Fire*. This is the beach on which the characters run in the movie's famous opening scene.

Just opposite the obelisk, across The Scores and next to the Alexander Restaurant, walk down the tiny **Gillespie Wynd alleyway.** It winds through the back gardens of the city's stone houses. Notice how the medieval platting gave landowners a little bit of street front and a long back garden. St. Andrews' street plan typifies that of a medieval pilgrimage town: All main roads lead to the cathedral; only tiny lanes, hidden alleys, and twisting "wynds" (rhymes with "minds") such as this one connect the main east-west streets.

• *The wynd pops you out onto North Street. Make like a pilgrim and head left toward the cathedral—look for its ruined facade in the distance. Walk about 100 yards to the small cinema from where you'll see*

ST. ANDREWS

the church tower with the red clock face (our next stop). It's on the corner of North Street and **Butts Wynd** *(no joke). For some reason, this street sign often goes missing.*

At Butts Wynd, you're standing outside St. Salvator's Chapel and St. Salvator's College. If you're a student, be careful not to stand on the initials PH *in the cobbles. They mark the spot where St. Andrews alum and professor Patrick Hamilton—the Scottish Reformation's most famous martyr—was burned at the stake. According to student legend, as he suffered in the flames, Hamilton threatened that any students who stood on this spot would fail their exams. (And you thought you had dramatic professors.)*

Enter the grounds by walking through the arch under the tower with the red clock. (If the entrance is closed, you can go halfway down Butts Wynd and enter, or at least look, through the gate to the green square.)

ST. ANDREWS

St. Salvator's College

This grassy square, known to students as **Sally's Quad,** is the heart of the university. As most of the university's classrooms, offices, and libraries are spread out across the medieval town, this quad is the one focal point for student gatherings. It's where graduation is held every July, where the free-for-all food fight of Raisin Monday takes place in November, and where almost the entire student body gathered to celebrate the wedding day of their famous alumni couple—Prince William and Princess Kate—complete with military flybys.

On the outside wall of **St. Salvator's Chapel** are cases holding notices and university information; if you're here in spring, you might see students nervously clustered here, looking to see if they've passed their exams.

Go through the simple wooden door and into the chapel. Dating from 1450, this is the town's most beautiful medieval church. It's a Gothic gem, with a wooden ceiling, 19th-century stained glass, and (supposedly) the pulpit of reformer John Knox.

Stroll around Sally's Quad counterclockwise. If you're feeling curious, push a few doors (some seemingly off-limits university buildings, many marked by blue doors, are actually open to the public). On the east (far) side, stop to check out the crazy faces on the heads above the second-floor windows. Find the **university's shield** over the door marked *School Six.* The diamonds are from the coat of arms of the bishop who issued the first university charter in 1411; the crescent moon is a shout-out to Pope Benedict XIII, who gave the OK in 1413 to found the university (his given name was Peter de Luna); the lion is from the Scottish coat of arms; and the X-shaped cross is a stylized version of the Scottish flag (a.k.a. St.

The Scottish Reformation

It's easy to forget that during the 16th-century English Reformation—when King Henry VIII split with the Vatican and formed the Anglican Church (so he could get an officially recognized divorce)—Scotland was still its own independent nation. Like much of northern Europe, Scotland eventually chose a Protestant path, but it was more gradual and grassroots than Henry VIII's top-down, destroy-the-abbeys approach. While the English Reformation resulted in the Church of England (a.k.a. the Anglican Church, called "Episcopal" outside of England), with the monarch at its head, the Scottish Reformation created the Church of Scotland, which had groups of elected leaders (called "presbyteries" in church jargon).

One of the leaders of the Scottish Reformation was John Knox (1514-1572), who studied under the great Swiss Reformer John Calvin. Returning to Scotland, Knox hopped from pulpit to pulpit, and his feverish sermons incited riots of "born-again" iconoclasts who dismantled or destroyed Catholic churches and abbeys (including St. Andrew's Cathedral). Knox's newly minted Church of Scotland gradually spread from the Lowlands to the Highlands. The southern and eastern part of Scotland, around St. Andrews—just across the North Sea from the Protestant countries of northern Europe—embraced the Church of Scotland long before the more remote and Catholic-oriented part of the country to the north and west. Today about 40 percent of Scots claim affiliation with the Church of Scotland, compared with 20 percent who are Catholic (still mostly in the western Highlands). Glasgow and western Scotland are more Catholic, partly because of the Irish immigrants who settled here after fleeing the potato famine in the 1840s.

Andrew's Cross). On the next building to the left, facing the chapel, is St. Andrew himself (above door of building labeled *Upper & Lower College Halls*).

• *Exit the square at the west end, if the gate's open, and turn right into Butts Wynd (if the gate's closed, backtrack out the main gate and hang a right into Butts Wynd). When the alley ends, you're back at The Scores. Cross the street and head to the right. The turreted stone buildings along here are built in the Neo–Gothic Scots Baronial style, and most are academic departments. Head for the...*

Museum of the University of St. Andrews (MUSA)

This free museum is worth a quick stop. The first room has some well-explained medieval artifacts. Note the copy of the earliest-

ST. ANDREWS

Student Life in St. Andrews

Although most people associate St. Andrews with golf, it's first and foremost a university town—the home of Scotland's most prestigious university. Founded in 1411, it's the third-oldest in the English-speaking world; only Oxford and Cambridge have been around longer.

The U. of St. A. has about 6,000 undergrads and 1,000 grad students. Though Scots and most EU citizens attend for free, others (including students from England) must pay tuition. Some Scots resent the high concentration of upper-class English students (disparagingly dubbed "Yahs" for the snooty way they say "yes"), who treat St. Andrews as a safety school if rejected by Cambridge or Oxford. The school has even been called "England's northernmost university" because it has as many English students as Scottish ones. (Adding to the mix, about a quarter of the students come from overseas.) Its most famous recent graduate is Prince William (class of '05). Soon after he started here, the number of female applicants to study art history—his major—skyrocketed. (He later switched to geography.)

As with any venerable university, St. Andrews has its share of quirky customs—as if the university, like the town's street plan, insists on clinging to the Middle Ages. Most students own traditional red academic "gowns" (woolen robes). Today these are only worn for special occasions, such as graduation, but in medieval times, students were required to wear them always—supposedly so they could be easily identified in brothels and pubs. (In a leap of faith, divinity students—apparently beyond temptation—wear black.) The way the robe is worn indicates the student's progress toward graduation: First-year students (called

known map of the town, made in 1580—back when the town walls led directly to the countryside and the cathedral was intact. Notice that the street plan within the town walls has remained the same—but no golf course. The next room has some exhibits on student life. For a great view of the West Sands, climb to the rooftop terrace.

Cost and Hours: Free; April-Oct Mon-Sat 10:00-17:00, Sun 12:00-16:00; Nov-March Thu-Sun 12:00-16:00, closed Mon-Wed; 7 The Scores, tel. 01334/461-660, www.st-andrews.ac.uk/musa.

• *Leaving the museum, walk left toward the castle. The neighboring building is a fine example of that Neo-Gothic Scots Baronial style. About 100 yards farther along, the grand building (on the right, fronting The Scores) is St. Salvator's Hall, the most prestigious of the university residences and former dorm of Prince William. Just past St. Salvator's Hall, on a bluff overlooking the sea, are the remains of...*

"bejants") wear them normally, on the shoulders; second-years ("semi-bejants") wear them slightly off the shoulders; third-years ("tertians") wear them off one shoulder (right shoulder for "scientists" and left shoulder for "artists"); and fourth-years ("magistrands") wear them off both shoulders.

There's no better time to see these robes than during the Pier Walk on Sunday afternoons during the university term. After church services (around noon), students clad in their gowns parade out to the end of the lonesome pier beyond the cathedral ruins. The tradition dates so far back that no one's sure how it started (probably to bid farewell to a visiting dignitary). Today, students participate mostly because it's fun to be a part of the visual spectacle of a long line of red robes flapping in the North Sea wind.

St. Andrews also clings to an antiquated social-mentoring system, where underclassmen choose an "academic family." In mid-November comes Raisin Monday, named for the raisins traditionally given as treats to one's "parents" (but today students usually give wine to their "dad" and lingerie to their "mum"). After receiving their gifts, the upperclassmen "parents" dress up their "children" in outrageous costumes and parade them through town. The underclassmen are also obliged to carry around "receipts" for their gifts—often written on unlikely or unwieldy objects (e.g., plastic dinosaurs, microwave ovens, even refrigerators). Any upperclassmen they come across can demand a rendition of the school song in Latin. The whole scene invariably turns into a free-for-all food fight in St. Salvator's Quad (weapons include condiments, shaving cream, and, according to campus rumors, human entrails pilfered by med students).

▲St. Andrews Castle

Overlooking the sea, the castle is an evocative empty shell—another casualty of the Scottish Reformation. Built by a bishop to

entertain visiting diplomats in the late 12th century, the castle was home to the powerful bishops, archbishops, and cardinals of St. Andrews. In 1546, the cardinal burned a Protestant preacher at the stake in front of the castle. In retribution, Protestant Reformers took the castle and killed the cardinal. In 1547, the French came to attack the castle on behalf of their Catholic ally, Mary, Queen of Scots. During the ensuing siege, a young Protestant refugee named John Knox was captured and sent to France to row on a galley ship. Eventually he traveled to Switzerland and met the Swiss Protestant ringleader, John Calvin. Knox brought Calvin's ideas back home and became Scotland's greatest Reformer.

Your visit starts with a colorful, kid-friendly exhibit about the history of the castle. Afterward, head outside to explore. The most interesting parts are underground: the "bottle dungeon," where prisoners were sent, never to return (peer down into it in the Sea Tower); and the tight "mine" and even tighter "counter-mine" tunnels (follow the signs, crawling is required to reach it all; go in as far as your claustrophobia allows). This shows how the besieging French army dug a mine to take (or "undermine") the castle—but were followed at every turn by the Protestant counter-miners.

Just below the castle is a small beach called the Castle Sands, where university students take a traditional and chilly morning dip on May 1. Supposedly, doing this May Day swim is the only way to reverse the curse of having stepped on Patrick Hamilton's initials (explained earlier).

Cost and Hours: £5.50, £7.20 combo-ticket includes cathedral exhibit, daily April-Sept 9:30-17:30, Oct-March 9:30-16:30, last entry 30 minutes before closing, tel. 01334/477-196, www .historic-scotland.gov.uk.

• *Leaving the castle, turn left and continue along the bluff on The Scores, which soon becomes a pedestrian lane leading directly to the gate to the cathedral graveyard. Enter it to stand amid the tombstone-strewn ruins of...*

▲St. Andrew's Cathedral

Between the Great Schism and the Reformation (roughly the 14th-16th centuries), St. Andrews was the ecclesiastical capital of Scotland—and this was its showpiece church. Today the site features the remains of the cathedral and cloister (with walls and spires pecked away by centuries of scavengers), a graveyard, and a small exhibit and climbable tower.

Cost and Hours: Cathedral ruins-free; exhibit and tower-£4.50, £7.20 combo-ticket includes castle; daily April-Sept 9:30-17:30, Oct-March 9:30-16:30, last entry 30 minutes before closing, tel. 01334/472-563, www.historic-scotland.gov.uk.

Background: It was the relics of the Apostle Andrew that first put this town on the map and gave it its name. There are numerous legends associated with the relics. According to one version, in the fourth century, St. Rule was directed in a dream to bring the relics northward from Constantinople. When the ship wrecked offshore from here, it was clear that this was a sacred place. Andrew's bones (an upper arm, a kneecap, some fingers, and a tooth) were kept on this site, and starting in 1160, the cathedral was built and pilgrims began to arrive. Since St. Andrew had a direct connection to Jesus, his relics were believed to possess special properties, making them worthy of pilgrimages on par with St. James' relics in Santiago de Compostela, Spain (of Camino de Santiago fame). St. Andrew became Scotland's patron saint; in fact, the white "X" on the blue Scottish flag evokes the diagonal cross on which St. Andrew was crucified (he chose this type of cross because he felt unworthy to die as Jesus had).

◐ Self-Guided Tour: You can stroll around the cathedral **ruins**—the best part of the complex—for free. First walk between

the two ruined but still towering ends of the church, which used to be the apse (at the sea end, where you entered) and the main entry (at the town end). Visually trace the gigantic footprint of the former church in the ground, including the bases of columns—like giant sawed-off tree trunks. Plaques identify where elements of the church once stood.

Looking at the one wall that's still standing, you can see the architectural changes that were made over the 150 years the cathedral was built—from the rounded, Romanesque windows at the front to the more highly decorated, pointed Gothic arches near the back. Mentally rebuild the church, and try to imagine it in its former majesty, when it played host to pilgrims from all over Europe.

The church wasn't destroyed all at once, like all those ruined abbeys in England (demolished in a huff by Henry VIII when he broke with the pope). Instead, because the Scottish Reformation was more gradual, this church was slowly picked apart over time. First just the decorations were removed from inside the cathedral. Then the roof was pulled down to make use of its lead. Without a roof, the cathedral fell further and further into disrepair, and was quarried by locals for its handy precut stones (which you'll still find in the walls of many old St. Andrews homes). The elements—a big storm in the 1270s and a fire in 1378—also contributed to the

cathedral's demise.

The surrounding **graveyard,** dating from the post-Reformation Protestant era, is much more recent than the cathedral. In this golf-obsessed town, the game even infiltrates the cemeteries: Many notable golfers from St. Andrews are buried here (such as Young Tom—or "Tommy"—Morris, four-time British Open winner).

ST. ANDREWS

Go through the surviving wall into the former **cloister,** marked by a gigantic grassy square in the center. You can still see the cleats up on the wall, which once supported beams. Imagine the cloister back in its heyday, its passages filled with strolling monks.

At the end of the cloister is a small **exhibit** (entry fee required), with a relatively dull collection of old tombs and other carved-stone relics that have been unearthed on this site. Your ticket also includes entry to the surviving **tower of St. Rule's Church** (the rectangular tower beyond the cathedral ruins that was built to hold the precious relics of St. Andrew about a thousand years ago). If you feel like hiking up the 157 very claustrophobic steps for the view over St. Andrews' rooftops, it's worth the price. Up top, you can also look out to sea to find the pier where students traditionally walk out in their robes.

• *Leave the cathedral grounds on the town side of the cathedral. Angling right, head down North Street. Just ahead, on the left, is the adorable...*

▲St. Andrews Preservation Trust Museum and Garden

Filling a 17th-century fishing family's house that was protected from developers, this museum is a time capsule of an earlier, simpler era. The house itself seems built for Smurfs, but once housed 20 family members. The ground floor features replicas of a grocer's shop and a "chemist's" (pharmacy), using original fittings from actual stores. Upstairs are temporary exhibits. (To mark the centennial of the start of World War I, one of the rotating exhibits in 2014 will feature The Great War—from the perspective of its social history and impact on St. Andrews.) Out back is a tranquil garden (dedicated to the memory of a beloved professor) with "great-grandma's washhouse," featuring an exhibit about the history of soap and washing. Lovingly presented, this quaint, humble house provides a nice contrast to the big-money scene around the golf course at the other end of town.

Cost and Hours: Free but donation requested, generally open late May-late Sept daily 14:00-17:00, closed off-season, 12 North Street, tel. 01334/477-629, www.standrewspreservationtrust.org.

• *From the museum, hang a left around the next corner to South Castle Street. At the top of Market Street, look for the tiny white house on your left, with the cute curved staircase. What's that chase scene on the roof?*

Turn right down Market Street (which leads directly to the town's center, but we'll take a curvier route). Notice how the streets and even the buildings are smaller at this oldest end of town, as if the whole city is shrinking as the streets close in on the cathedral. Passing an antique bookstore on your right, take a left onto Baxter Wynd, a.k.a. Baker

Lane (unmarked). You'll pass a tiny garden on your right before land-ing on South Street. Turn right and head down South Street. After 50 yards, cross the street and enter a gate marked by a cute gray facade and a university insignia.

St. Mary's College

This is the home of the university's School of Divinity (theology). If the gate's open, find the peaceful quad, with its gnarled tree, purportedly planted by Mary, Queen of Scots. To get a feel of stu-dent life from centuries past, try poking your nose into one of the old classrooms.

• *Back on South Street, continue to your left. Some of the plainest build-ings on this stretch of the street have the most interesting history—sev-eral of them were built to fund the Crusades. Turn right on Church Street. You can end this walk at charming Church Square, where you'll find the library (with Internet access; see "Helpful Hints," earlier) and recommended Fisher and Donaldson bakery (closed Sun).*

But if you want to do more exploring, head to nearby Market Street (just a few yards down Church Street) to find the TI, grocery store, and...

Luvians Bottle Shop

Run by three brothers (**Lu**igi, **Vi**ncenzo, and **An**tonio), this might be the friendliest place in Scotland to talk, taste, and purchase whisky. The brothers and staff are so well-regarded that distill-eries bottle unique single-cask vintages just for them to celebrate the British Open every five years (ask about the recent 17-year-old Glenfarclas, or the 21-year-old Springbank they are expecting in 2015 to commemorate the tournament). With nearly 50 bottles open, a map of Scotland's whisky regions, and more-than-helpful team members, if you don't leave the shop enjoying whisky, you never will.

Cost and Hours: Daily 10:00-22:00, Sun open at 12:30, 66 Market Street, tel. 01334/477-752, www.luvians.com.
• *About a five-minute walk away in Kinburn Park is...*

St. Andrews Museum

This small, modest museum, which traces St. Andrews' history "from A to Zed," is an enjoyable way to pass time on a rainy day. It's situated in an old mansion in Kinburn Park, a five-minute walk from the old town (walk east down Market Street and St. Mary's Place, then through the roundabout onto Doubledykes Road; the museum is ahead on the right).

Cost and Hours: Free, daily April-Sept 10:00-17:00, Oct-March 10:30-16:00, café, Doubledykes Road, tel. 01334/659-380.

Golfing in St. Andrews

St. Andrews is the Cooperstown and Mecca of golf. While St. Andrews lays claim to founding the sport (the first record of golf being played here was in 1553), nobody knows exactly where and when people first hit a ball with a stick for fun. In the Middle Ages, St. Andrews traded with the Dutch; some historians believe they picked up a golf-like Dutch game on ice, and translated it to the bonnie rolling hills of Scotland's east coast. Since the grassy beachfront strip just outside St. Andrews was too poor to support crops, it was used for playing the game—and, centuries later, it still is. Why do golf courses have 18 holes? Because that's how many fit at the Old Course in St. Andrews, golf's single most famous site.

The Old Course

The Old Course hosts the British Open every five years (next in 2015). At other times it's open to the public for golfing. Fortunately for women golfers, the men-only Royal and Ancient Golf Club (R&A) doesn't actually own the course, which is public and managed by the St. Andrews Links Trust. Drop by their clubhouse, overlooking the beach near the Old Course (hours roughly May-Aug daily 7:00-21:00, progressively shorter until 7:30-16:00 in Dec, www.standrews.org.uk).

Teeing Off at the Old Course: Playing at golf's pinnacle course is pricey (£155/person, less off-season), but accessible to the public—subject to lottery drawings for tee times and reserved spots by club members. You can play the Old Course only if you have a handicap of 24 (men) or 36 (women); bring along your certificate or card. If you don't know your handicap—or don't know what "handicap" means—then you're not good enough to play here (they want to keep the game moving, rather than wait for novices to spend 10 strokes on each hole). If you play, you'll do nine holes out, then nine more back in—however, all but four share the same greens.

Reserving a Tee Time: To ensure a specific tee time at the Old Course, it's smart to reserve a full year ahead. Call 01334/466-666 or email reservations@standrews.org.uk. Otherwise, some tee times are determined each day by a lottery called the "daily ballot." Call or visit in person by 14:00 two days before to put your name in (2 players minimum, 4 players max)—they post the results online at 16:00. Note that no advance reservations are taken on Saturdays or in September, and the courses are closed on Sundays—which is traditionally the day reserved for townspeople.

Other Courses: The trust manages six other courses (including two right next to the Old Course—the New Course and the Jubilee Course), plus the modern cliff-top Castle Course just outside the city. These are cheaper, and it's much easier to get a tee time (£70 for New and Jubilee, £120 for Castle Course, £15-45 for others). It's usually possible to get a tee time for the same day or next day (if you want a guaranteed reservation, make it at least 2 weeks in advance). The Castle Course has great views overlooking the town, but even more wind to blow your ball around.

▲The Himalayas

Named for its dramatically hilly terrain, "The Himalayas" is basically a very classy (but still relaxed) game of mini-golf. Technically

the "Ladies' Putting Green," this cute little patch of undulating grass presents the perfect opportunity for non-golfers (female or male) to say they've played the links at St. Andrews—for less than the cost of a Coke. It's remarkable how the contour of the land can present even more challenging obstacles than the tunnels, gates, and distractions of a corny putt-putt course back home. Flat shoes are required (no high heels). You'll see it on the left as you walk toward the clubhouse from the R&A.

ST. ANDREWS

Cost and Hours: £2 for 18 holes. The putting green is open April-Oct daily 10:30-18:00 or 19:00, closed Nov-March. While most hours are reserved for members, non-members (tourists like you) are welcome to play Mon-Tue and Fri (10:30-17:00), Wed (10:30-12:00 & 16:00-18:00), Thu (11:00-18:00), and Sun (10:00-12:00). Tel. 1334/475-196.

British Golf Museum

This exhibit, which started as a small collection in the R&A across the street, is the best place in Britain to learn about the Scots' favorite sport. It's fascinating for golf lovers.

The compact, one-way exhibit reverently presents a meticulous survey of the game's history—from the monarchs who loved and hated golf (including the king who outlawed it because it was distracting men from church and archery practice), right up to the "Golden Bear" and a randy Tiger. A constant 2-hour loop film shows highlights of the British Open from 1923 to the present, and other video screens show scratchy black-and-white highlights from the days before corporate sponsorship. At the end, find items donated by the golfers of today, including Tiger Woods' shirt, hat, and glove.

Cost and Hours: £6.50, includes informative book about the history of golf; April-Oct Mon-Sat 9:30-17:00, Sun 10:00-17:00; Nov-March daily 10:00-16:00; last entry 45 minutes before closing; free 45-minute guided tours June-Sept daily at 11:15 and 15:45; Bruce Embankment, in the blocky modern building squatting behind the R&A by the Old Course, tel. 01334/460-046, www .britishgolfmuseum.co.uk.

Sleeping in St. Andrews

Owing partly to the high-roller golf tourists flowing through the town, St. Andrews' accommodations are expensive. During graduation week in June, hotels often require a four-night stay and book up quickly. Solo travelers are at a disadvantage, as many B&Bs don't have singles—and charge close to the double price for one person (I've listed "S" or "Sb" below for those that actually have single rooms). But the quality at my recommendations is high, and budget alternatives—including a hostel—are workable. All of these, except the hostel and the dorms, are on the streets called Murray Park and Murray Place, between North Street and The Scores in the old town. If you need to find a room on the fly, head for this same neighborhood, which has far more options than just the ones I've listed below.

$$ Cameron House has five old-fashioned, paisley, masculine-feeling rooms—including two nice singles that share one bathroom—around a beautiful stained-glass atrium (S-£45, Db-£90, discount for longer stays, prices soft and sometimes closed Nov-Easter, free Wi-Fi, lounge, 11 Murray Park, tel. 01334/472-306, www.cameronhouse-sta.co.uk, info@cameronhouse-sta.co.uk, Donna and Yvonne).

$$ Lorimer Guest House has five comfortable, tastefully decorated rooms, including one on the ground floor (Db-£88-104, deluxe Db-£94-120, higher prices are for July-Sept, ask about discount for longer stays, guest computer, free Wi-Fi, 19 Murray Park, tel. 01334/476-599, www.lorimerhouse.com, info@lorimerhouse.com, Mick and Chris Cordner).

$$ Doune Guest House is golfer-friendly, with six comfortable, plaid-heavy rooms. The helpful owners are happy to arrange early breakfasts and airport transfers (S-£40-49, Db-£80-98, price depends on season, cheaper off-season, cash only, guest computer, free Wi-Fi, 5 Murray Place, tel. 01334/475-195, www.dounehouse.com, info@dounehouse.com).

$$ Arran House has nine modern rooms, including a single with a private bathroom across the hall (S-£50, Sb-£60, Db-£85-90, three ground-floor rooms, two family rooms, free Wi-Fi, 5 Murray Park, tel. 01334/474-724, mobile 07768-718-237, www.arranhousestandrews.co.uk, info@arranhousestandrews.co.uk, Anne and Jim McGrory).

$$ Glenderran Guest House offers five plush rooms (including two true singles) and a few nice breakfast extras (Sb-£40-60, Db-£80-120, free Wi-Fi, same-day laundry-£10, 9 Murray Park, tel. 01334/477-951, www.glenderran.com, info@glenderran.com, Ray and Maggie).

> # Sleep Code
>
> **(£1 = about $1.60, country code: 44, area code: 01334)**
> **S** = Single, **D** = Double/Twin, **T** = Triple, **Q** = Quad, **b** = bathroom,
> **s** = shower only. Unless otherwise noted, credit cards are
> accepted and breakfast is included.
>   To help you sort easily through these listings, I've divided
> the accommodations into two categories based on the price
> for a standard double room with bath (during high season):
>
> **$$ Higher Priced**—Most rooms £70 or more.
> **$ Lower Priced**—Most rooms less than £70.
>
> Prices can change without notice; verify the hotel's cur-
> rent rates online or by email. For the best prices, always book
> direct.

$$ Hoppity House is a bright and contemporary place, with neutral tones and built-in furniture that makes good use of space. You may find a stuffed namesake bunny or two hiding out among its six rooms. Golfers appreciate the golf-bag lockers on the ground floor (Sb-£45-55, Db-£75-90, deluxe Db-£90-110, family room, lower prices off-season, fridges in rooms, free Wi-Fi, 4 Murray Park, tel. 01334/461-116, mobile 07701-099-100, www.hoppity house.co.uk, enquiries@hoppityhouse.co.uk, helpful Gordon and Heather).

Hostel: **$ St. Andrews Tourist Hostel** has 44 beds in colorful 4- to 8-bed rooms about a block from the base of Market Street. The high-ceilinged lounge is a comfy place for a break, and the friendly staff is happy to recommend their favorite pubs (£16-20/bed, includes sheets, no breakfast, kitchen, free Wi-Fi, self-service laundry-£4, towels-£2, office open 7:00-23:00, office closed 15:00-18:00 outside of summer, no curfew, St. Mary's Place, tel. 01334/479-911, www.standrewshostel.com, standrewshostel @gmail.com).

University Accommodations

In the summer (mid-June-Aug), two of the University of St. Andrews' student-housing buildings are tidied up and rented out to tourists (website for both: www.discoverstandrews.com; pay when reserving).

$$ Agnes Blackadder Hall has double beds and private bathrooms; it's more comfortable, but also more expensive and less central (Sb-£39-59, Db-£68-85, family Qb-£89-102, includes breakfast, tel. 01334/467-000, agnes.blackadder@st-andrews.ac.uk).

$ McIntosh Hall is cheaper and more central, but it only has twin beds and shared bathrooms (S-£39, D-£68, tel. 01334/467-035, mchall@st-andrews.ac.uk). Because true single rooms are rare in St. Andrews' B&Bs, these dorms are a good option for solo travelers.

Eating in St. Andrews

The first three listings—owned by the same group—are popular and serve up reliably good international cuisine. Comparing their early-dinner specials may help you choose (www.houserestaurants.com).

The Doll's House offers cuisine with a French flair, with two floors of indoor seating and a cozy, colorful, casual atmosphere; the sidewalk seating out front is across from Holy Trinity Church (£7-11 lunches, £14-18 dinners, £12 two-course early-bird special 17:00-19:00, open daily 12:00-15:00 & 17:00-22:00, a block from the TI at 3 Church Square, tel. 01334/477-422).

The Glass House serves pizza, pasta, and salads in a two-story glass building with an open-style layout (£7 lunches 12:00-17:00, £9-11 dinners, £10 two-course early-bird special 17:00-18:30, open daily 12:00-22:00, second-floor outdoor patio, near the castle on 80 North Street, tel. 01334/473-673).

The Grill House offers Mexican-style food in a vibrantly colored space (£6 lunches 12:00-16:00, £11-17 dinners, £10 two-course early-bird special 16:00-18:30, open daily 12:00-22:00, St. Mary's Place, tel. 01334/470-500).

The Seafood Restaurant is St. Andrews' favorite splurge. Situated in a modern glassy building overlooking the beach near the Old Course, it's like dining in an aquarium. The place serves locally caught seafood to a room full of tables that wrap around the busy open kitchen. Dinner reservations are recommended (£13-26 lunches, £48.50 three-course dinner, daily 12:00-14:30 & 18:00-22:00, The Scores, tel. 01334/479-475, www.theseafoodrestaurant.com).

On Market Street: In the area around the TI, you'll find a concentration of good restaurants—pubs, grill houses, coffee shops, Asian food, fish-and-chips (see later), and more...take your pick. Also on Market Street, you can stock up for a picnic at **Greggs, Tesco,** and **Sainsbury's Local.**

Pubs: There's no shortage in this college town. **Aikmans,** run by Barbara and Malcolm (two graduates from the university who couldn't bring themselves to leave), features a cozy wood-table ambience, live music (traditional Scottish music upstairs once a month, other live music Fri-Sat) and simple soups, sandwiches, and snacks. This place knows its ales—it's been featured for the past quarter-century in the *Good Beer Guide* (£3-5 grub, open daily 11:00-24:00, 32 Bell Street, tel. 01334/477-425). **The Central** is a St. Andrews standby, with old lamps and lots of brass (£5 sandwiches, £8-10 burgers, Mon-Sat 11:00-23:45, Sun 12:30-23:45, food until 21:00, 77 Market Street, tel. 01334/478-296). **Ma Bells** is a sleek but friendly place that clings to its status as one of Prince William's favorites (£5-10 pub grub, pricier bistro meals, Mon-Sat 12:00-24:00, Sun 12:30-24:00, food served until 21:00, two blocks from the Old Course and R&A at 40 The Scores, tel. 01334/472-622). **Greyfriars** is in a classy, modern hotel near the Murray Park B&Bs (£5 light meals, £8-15 main dishes, daily 12:00-24:00, 129 North Street, tel. 01334/474-906).

Fish-and-Chips: **Fritto** is a local favorite for take-away fish-and-chips, centrally located on Market Street near the TI (£6 fish-and-chips, £4 burgers, daily 12:00-21:00, can be later Fri-Sat and when the weather's good, at the corner of Union and Market, tel. 01334/475-555). Brave souls will order a can of Irn-Bru with their fish (warning: It doesn't taste like orange soda). For what's considered the country's best chippie, head for the Anstruther Fish Bar in the East Neuk (described at the end of this chapter).

Dessert: **Fisher and Donaldson** is beloved for its rich, affordable pastries and chocolates. Listen as the straw-hatted bakers chat with their regular customers, then try their Coffee Tower—like a giant cream puff filled with rich, lightly coffee-flavored cream—or their number-one seller, the fudge doughnut (£1-2 pastries, Mon-Fri 6:00-17:15, Sat until 17:00, closed Sun, just around the corner from the TI at 13 Church Street, tel. 01334/472-201). **B. Jannettas,** which has been around for more than a century, features a wide and creative range of 52 tasty ice-cream flavors (£1.60 single scoop, £2.90 double scoop, daily 9:00-22:00, 31 South Street, tel. 01334/473-285, www.jannettas.co.uk).

St. Andrews Connections

Trains don't go into St. Andrews—instead, use the Leuchars station (5 miles from St. Andrews, connected by buses coordinated to meet most trains, 2-4/hour). The TI has useful train schedules, which also list bus departure times from St. Andrews.

From Leuchars by Train to: Edinburgh (1-2/hour, 1 hour), **Glasgow** (2/hour, 2 hours, transfer in Haymarket), **Inverness** (roughly hourly, 3.25-4 hours, 1-2 changes). Trains run less frequently on Sundays. Train info: Tel. 0845-748-4950, www.national rail.co.uk.

The East Neuk

On the lazy coastline meandering south from St. Andrews, the cute-as-a-pin East Neuk (pronounced "nook") is a collection of tidy fishing villages. While hardly earth-shattering, the East Neuk is a pleasant detour if you've got the time. The villages of Crail and Pittenweem have their fans, but Anstruther is worth most of your attention. The East Neuk works best as a half-day side-trip (by either car or bus) from St. Andrews, though drivers can use it as a scenic detour between Edinburgh and St. Andrews.

Getting There: It's an easy **drive** from St. Andrews. For the scenic route, follow the A-917 south of town along the coast, past Crail, on the way to Anstruther and Pittenweem. For a shortcut directly to Anstruther, take the B-9131 across the peninsula (or return that way after driving the longer coastal route there). **Buses** connect St. Andrews to the East Neuk: Bus #95 goes hourly from St. Andrews to Crail and Anstruther (50 minutes to Anstruther, catch bus at St. Andrews bus station or from Church Street, around the corner from the TI). The hourly #X60 bus goes directly to Anstruther, then on to Edinburgh (25 minutes to Anstruther, 2.25 hours more to Edinburgh). Bus info: Tel. 0871-200-2233, www.travelinescotland.com.

▲Anstruther

Stretched out along its harbor, colorful Anstruther (AN-stru-ther; pronounced ENT-ster by locals) is the centerpiece of the East Neuk. The main parking lot and bus stop are both right on the harbor. Anstruther's handy **TI,** which offers lots of useful information for the entire East Neuk area, is located next door to the town's main sight, the Scottish Fisheries Museum (April-Oct Mon-Sat 10:00-17:00, Sun 11:00-16:00, closed Nov-March, tel. 01333/311-073, www.visitfife.com). Stroll the harborfront to the end, detouring inland around the little cove (or crossing the causeway at low tide) to reach some colorful old houses, including one encrusted with seashells.

Anstruther's **Scottish Fisheries Museum** is true to its slogan: "We are bigger than you think!" The endearingly hokey exhibit sprawls through several harborfront buildings, painstakingly tracing the history of Scottish seafaring from primitive dugout dinghies to modern vessels. You'll learn the story of Scotland's "Zulu" fishing boats and walk through vast rooms filled with boats. For a glimpse at humble fishing lifestyles, don't miss the Fisherman's Cottage, hiding upstairs from the courtyard (£7; April-Sept Mon-Sat 10:00-17:30, Sun 11:00-17:00; Oct-March Mon-Sat 10:00-16:30, Sun 12:00-16:30; last entry one hour before closing, tearoom, Harbourhead, tel. 01333/310-628, www.scotfishmuseum .org).

Eating in Anstruther: Anstruther's claim to fame is its fish-and-chips, considered by many to be Scotland's best. Though there are several good chippies in town, the famous one is the **Anstruther Fish Bar,** facing the harbor just a block from the TI and Fisheries Museum. As you enter, choose whether you want to get takeout or dine in for a few pounds more. While more expensive than most chippies, the food here is good—so good the place has officially been named "UK's Fish and Chip Shop of the Year" multiple times. For those who don't like fish, they also have pizza, burgers, and—for the truly brave—deep-fried haggis (£6-8 take-out, £8-11 to dine in, dine-in prices include bread and a drink, daily 11:30-21:30, until 22:00 for take-away, 42-44 Shore Street, tel. 01333/310-518).

ST. ANDREWS

GLASGOW

Glasgow (GLAS-goh)—astride the River Clyde—is a surprising city. A century ago it had 1.2 million people, twice the size (and importance) of today. It was an industrial powerhouse producing 25 percent of the world's oceangoing ships. In its heyday, Glasgow was one of Europe's biggest cities and the second-largest in Britain, right behind London. But in the mid-20th century, tough times hit Glasgow, giving it a rough edge and a run-down image.

Today Glasgow is on the rise again. Its industrial heritage, combined with its flair for art and its unpretentious friendliness, make it more popular than ever to visit. And the city is spiffing up its image and offering a warm welcome. You'll enjoy free admission to all city museums, and have your choice of more music venues than you'll find anywhere north of London. The shopping is great—Glasgow likes to brag that it's Britain's number two shopping town.

Yet there still is a rough side to the culture, and locals seem to come in two stripes: heavy-drinking football (soccer) fans...and the rest. Historically, you could get beat up for wearing the wrong football club colors into the wrong pub. The two rival Glasgow teams (sort of like the Cubs and White Sox in Chicago) each have a rabid following. But assaults on tourists are very rare.

In 2014, all eyes will be on Glasgow as it hosts the Commonwealth Games—something like the Olympics—for the 53 countries of the former British Empire. More than 6,000 athletes will compete from July 23 to August 3. Just as London did when choosing the site for its 2012 Olympics, Glasgow has chosen to invest in its poor East End. (In Industrial Age cities, the wealth-

When the Great Ships of the World Were "Clyde-Built"

Glasgow's River Clyde shipyards were the mightiest in the world, famed for building the largest moving manmade objects on earth. The shipyards, once 50 strong, have dwindled to just three. Yet a few giant cranes still stand to remind locals and visitors that from 1880 to 1950, a quarter of the world's ships were built here and "Clyde-built" meant reliability and quality. For 200 years, shipbuilding was Glasgow's top employer—as many as 100,000 workers at its peak, producing a new ship every two days. The glamorous Cunard ships were built here—from the *Lusitania* in 1906 (infamously sunk by a German U-boat in World War I, which brought the US into the war) to the *Queen Elizabeth II* in 1967. People still talk about the day when over 200,000 Glaswegians gathered for the launch, the queen herself smashed the Champagne bottle on the prow, and the magnificent ship slid into the harbor. To learn lots more about shipbuilding in Glasgow, visit the excellent Riverside Museum of Transport and Travel.

ier people lived upwind, while the poor lived in slums downwind of the factories.) Glasgow's struggling East End will come out of the games with a nice souvenir—a modernized infrastructure.

Glasgow is both a workaday Scottish city as well as a cosmopolitan destination, with an energetic dining and nightlife scene. It's also a pilgrimage site of sorts for architecture buffs, thanks to a cityscape packed with Victorian architecture, early 20th-century touches, and modern flair. Most beloved are the works by hometown boy Charles Rennie Mackintosh, the visionary—and now very trendy—architect who left his mark all over Glasgow during the turn of the 20th century.

Many more tourists visit Edinburgh, a short train trip away. And, even though Glasgow is bigger than Edinburgh, it lives forever in the shadow of its more popular neighbor. (In Edinburgh, people identify with the quality of the school they attended; in Glasgow, it's their soccer team allegiance.)

Edinburgh may have the royal aura, but Glasgow's down-to-earth appeal is captivating. One Glaswegian told me, "The people of Glasgow have a better time at a funeral than the people of Edinburgh have at a wedding." In Glasgow, there's no upper-crust history, and no one puts on airs. Locals call sanded and polished concrete "Glasgow marble." In this revitalized city, friendly locals do their best to introduce you to the fun-loving, laid-back Glaswegian (rhymes with "Norwegian") way of life.

Planning Your Time

While many visitors just blitz Glasgow as a day trip from Edinburgh (and a first day in Glasgow is certainly more exciting than a fourth day in Edinburgh), the city can easily fill two days of sightseeing. The sights and museums seem to represent a city greater than it is today—a reminder of its former industrial importance.

My self-guided walk of the city (described later) covers the core of Glasgow, tying together the most important sights in the center. The two-hour hop-on, hop-off bus tour is perfect for getting the bigger picture and visiting the three important sights away from the center (the Cathedral Precinct, the Riverside Museum of Transport and Travel, and the Kelvingrove Art Gallery and Museum).

If you're a fan of Art Nouveau and Charles Rennie Mackintosh, you can lace together a busy day's worth of sightseeing (the TI has a brochure laying it out). At a minimum, those interested in Mackintosh should tour the Glasgow School of Art (which he designed and is only open via tour) and see the Mackintosh exhibit at the Kelvingrove Gallery.

If you just have one evening in town, the West End is most enjoyable.

Day Trip from Edinburgh: For a full day, catch the 9:30 train to Glasgow (morning trains every 15 minutes; £13 same-day round-trip if leaving after 9:15 or on weekend); it arrives at Queen Street Train Station at 10:30. To fill your Glasgow hours smartly, I'd do the entire hop-on, hop-off bus tour circuit (two hours). Then I'd follow my self-guided walk (finishing with the Glasgow School of Art tour and the Tenement House).

The four major interiors to consider, depending on your interests and time limits, are: The Glasgow School of Art (one-hour tours need to be booked in advance); The Tenement House (last entry at 16:30); the Riverside Museum (closes at 17:00); and the Kelvingrove Gallery (closes at 17:00).

For dinner, consider heading out to the thriving West End restaurant scene, then hop the subway back to Queen Street Station (use the Buchanan Street stop) and catch the 21:00 train back to Edinburgh (evening trains depart every 30 minutes).

Orientation to Glasgow

With a grid street plan, a downtown business zone, and more than its share of boxy office buildings, Glasgow feels more like a mid-sized American city than a big Scottish one—like Cleveland or Cincinnati with shorter skyscrapers, more sandstone, and more hills. (In fact, the film *Cloud Atlas,* set in San Francisco and starring Halle Berry, was filmed here.) The tourist's Glasgow has three main parts: the city center; the Cathedral Precinct (a cluster of minor sights near the cathedral in the east); and the West End restaurant/nightlife/shopping zone.

The easily walkable city center has two main drags, both lined with shops and crawling with shoppers: Sauchiehall Street (pronounced "Suckyhall," running west to east) and Buchanan Street (running north to south). These two pedestrian malls, part of what's nicknamed the Golden Zed (Golden Z), make a big zig and zag through the heart of town. Three streets make up the full Golden Zed: Sauchiehall Street is the top of the Z, Buchanan Street the middle part, and Argyle Street the bottom of the Z.

GLASGOW

Tourist Information

The TI is outside Queen Street Station opposite the Buchanan Street subway station (at #170 Buchanan Street). They hand out an excellent free map, stock other Glasgow brochures, and can book you a room for a £4 fee plus 10 percent deposit. They also have information on the rest of Scotland (Mon-Sat 9:00-18:00, Sun 10:00-17:00, until 16:00 Oct-April, www.visitscotland.com).

Mackintosh Trail Ticket: Ask about this ticket at the TI. If it's available, it covers entry to all "Charles Rennie Mac" sights and public transportation to those outside the city limits (£16/day, www.crmsociety.com).

Arrival in Glasgow

By Train: Glasgow, a major Scottish transportation hub, has two main train stations, which are just a few blocks apart in the heart of town: **Central Station** (with a grand, genteel interior under a vast steel-and-glass Industrial Age roof) and **Queen Street Station** (more functional, with better connections to Edinburgh, and closer to the TI—take the exit marked *Dundas Street* and head one block straight ahead to Buchanan Street). Both stations have pay WCs and baggage storage (about £7 per bag). You can walk the five minutes between the stations or take the roundabout "RailLink" bus #398 (£0.80, or free if you have a ticket for a connecting train).

By Bus: Buchanan bus station is at Killermont Street, two blocks up the hill behind Queen Street train station.

By Car: The M-8 motorway, which slices through downtown Glasgow, is the easiest way in and out of the city. Ask your hotel for directions to and from the M-8, and connect with other highways from there.

By Air: For information on Glasgow's two airports, see "Glasgow Connections," at the end of this chapter.

Helpful Hints

Safety: The city center, which is packed with ambitious career types during the day, can feel deserted at night. Avoid the area near the River Clyde (hookers and thugs), and confine yourself to the streets north of Argyle Street if you're in the downtown quarter. The Merchant City area (east of the train stations) and the West End bustle with crowded restaurants well into the evening and feel well-populated in the wee hours.

If you've picked up a football (soccer) jersey or scarf as a souvenir, don't wear it in Glasgow; passions run very high, and most drunken brawls in town are between supporters of Glasgow's two rival soccer clubs: Celtic in green, and Rangers in blue and red. (For reasons no one can explain, the Celtic team name is pronounced "sell-tic"—like it is in Boston. In all other cases, such as when referring to music, language, or culture, this word is pronounced "kell-tic".)

Sightseeing: Glasgow's city-owned museums—including the big museums and the sights near the cathedral—are free, but request £1-3 donations (www.glasgowmuseums.com).

Sunday Travel: Bus and train schedules are dramatically reduced on Sundays—most routes have only half the departure times they have during the week. And trains run less frequently in the off-season; so if you want to get to the Highlands by bus on a Sunday in winter, forget it.

Internet Access: Many pubs and coffee shops offer free Wi-Fi. You'll see signs advertising Internet cafés around the city core (near Central Station and Buchanan Street).

Local Guides: Joan Dobbie, a native Glaswegian and registered Scottish Tourist Guide, will give you the insider's take on Glasgow's sights (£95/half-day, £140/day, tel. 01355/236-749, mobile 07773-555-151, joan.leo@lineone.net). **Colin Mairs**, who was the youngest licensed guide in town, is also good and is licensed to drive while guiding (£100/half-day, £150/day, more by car, mobile 07716-232-001, www.excursionscotland.com, colin_mairs@yahoo.co.uk).

Getting Around Glasgow

By City Bus: Most city-center routes are operated by First Bus Company (£1.90/ride, £4 for all-day ticket—good only on First buses, buy tickets from driver, exact change required). Buses run every few minutes down Glasgow's main thoroughfares (such as Sauchiehall Street) to the downtown core (train stations). If you're waiting at a stop and a bus comes along, put out your hand to signal it to stop. Ask the driver if the bus is headed to Central Station; chances are the answer is yes.

By Hop-On, Hop-Off Bus Tour: This tour connects Glasgow's far-flung historic sights in a two-hour loop and lets you hop on and off as you like for two days. Buses are frequent (every 15 to 20 minutes) and punctual, and alternate between live guide and recorded narration (both are equally good). It works great for Glasgow, covering the city very well, and the guide does a fine job of describing activities at each stop. While the first stop is on George Square, you can hop on and pay the driver anywhere along the route (£12, daily 9:30-16:00, July-Aug 4/hour, spring and fall 3/hour, winter 2/hour, tel. 0141/204-0444, www.citysightseeing glasgow.co.uk).

By Taxi: Taxis are affordable, plentiful, and often come with nice, chatty cabbies—all speaking in the impenetrable Glaswegian accent. (Scottish English is considered its own language—as you'll hear in a cab.) Just smile and nod. Most taxi rides in the downtown area cost about £5; to the West End about £7. Use taxis or public transport to connect Glasgow's more remote sights; splurge for a taxi (for safety) any time you're traveling late at night.

By Subway: Glasgow's cute little single-line subway system, nicknamed Clockwork Orange, makes a six-mile circle that has 15 stops. While simple today, when it opened in 1896 it was the bee's knees (it's the world's third-oldest subway system, after London and Budapest). Though the subway is essentially useless for connecting city-center sightseeing (Buchanan Street and St. Enoch are the only downtown stops), it's handy for reaching sights farther out, including the Kelvingrove Gallery (Kelvinhall stop) and West End restaurant/nightlife neighborhood (Hillhead stop; £1.40 single trip, £3.80 for all-day ticket, subway runs Mon-Sat 6:30-23:45, Sun 10:00-18:00, www.spt.co.uk/subway).

Self-Guided Walk

Get to Know Glasgow

Glasgow isn't romantic, but it has an earthy charm, and architecture buffs love it. The longer you spend here, the more you'll feel the edgy, artsy vibe. The trick to sightseeing here is to always look up—above the chain restaurants and mall stores, you'll see a wealth of imaginative facades, complete with ornate friezes and expressive sculptures. These buildings transport you to the heady days around the turn of the 20th century—when the rest of Great

Glasgow Walk

1. Buchanan Street
2. Royal Exchange Square & Glasgow Gallery of Modern Art
3. George Square & Queen Victoria Statue
4. Nelson Mandela Place
5. More of the Golden Zed
6. Celtic Shop
7. Willow Tea Rooms (2)
8. Glasgow School of Art
9. Tenement House
10. Bus to Central Station

TO EDINBURGH

TENEMENT HOUSE

WEST
M-8
GARN.
HILL
RENFREW
B 10
SAUCHIEHA
FINISH
CHARING
CROSS
STN.
BATH
TO
KELVINGROVE
MUSEUM
MOTORWAY
M-8
NEWTON
ST.
ELMBANK
HOLLAND
WEST
WEST
BOTH-
PIT
FOOT-
BRIDGE
WATER-
CA
A-814
ARGYLE
S SUBWAY STOP
B BUS STOP
P PARKING
PEDESTRIAN ZONE
TO
RIVERSIDE
MUSEUM OF
TRANSPORT
KINGSTON BRIDGE
BROOMIE
200 YARDS
200 METERS
RIVER
TO
AIRPORT & OBAN
VIA A-82

GLASGOW

Britain was enthralled by Victorianism, but Glasgow set its own course, thanks largely to the artistic bravado of Charles Rennie Mackintosh and his friends (the "Glasgow Four"). This walking tour takes a couple of hours—more if you tour the Glasgow School of Art along the way.

• Start at the St. Enoch subway station, at the base of the pedestrian shopping boulevard, Buchanan Street. (This is a short walk from the Central Station, a longer walk or quick cab ride from Queen Street Station.) Begin strolling up...

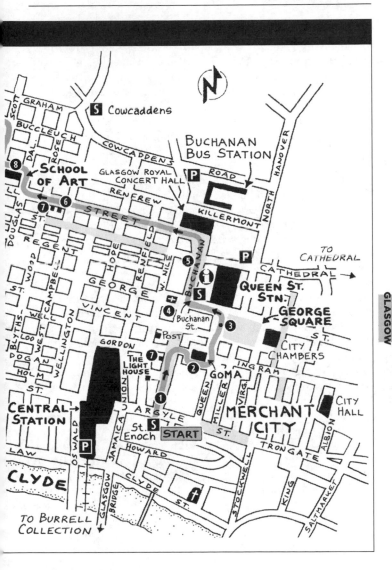

❶ Buchanan Street

The Golden Zed is the nickname for a Z-shaped pedestrian boulevard made of three streets: Sauchiehall, Buchanan, and Argyle. Always coming up with marketing slogans to goose the shopping metabolism of the city, this district (with the top shops in town) is also called the "Style Mile." City officials have cleverly co-opted graffiti artists by sanctioning huge, fun, and edgy graffiti murals that you can see if you side-trip down alleys in the Style Mile.

Buchanan Street has a friendly Ramblas-style vibe with an

abundance of street musicians. As you stroll uphill, keep an eye out for: The **Argyll Arcade** (#30, opposite Frasers), dating from 1827, is the oldest arcade in town. It's filled with mostly jewelry and comes with security guards dressed in Victorian-era garb. Eager couples—whether they're engaged or about to be—can be heard to say, "Let's take a shortcut through here." **Frasers** (#45) is a vast and venerable department store, considered the Harrods of Glasgow. **Princes Square** (#48) is a classic old building dressed with a modern steel peacock and foliage. Step inside to see the delightfully modernized Art Nouveau atrium.

At #97 (on the left) is one of two Mackintosh-designed **Willow Tea Rooms** (other location described later in this walk).

• *Cross the street and leave the big pedestrian boulevard by turning down the second alley on the right, called Exchange Place. You'll pass windows full of old sewing machines on the left and the recommended Rogano restaurant on your right before emerging onto...*

❷ Royal Exchange Square

The centerpiece of this square—which marks the entrance to the shopping zone called Merchant City—is a stately, Neoclassical, bank-like building. This was once the **private mansion** of one of the tobacco lords, the super-rich businessmen who reigned here through the 1700s, stomping through the city with gold-tipped canes. During the port's heyday, these entrepreneurs helped Glasgow become Europe's sixth-biggest city—number two in the British Empire.

Today the mansion houses the **Glasgow Gallery of Modern Art,** nicknamed GoMA. Walk to the main entry (at the eques-

trian statue of the Duke of Wellington, often creatively decorated as Glasgow's favorite cone-head), and step back to take in the full Neoclassical facade. On the pediment, notice the funky, mirrored mosaic celebrating the miracles of St. Mungo—an example of how Glasgow refuses to take itself too seriously. The temporary exhibits inside GoMA are generally forgettable, but the museum does have an unusual charter: It displays only the work of living artists (free, £2 suggested donation, Mon-Wed and Sat 10:00-17:00, Thu 10:00-20:00, Fri and Sun 11:00-17:00, free guided tours Sat-Sun at 12:00 and 14:00, tel. 0141/287-3050).

• *Facing the fanciful GoMA facade, turn right onto Queen Street. Within a block, you'll reach...*

❸ George Square

This square, the centerpiece of Glasgow, is filled with statues and lined with notable buildings, such as the Queen Street train station

and the Glasgow City Chambers (the big Neoclassical building standing like a secular church to the east, open by tour, generally Mon-Fri 10:30 and 14:30, free). In front of the City Chambers stands a monument to Glaswegians killed fighting in the World Wars. The square is decorated with a *Who's Who* of statues depicting great Glaswegians. Find James Watt (who perfected the steam engine that helped power Europe into the Industrial Age), as well as Scotland's two top poets: Robert Burns and Sir Walter Scott (capping the tallest pillar in the center). The two equestrian statues are of Prince Albert and a surprisingly skinny **Queen Victoria**—a rare image of her in her more svelte youth.

• *If you're hungry, pop into Wetherspoon, a big, cheap pub with good basic meals that fills a former bank building facing the square. Next, just past skinny Vic and Robert Peel, turn left onto West George Street, and cross busy Buchanan Street to the tall church in the middle of...*

❹ Nelson Mandela Place

This is the first public space named for Nelson Mandela—honoring the man who, while still in prison, helped bring down apartheid in South Africa. Glasgow, nicknamed Red Clyde Side for its socialist politics and empathy for the working class, has been quick to jump on progressive causes—like ending apartheid.

The area around this church features some interesting bits of architectural detail. Standing along the left side of the church, look up across from the church to find the three circular friezes of the former **Stock Exchange** (built in 1875). These idealized heads represent the industries that made Glasgow prosperous during its heyday: building, engineering, and mining.

Around the back of the church find the Athenaeum, the sandy-colored building at #8 (notice the low-profile label over the door). Now a law office, this was founded in 1847 as a school and city library during Glasgow's Golden Age. (Charles Dickens gave the building's inaugural address.) Like Edinburgh, Glasgow was at the forefront of the 17th-century Scottish Enlightenment, a celebration of education and intellectualism. The Scots were known for their extremely practical brand of humanism; all members of society, including the merchant and working classes, were expected to be well-educated. (Tobacco lords, for example, often knew Latin and Greek.) Look above the door to find the symbolic statue of a reader sharing books with young children, an embodiment of this ideal.

• *Return to the big, busy pedestrianized Buchanan Street in front of the church. Just downhill, to the right, is a huge Apple Store in a grand old building. Turn left and start up...*

❺ Buchanan Street to Sauchiehall Street (More of the Golden Zed)

A short distance uphill is the glass entry to Glasgow's subway (from here you could ride directly to the Hillhead stop for the West End restaurant district; see "Eating in Glasgow," later). Across the street is the TI, with information on Glasgow and all of Scotland. And just up the street from the TI is the Buchanan Galleries, a big indoor mall (offering a refuge if it's raining).

At the top of Buchanan Street stands the Glasgow Royal Concert Hall. Its steps are a favorite perch where local office workers munch lunch and enjoy the street scene. The statue is of Donald Dewar, who served as Scotland's first ever "First Minister" after the Scottish Parliament reconvened in 1999 (previously they'd been serving in London—as part of the British Parliament—since 1707).

• *From here, the Golden Zed zags left, Buchanan Street becomes Sauchiehall Street, and the shopping gets cheaper and less elegant. While there's little of note to see, it's still an enjoyable stroll. Walk a few blocks and enjoy the people-watching. Just before the end of the pedestrian zone are two final attractions (both on the left): a sports club store and a tea house (at #217).*

❻ The Celtic Shop

This shop is extreme green. That's the color of Glasgow's dominant (for now) soccer team. It's hard to fathom the intensity of the rivalry between Glasgow's Celtic and Rangers. Celtic, founded by an Irish Catholic priest to raise money for poor Irish immigrants in the East End, is—naturally—green and favored by Catholics. The Rangers, with team colors of the Union Jack (red, white, and blue), are more likely to be supported by Unionist and Protestant families. Today Celtic is in the major league and the Rangers (wracked recently by scandals) have fallen into a lower division. Wander into the shop (minimizing or hiding any red or blue you might be wearing). Check out the energy in the photos and shots of the stadium filled with 60,000 fans. Walk to the back and look for red or blue. You're in a world where those colors don't exist.

• *The Willow Tea Rooms, a smartly designed, affordable restaurant, is next door.*

Charles Rennie Mackintosh
(1868-1928)

During his lifetime, Charles Rennie Mackintosh brought an exuberant Art Nouveau influence to the architecture of his hometown. His designs challenged the city planners of this otherwise practical, working-class port city to create beauty in the buildings they commissioned. A radical thinker, he freely shared credit with his artist wife, Margaret MacDonald. (He once famously said, "I have the talent...Margaret has the genius.")

When Mackintosh was a young student at the Glasgow School of Art, the Industrial Age dominated life here. Factories belched black soot into the city as they burned coal and forged steel. Mackintosh and his circle of artist friends drew their solace and inspiration from nature (just as the Romantics had before them) and created some of the original Art Nouveau buildings, paintings, drawings, and furniture.

As a student traveling abroad in Italy, Mackintosh ignored the famous Renaissance paintings inside the museum walls and set up his easel to paint the exteriors of churches and buildings instead. He rejected the architectural traditions of ancient Greece and Rome. In Venice and Ravenna, he fell under the spell of Byzantine design, and in Siena he saw a unified, medieval city design he would try to import—but with a Scottish flavor and Glaswegian palette—to his own hometown.

His first commission came in 1893, to design an extension to the Glasgow Herald building. More work soon followed, including the Glasgow School of Art and the Willow Tea Rooms 10 years later. Mackintosh envisioned a world without artistic borders, where an Islamic flourish could find its way onto a workaday building in a Scottish city. Inspired by the great buildings of the past and by his Art Nouveau peers, he in turn influenced others, such as painter Gustav Klimt and Bauhaus founder Walter Gropius. As is the fate of many artists, his vision was not as appreciated in his own time as it is now. When he died, he had only £88 to his name. But today, a century after Scotland's greatest architect set pencil to paper, his hometown is at last celebrating his unique vision.

❼ Willow Tea Rooms

This delightful black-and-white space is an Art Nouveau masterpiece by Charles Rennie Mackintosh. Visitors are welcome to browse.

Mackintosh made his living from design commissions, including multiple tearooms for businesswoman Kate Cranston. A well-known control freak, Mackintosh designed everything here—down to the furniture, lighting, and cutlery. He took his theme for the café from the name of the street it's on—*saugh* is Scots for willow, and *haugh* for meadow.

In the design of these tearooms, there was a meeting of the (very modern) minds. Cranston wanted a place for women to be able to gather while unescorted, in a time when traveling solo could give a woman a less-than-desirable reputation. An ardent women's rights supporter, Cranston requested that the rooms be bathed in white, the suffragettes' signature color.

On the ground floor peruse the Mackintosh-inspired jewelry and the exhibit about his design in back. Then climb the stairs to find 20 tables run like a diner from a corner kitchen, serving simple meals to middle-class people—just as this place has since it opened in 1903. Then look for the almost-hidden Room de Luxe dining room (upstairs). While some parts of the Room de Luxe are reproductions (such as the chairs and the doors, which were too fragile to survive), the rest is just as it was in Mackintosh's day (same menu no matter where you eat: £5-9 meals, £13 tea, and more; Mon-Sat 9:00-17:00, Sun 11:00-16:15).

• *From here it's a five-minute, mostly uphill walk to the must-see Mackintosh sight in the town center. Continue a block and a half on Sauchiehall (with traffic), and make a right onto Dalhousie Street; the big, blond sandstone building on the left at the top of the hill is the Glasgow School of Art (described next). Tickets for the school tour are sold across the street in the new Reid Building (where tours start).*

If you have time to kill before your tour starts, consider eating lunch at the nearby **CCA Saramago Bar and Courtyard Café** *(on Sauchiehall). Or, if you have an hour before your tour, you can head to the* **Tenement House** *(listed at the end of this walk), a preserved home from the early 1900s— right when Mackintosh was doing his most important work.*

❽ Glasgow School of Art

A pinnacle of artistic and architectural achievement—worth ▲—the Glasgow School of Art presented a unique opportunity for Charles Rennie Mackintosh to design a massive project entirely to his own liking, down to every last detail. Those details—from a fireplace that looks like a kimono to windows that soar for multiple stories—are the beauty of the Glasgow School of Art.

Because the Glasgow School of Art is still a working school, the interior can only be visited by one-hour guided tour. The tour fees help fund the conservation of Mackintosh's work and, as a bonus, you get to meet and enjoy the accent of a smart, young Glasgow art student.

Each year in early June, the **Degree Show** opens the entire building to the public—for free—for a week. This is when tomorrow's stars in design—graduating art students—show their work. While there are no guided tours during this period, it is the best time to see the art school, with the building used as it was intended.

Cost and Hours: £10 guided tour, usually daily at 11:00, 13:00, and 15:00, hourly at busy times. Tip the starving student guides a pound or two if they give a good spiel. In the summer, tours run more frequently but fill up quickly (confirm times and reserve a spot by booking online, calling, or emailing the shop, open daily April-Sept 10:30-18:30, Oct-March 10:30-17:00; tel. 0141/353-4526—provide call-back number if leaving a message, www.gsa.ac.uk/visit-gsa/tours, tours@gsa.ac.uk). No photos are allowed on the tour. Serious admirers may also want to ask about the 2.5-hour Mackintosh-themed city walking tours given by students (£20, both tours £24, July-Aug only).

Visiting the School: Mackintosh loved the hands-on ideology of the Arts and Crafts movement, but he was also a practical Scot. Study the outside of the building. Those protruding wrought-iron brackets that hover outside the multi-paned windows were a new invention during the time of the Industrial Revolution; they reinforce the big, fragile glass windows, allowing natural light to pour in to the school. Mackintosh brought all the most recent technologies to this work and added them to his artistic palate—which also merged clean Modernist lines, Asian influences, and Art Nouveau flourishes.

When the building first opened, it was modern and minimalist. Other elements were added later, such as the lobby's tile mosaics depicting the artistic greats, including mustachioed Mackintosh (who hovers over the gift shop).

As you tour the school, you'll see how Mackintosh—who'd been a humble art student himself not too long before he designed this building—strove to create a space that was both artistically innovative and completely functional for students. The plaster replicas of classical sculptures lining the halls were part of Mackintosh's vision to inspire students by the greats of the past. You'll likely see students and their canvases lining the halls.

Linking these useable spaces are clever artistic patterns and puzzles that Mackintosh embedded to spur creative thought. If you notice a design that looks like it is repeated elsewhere, look again. No two motifs are exactly alike, just as nothing is exactly the same in nature.

Mackintosh cleverly arranged the school so that the cellar studios are bathed in intense natural light. And yet, as you climb to the top of the building—which you'd expect be the brightest, most light-filled area—the space becomes dark and gloomy, and the stairwell is encumbered by a cage-like structure.

During the tour, you'll be able to linger a few minutes in the major rooms, such as the remarkable forest-like library and the furniture gallery (including some original tables and chairs from the Willow Tea Rooms). Walking through the GSA, remember that this work was the Art Nouveau original, and that Frank Lloyd Wright, the Art Deco Chrysler Building, and everything that resembles it came well after Charles Rennie Mack's time.

• To finish this walk, head north from the Glasgow School of Art on Scott Street. Just past the crest of the hill, make a left onto Buccleuch Street. After three blocks, the last house on the left is the...

❾ Tenement House

Here's a chance to drop into a perfectly preserved 1930s-era middle-class residence. The National Trust for Scotland bought this otherwise ordinary row home, located in a residential neighborhood, because of the peculiar tendencies of Miss Agnes Toward (1886-1975). For five decades, she kept her home essentially unchanged. The kitchen calendar is still set for 1935, and canisters of licorice powder (a laxative) still sit on the bathroom shelf. It's a time-warp experience, where Glaswegian old-timers enjoy coming to reminisce about how they grew up.

Buy your ticket on the main floor, and poke around the little museum on the ground floor. You'll learn that in Glasgow, a "tenement" isn't a slum—it's simply an apartment house. In fact, tenements like these were typical for every class except the richest.

Head upstairs to the apartment, which is staffed by caring volunteers. Ring the doorbell to be let in. Ask them why the bed is in the kitchen or why the rooms still smell like natural gas. As you look through the rooms laced with Victorian trinkets—such as the ceramic dogs on the living room's fireplace mantle—consider how different they are from Mackintosh's stark, minimalist designs from the same period.

Cost and Hours: £6.50, £3.50 guidebook, March-Oct daily 13:00-17:00, last entry 30 minutes before closing, closed Nov-Feb, no photos allowed, 145 Buccleuch Street (pronounced "ba-KLOO") down off the top of Garnethill, tel. 0844-493-2197, www.nts.org.uk.

GLASGOW

• *Our walk is finished. To get to Sauchiehall Street (with the nearest bus stop and taxis), exit the Tenement House, cross the street, go left, and follow the sidewalk down the hill toward the traffic noise. Pass under the pedestrian bridge and curve around to arrive at the far end of Sauchiehall.*

More Sights in Glasgow

Cathedral Precinct, with a Hint of Medieval Glasgow

Very little remains of medieval Glasgow, but when you visit the cathedral and the area around it, you're visiting the birthplace of the city. The first church was built here in the seventh century. Today's towering cathedral is mostly 13th-century—the only great Scottish church to survive the Reformation intact. In front you'll see an attention-grabbing statue of David Livingstone (1813-1873). Livingstone—the Scottish missionary/explorer/cartographer who discovered a huge waterfall in Africa and named it in honor of his queen, Victoria—was born eight miles from here.

Nearby, the Provand's Lordship is Glasgow's only secular building dating from the Middle Ages. The St. Mungo Museum of Religious Life and Art, built on the site of the old Bishop's Castle, is a unique exhibit covering the spectrum of religions. And the Necropolis, blanketing the hill behind the cathedral, provides an atmospheric walk through a world of stately Victorian tombstones. From there you can scan the city and look down on the brewery where Tennent's Lager (a longtime Glasgow favorite) has been made since 1885.

The four main sights, including the cathedral, are within close range of each other. As you face the cathedral, the St. Mungo Museum is on your right (with handy public WCs), the Provand's Lordship is across the street from St. Mungo, and the Necropolis is behind the cathedral and toward the right.

To reach these sights from the TI, head up Buchanan Street and turn right on Bath Street, which soon becomes Cathedral Street, and walk about 15 minutes (or hop a bus along the main drag—try bus #38, or #57, confirm with driver that the bus stops at the cathedral). If you'll be heading to the Kelvingrove Gallery after your visit: From the cathedral, walk two blocks up Castle Street and catch bus #19 (on the cathedral side) to the gallery.

▲Glasgow Cathedral

This blackened, Gothic cathedral is a rare example of an intact pre-Reformation Scottish cathedral. (It was once known as "the Pink Church" for the tone of its stone. But with Industrial Age soot and modern pollution, it blackened. Cleaning would damage the integrity of the stone structure so it was left black.) While the zealous Reformation forces of John Knox ripped out the stained glass and the ornate chapels of the Catholic age, they left the church standing. Look up to see the wooden barrel-vaulted ceiling, and take in the beautifully decorated section over the choir ("quire"). The choir screen is the only pre-Reformation screen surviving in Scotland. It divided the common people from the priests and big shots of the day, who got to worship closer to the religious action. Standing at the choir, turn around to look down the nave at the west wall, and notice how the right wall lists. (Don't worry; it's been listing—and still standing—for 800 years.) The cathedral's glass dates mostly from the 19th century. One window on the right side of the choir, celebrating the 14 trades of Glasgow, dates from 1951.

Step into the lower church (down stairs on right as you face the choir), where the central altar sits upon St. Mungo's tomb. Mungo was the seventh-century Scottish monk and mythical founder of Glasgow who established the first wooden church on this spot and gave Glasgow its name. Notice the ceiling bosses (decorative caps where the ribs come together) with their colorfully carved demons, dragons, and skulls.

Cost and Hours: Free, suggested donation £3; April-Sept Mon-Sat 9:30-17:30, Sun 13:00-17:00; Oct-March Mon-Sat 9:30-16:30, Sun 13:00-16:30, ask about free guided tours; last entry 30 minutes before closing, near junction of Castle and Cathedral Streets, tel. 0141/552-8198, www.glasgowcathedral.org.uk.

Necropolis

From the cathedral, a lane leads over the "bridge of sighs" into the park filled with grand tombstones. Glasgow's huge burial hill has a wistful, ramshackle appeal. A stroll among the tombstones of the eminent Glaswegians of the 19th century gives a glimpse of Victorian Glasgow and a feeling for the confidence and wealth of the second city of the British Empire in its glory days.

With the Industrial Age (in the early 1800s), Glasgow's population tripled to 200,000. The existing churchyards were jammed and unhygienic. The city needed a beautiful place in which to bury its beautiful citizens, so this grand necropolis was established. As Presbyterians are more into simplicity, the statuary is simpler than in a Catholic cemetery. Wandering among the disintegrating memorials to once important people, I thought about how, someday, everyone's tombstone will fall over and no one will care.

The highest pillar in the graveyard is a memorial to John Knox. The Great Reformer (who's actually buried in Edinburgh) looks down at the cathedral he wanted to strip of all art, and even tear down. (The Glaswegians rallied to follow Knox, but saved the church.) If the cemetery's main black gates are closed, see if you can get in and out through a gate off the street to the right.

▲St. Mungo Museum of Religious Life and Art

This interesting museum, next to the cathedral, aims to promote religious understanding. Built in 1990 upon the site of the old Bishop's Castle, it provides a handy summary of major and minor world religions, showing how each faith handles various rites of passage across the human life span: birth, puberty, marriage, death, and everything in between and after. Start with the 10-minute video overview on the first floor, and finish with a great view from the top floor of the cathedral and Necropolis.

Cost and Hours: Free, suggested donation £3, Tue-Thu and Sat 10:00-17:00, Fri and Sun 11:00-17:00, closed Mon, free WCs downstairs, cheap ground-floor café, 2 Castle Street, tel. 0141/276-1625, www.glasgowmuseums.com.

Provand's Lordship

With low beams and medieval decor, this creaky home—supposedly the "oldest house in Glasgow"—is the only secular building surviving in Glasgow from the Middle Ages. It displays the *Lifestyles of the Rich and Famous*...circa 1471. The interior, while sparse and stony, shows off a few pieces of furniture from the 16th, 17th, and 18th centuries. Out back, explore the St. Nicholas Garden, which was once part of a hospital that dispensed herbal remedies. The plaques in each section show the part of the body each plant is used to treat.

Cost and Hours: Free, small donation requested, Tue-Thu and Sat 10:00-17:00, Fri and Sun 11:00-17:00, closed Mon, across the street from St. Mungo Museum at 3 Castle Street, tel. 0141/552-8819, www.glasgowmuseums.com.

Away from the Center

▲▲Riverside Museum of Transport and Travel

Located along the River Clyde, this high-tech, extremely kid-friendly museum is dedicated to all things transportation-related. Named the European museum of the year in 2013, a visit here is a must for anyone interested in transportation and how it has shaped society. Highlights of its vast collection include the world's oldest bicycle, stagecoaches, locomotives, a re-creation of a circa-1900 street (with video clips of local seniors in time-warp shops reminiscing—like about the time the little girl noticed her daddy was selling things to the pawn shop to pay the rent).

A highlight is the shipping section, commemorating Glasgow's shipbuilding era. Exhilarating newsreels show that proud moment when "the band plays, the minister prays, the lady sponsor gives the name, the crowds cheer, and seconds later a new ship takes to the water for the first time."

Upon entering, find out about upcoming tours and activities (free, ask at info desk—to the right as you enter, near the shop—or listen for announcements). Be sure to pick up a map from the info desk, as the museum's open floor plan, spread over two levels and packed with original vehicles, can feel a bit like a traffic jam at rush hour.

Cost and Hours: Free, £1-2 suggested donation, Mon-Thu and Sat 10:00-17:00, Fri and Sun 11:00-17:00, restaurant (£6-9 meals, daily 12:00-16:00), first-floor coffee shop with basic drinks and snacks, 100 Pointhouse Place, tel. 0141/287-2720, www.glasgowmuseums.com.

Getting There: It's on the riverfront promenade, two miles west of the city center. **Bus #100** runs between the museum and George Square (2/hour, last departure from George Square at 15:02, operated by McColl's), or you can take a **taxi** (£6, 10-minute ride from downtown). The museum is also included on the **hop-on, hop-off sightseeing bus** route (described earlier, under "Getting Around Glasgow").

Nearby: The *Glenlee*, one of five remaining tall ships built in Glasgow in the 19th century, is moored just outside the museum on the River Clyde (free, daily 10:00-17:00, Nov-Feb until 16:00, tel. 01413/573-699, www.thetallship.com).

▲▲Kelvingrove Art Gallery and Museum

This museum is like a Scottish Smithsonian—with everything from a stuffed elephant to fine artwork by the great masters. The

well-described contents are impressively displayed in a grand, 100-year-old, Spanish Baroque-style building. Purpose-built to house the city collection in 1902, it's divided into two sections. The "Life" section, in the West Court, features a menagerie of stuffed animals (including a giraffe, kangaroo, ostrich, and moose) with a WWII-era Spitfire fighter plane hovering overhead. Branching off are halls with exhibits ranging from Ancient Egypt to "Scotland's First Peoples" to weaponry ("Conflict and Consequence"). The more serene "Expression" section, in the East Court, focuses on artwork, including Dutch, Flemish, French, and Scottish Colorists. On the second floor near the main hall, you'll find its most famous painting, Salvador Dalí's *Christ of St. John of the Cross,* which brought visitors to tears when it was first displayed here in the 1950s. This section also has exhibits on "Scottish Identity in Art" (letting you tour the country's scenic wonders and history on canvas) and on Charles Rennie Mackintosh and the Glasgow School. The Kelvingrove claims to be one of the most-visited museums in Britain—presumably because of all the field-trip groups you'll see here. Watching all the excited Scottish kids—their imaginations ablaze—is as much fun as the collection itself.

Cost and Hours: Free, suggested donation £3, Mon-Thu and Sat 10:00-17:00, Fri and Sun 11:00-17:00, free tours at 11:00 and 14:30, Argyle Street, tel. 0141/276-9599, www.glasgowmuseums .com.

Getting There: Ride the **subway** to the Kelvinhall stop; when you exit, turn left and walk five minutes. **Buses** #3, #7, and #19 all stop nearby—when you get off the bus, look for the huge red-brick building. It's also on the hop-on, hop-off bus route.

Organ Concerts: At the top of the main hall, the huge pipe organ booms with a daily recital at 13:00 (15:00 on Sunday, 30-45 minutes).

▲Burrell Collection

This eclectic art collection of a wealthy local shipping magnate is one of Glasgow's top destinations, but it's three miles outside the

city center. If you'd like to visit, plan to make an afternoon of it, and leave time to walk around the surrounding park, where Highland cattle graze. The diverse contents of this museum include sculptures (from Roman to Rodin), stained glass, tapestries, furniture, Asian and Islamic works, and halls of paintings—starring Cézanne, Renoir, Degas, and a Rembrandt self-portrait.

Cost and Hours: Free, Mon-Thu and Sat 10:00-17:00, Fri and Sun 11:00-17:00, Pollok Country Park, 2060 Pollokshaws Road, tel. 0141/287-2550, www.glasgowmuseums.com.

Getting There: From downtown, take **bus** #57 to Pollokshaws Road, or take a train to the Pollokshaws West train station; the entrance is a 10-minute walk from the bus stop and the train station. By **car**, follow the M-8 to exit at Junction 22 onto the M-77 Ayr; exit Junction 1 on the M-77 and follow signs.

Nightlife in Glasgow

Glasgow has a youthful vibe, and its nightlife scene is renowned. The city is full of live music acts and venues. Walking through the city center, you'll pass at least one club or bar on every block. For the latest, pick up a copy of *The List* (sold at newsstands) or the *Gig Guide*. For nightlife suggestions in the West End, see that section under "Eating in Glasgow," later.

GLASGOW

Sleeping in Glasgow

Near the Glasgow School of Art

The area just west of the school has a few decent accommodations options, including a fine guesthouse in a church building (Adelaides), an Ibis chain hotel, and a buffet line of tired, basic B&Bs along Renfrew Street. From here you can walk downhill into the downtown core in about 10 to 15 minutes (or take a £5 taxi). If approaching by car, you can't drive down one-way Renfrew Street from the city center. Instead, from busy Sauchiehall Street, go up Scott Street or Rose Street, turn left onto Buccleuch Street, and circle around to Renfrew Street.

South of Sauchiehall Street

$$ Adelaides Guest House rents eight clean and cheerful rooms in a multitasking church building that also houses a theater and nursery school. Ted and Lisa run the place with warmth and quirky humor (S-£37, Sb-£55, Db-£69, family deals, includes very basic breakfast, £5.50 cooked breakfast available Mon-Fri, guest computer, 209 Bath Street, tel. 0141/248-4970, www.adelaides .co.uk, reservations@adelaides.co.uk).

$$ Ibis Glasgow, part of the modern hotel chain, has 141 cookie-cutter rooms with blond wood and predictable comfort (Sb/Db-£56 on weeknights, £69 on weekends, £85 "event rate" during festivals and in Aug, breakfast-£8, air-con, pay guest computer, free Wi-Fi in lobby, elevator, restaurant, hiding behind a big Novotel at 220 West Regent Street, tel. 0141/225-6000, www .ibishotel.com, h3139@accor.com).

North of Sauchiehall, on Renfrew Street

These places, all on Renfrew Street, offer instant immersion into Glasgow's working-class roots. Adjust your expectations: Each comes with tired public spaces, past-their-prime rooms, and a touch of indifference. But breakfast is included and the prices are competitive.

$$ Rennie Mackintosh Art School Hotel has 24 rooms—some redecorated—and hints of Glasgow's favorite architect (slippery rates change with demand, but generally Sb-£40-55; Db-£55-60 Sun-Thu, £55 Fri-Sat; family rooms around £100, free Wi-Fi, 218-220 Renfrew Street, tel. 0141/333-9992, www.rmg hotels.com, rennie@rmghotels.com).

$$ Victorian House Hotel is a crank-'em-out place with a friendly staff and 58 worn but workable rooms sprawling through several old townhouses (S-£32, Sb-£39, Db-£60, lots of stairs and no elevator, free Wi-Fi, 212 Renfrew Street, tel. 0141/332-0129, www.thevictorian.co.uk, info@thevictorian.co.uk).

Sleep Code

(£1 = about $1.60, country code: 44, area code: 0141)
S = Single, **D** = Double/Twin, **T** = Triple, **Q** = Quad, **b** = bathroom,
s = shower only. You can assume credit cards are accepted
unless otherwise noted.

To help you sort easily through these listings, I've divided
the accommodations into two categories based on the price
for a standard double room with bath (during high season):

$$ Higher Priced—Most rooms £50 or more.
$ Lower Priced—Most rooms less than £50.

Prices can change without notice; verify the hotel's cur-
rent rates online or by email. For the best prices, always book
direct.

$$ Willow Guest House feels the most boutique, with 39
rooms—all with private bath (Sb-£40-45, Db-£60-70, family
rooms-£95, free Wi-Fi, 228 Renfrew Street, tel. 0141/332-2332,
www.willowguesthouseglasgow.com).

$$ Alba Lodge Guest House, at the end of the Renfrew row,
has 15 mostly en suite rooms and featureless common areas (Sb-
£35, Db-£52, Tb-£72, Qb-£89, free Wi-Fi, 232 Renfrew Street,
tel. 0141/332-2588, www.albalodge.co.uk, info@albalodge.co.uk).

$ Hampton Court Guest House, with 18 basic rooms (most
set up for families), drapes visitors in tartan. Run by the hard-
working Purewal family, who offer a warm welcome and friendly
respite, their house is the pearl on this oyster of a street (Sb-£36,
Db-£55-59, family rooms-£78-129, free Wi-Fi, 230 Renfrew
Street, tel. 0141/332-6623, info@hamptoncourtguesthouse.com).

Elsewhere in Central Glasgow

$$ Premier Inn George Square is a family-friendly
chain hotel in the Merchant City district, close to Queen
Street Station (Sb/Db-£61, Db for up to 2 adults and 2
kids-£69-100, cheaper midweek and in winter, elevator, pay Wi-Fi, 187 George Street, tel. 08715-278-440, www
.premierinn.com).

$$ Babbity Bowster, named for a traditional Scottish dance,
is a pub and restaurant renting six simple, mod rooms up top.
It's located in the trendy Merchant City on the eastern fringe of
downtown, near several clubs and restaurants (Sb-£45, Db-£60,
breakfast-£6, lots of stairs and no elevator, 10-minute walk from
Central Station, 16-18 Blackfriars Street, tel. 0141/552-5055,

GLASGOW

Central Glasgow Hotels & Restaurants

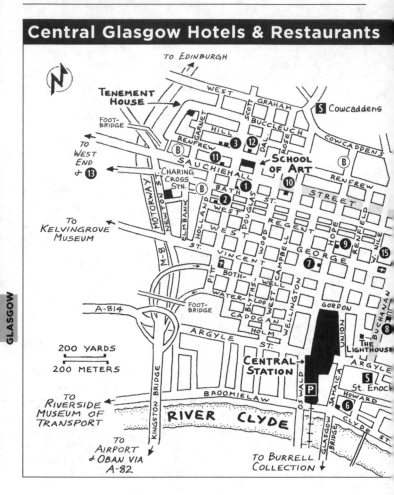

www.babbitybowster.com, babbity@btinternet.com). The ground-floor pub serves £5-9 pub grub (daily 12:00-22:00); the first-floor restaurant, run by a French chef, offers £14-17 main dishes (Fri-Sat only 18:30-21:30, closed Sun-Thu).

$ Euro Hostel is the best bet for hostel beds in the city center. Part of a chain, this place is a lively hive of backpacker activity, with 364 beds on nine floors, plus pay guest computer, free Wi-Fi in the bar, a kitchen, and friendly staff (request a room on a higher floor and in the back for maximum quiet; very slippery rates, but figure £13-20 bunk in 4- to 14-bed dorm with bathroom, Sb-£29-40, Db-£36-52, couples should request a double or else end up with a bunk-bed, includes continental breakfast, elevator, laundry-£4/load, 318 Clyde Street, tel. 08455-399-956, www.euro-hostels.co.uk, reservations@euro-hostels.co.uk). It's on the busy

1. Adelaides Guest House
2. Ibis Glasgow
3. Renfrew Street Accommodations
4. Premier Inn George Square
5. Babbity Bowster Rooms
6. Euro Hostel
7. Mussel Inn Restaurant
8. Rogano Restaurant
9. The Pot Still Bar
10. Willow Tea Rooms
11. CCA Saramago Bar & Courtyard Vegetarian Café
12. Where the Monkey Sleeps Cafeteria
13. To West End Eateries & Nightlife
14. Bus to West End

main thoroughfare past Central Station, along the River Clyde, near some seedy areas.

Eating in Glasgow

Many of Glasgow's fancier eateries serve "pre-theatre menus"—affordable, fixed-price meals served before 19:00.

In the City Center

Mussel Inn offers light, good-value fish dinners and seafood plates in an airy, informal environment. The restaurant is a cooperative, owned and run by shellfish farmers. Their £10 "kilo pot" of Scottish mussels is popular with locals and big enough to share (£7-8 small grilled platters, £11-18 meals, Mon-Fri 12:00-14:30 &

17:00-22:00, Sat 12:00-22:00, Sun 12:30-22:00, 157 Hope Street, between St. Vincent and West George Streets, tel. 0141/572-1405).

Rogano is a time-warp Glasgow institution that retains much of the same classy Art Deco interior it had when it opened in 1935. You half-expect to see Bacall and Bogart at the next table. The restaurant has three parts. The bar in front has outdoor seating (£6 lunch sandwiches, £12-15 meals). The fancy dining room at the back of the main floor smacks of the officers' mess on the *Queen Mary*, which was built here on the Clyde during the same period (£20-24 meals with a focus on seafood). A more casual yet still dressy bistro in the cellar is filled with 1930s-Hollywood glamour (£11-14 meals, £15 afternoon tea; daily 12:00-21:30, fancy restaurant closed 14:30-18:00, 11 Exchange Place—just before giant archway from Buchanan Street, reservations smart, tel. 0141/248-4055).

And More: Dozens of restaurants line the main commercial areas of town: Sauchiehall Street, Buchanan Street, and the Merchant City area. Many are similar, with trendy interiors, Euro disco-pop soundtracks, and dinner for about £15-20 per person.

For Your Whisky: **The Pot Still** is an award-winning malt whisky bar from 1835 that boasts a formidable array of more than 300 choices. You'll see locals of all ages sitting in its leathery interior, watching football (soccer), and discussing their drinks. They have whisky aged in sherry casks, whisky preferred by wine drinkers, and whisky from every region of Scotland. Give the friendly bartenders a little background on your beverage tastes, and they'll narrow down a good choice for you from their long list (whisky runs £2-55 a glass, average price £4-5, £2.50 pasties and pies, daily 11:00-24:00, 154 Hope Street, tel. 0141/333-0980).

Budget Options near the Glasgow School of Art

The **Willow Tea Rooms,** designed by Charles Rennie Mackintosh, has a diner-type eatery and a classy Room de Luxe dining room. The cheap and cheery menu covers both dining areas (£4-7 breakfasts, £5 sandwiches, £7-9 salads and main dishes, £13 afternoon tea served all day, gluten-free options, Mon-Sat 9:00-17:00, Sun 11:00-16:15, 217 Sauchiehall Street, tel. 0141/332-0521, www.willowtearooms .co.uk).

CCA Saramago Bar and Courtyard Vegetarian Café, located on the first floor of Glasgow's edgy contemporary art museum, charges art-student prices for its designer, animal-free food (such as tasty roast beetroot and avocado salads). An 18th-century facade, discovered when the site was excavated to build the gallery, looms over the courtyard restaurant (£3-4 small plates,

£7-9 main courses, food served Mon-Sat 12:00-22:00, closed Sun, free Wi-Fi, 350 Sauchiehall Street, tel. 0141/332-7959).

Where the Monkey Sleeps is the Glasgow School of Art's cheap student cafeteria. It's your chance to mingle with the city's next generation of artists and hear more of that lilting Glaswegian accent (if open, generally Sept-June Mon-Fri 8:00-17:00, closed Sat-Sun, tel. 0141/353-4728).

In the West End

The hip, lively residential neighborhood/university district called the West End is worth exploring, particularly in the evening. A collection of fun eateries and bars lines Ashton Lane, just off bustling Byres Road (the scene continues to the left along Cresswell Lane). It's a short 10-minute walk from the nearby Kelvingrove Gallery and convenient to downtown as it's right at the Hillhead subway station.

Before choosing a place, take a stroll and scout the whole scene. The subway station is on Byres Road. Across the street is Ruthven Lane (with two good restaurants) and around the corner is the popular, quaint, and cobbled Ashton Lane—lined with an array of restaurants and bars. Most have tables out front positioned nicely so you can watch the parade of people, and also have convivial gardens in the back.

Along Ashton Lane you'll find: **Ketchup** (an American-style diner), **Brel** (a Belgian beer bar), **The Wee Curry Shop** (£7-14 Scottish-Indian fusion main dishes, tel. 0141/357 5280), and **Jinty McGuinty's** Irish pub and beer garden.

Other favorites nearby include: The landmark **Ubiquitous Chip,** which has various pubs and restaurants sprawling through a deceptively large building (£5-9 pub grub, £6-9 starters, £16-28 restaurant meals, tel. 0141/334-5007), and **La Vallée Blanche,** which serves French cuisine with a Scottish twist, in a romantic dining area that resembles an upscale mountain lodge (£12 two-course early dinner specials, £11-18 main courses, closed Mon, 360 Byres Road, tel. 0141/334-3333).

On nearby Cresswell Lane, consider **Café Andaluz,** which offers £4-9 tapas and sangria behind lacy wooden screens, as the waitstaff clicks past on the cool tiles (2 Cresswell Lane, tel. 0141/339-1111).

Along Ruthven Lane (across Byre's Road from the subway station) are two fine options: one Scottish and one Vietnamese, both with inside and outside seating.

Bothy Restaurant offers tasty, traditional Scottish fayre and a warm welcome (mains £10-18, 11 Ruthven Lane, tel. 0141/334-4040).

The Hanoi Bike Shop, a rare Vietnamese restaurant (opened

2013), serves Asian tapas that are healthy and tasty, using local produce. With tight seating and friendly service, the place has a nice energy (small plates for around £5 each, homemade desserts, kitchen open daily 12:00-23:00, 8 Ruthven Lane, tel. 0141/334-7165).

West End Nightlife: Òran Mòr, a converted 1862 church overlooking a busy intersection, is one of Glasgow's most popular hangouts. It's a five-minute walk from the recommended restaurants (at the intersection of Byres and Great Western Road). In addition to hosting an atmospheric bar, outdoor beer garden, and brasserie, the building's former nave (now decorated with funky murals) has a downstairs nightclub featuring everything from rock shows to traditional Scottish music nights (brasserie serves £7-18 main dishes; pub with dressy conservatory or outdoor beer garden serves £3-10 pub grub; daily 9:00-very late, food served Mon-Wed 9:00-21:00, Thu-Sat 9:00-19:00, Sun 10:00-21:00, top of Byres Road at 731-735 Great Western Road, tel. 0141/357-6200).

Hillhead Bookclub Bar is a historic building cleared out to make room for fun, disco, pub grub, and lots of booze. It's a youthful and quirky art-school scene, with lots of beers on tap, creative cocktails, retro computer games, ping-pong, and theme evenings (just off Byres Road at 17 Vinicombe Street, tel. 0141/576-1700).

Getting to the West End: It's easiest to take the subway to Hillhead, which is a one-minute walk from Ashton Lane (exit the station to the left, then take the first left to find the lane). From the city center, you can also take a £5-6 taxi.

Glasgow Connections

Traveline Scotland has a journey planner that's linked to all of Scotland's train and bus schedule info. Go online (www.travelinescotland.com); call them at tel. 0871-200-2233; or use the individual websites listed below. If you're connecting with Edinburgh, note that the train is faster but the bus is cheaper.

By Train
From Glasgow's Central Station by Train to: Keswick in the Lake District (roughly hourly, 1.5 hours to Penrith, then catch a bus to Keswick, 45 minutes), **Cairnryan** and ferry to Belfast (take train to Ayr, 2/hour, 1 hour; then ride bus to Cairnryan, 1 hour), **Blackpool** (hourly, 3.5-4 hours, transfer in Preston), **Liverpool** (1-2/hour, 3.5-4 hours, change in Wigan or Preston), **Durham** (2/hour, 3 hours, may require change in Edinburgh), **York** (2/hour, 3.5 hours, may require change in Edinburgh), **London** (1-2/hour,

4.5-5 hours direct). Train info: Tel. 0845-748-4950, www.national-rail.co.uk.

From Glasgow's Queen Street Station by Train to: **Oban** (3-4/day, just 1/day Sun in winter, 3 hours), **Inverness** (10/day, 3 hours, 4 direct, the rest change in Perth), **Edinburgh** (4/hour, 50 minutes), **Stirling** (3/hour, 30-45 minutes), **Pitlochry** (9/day, 1.75-2 hours, some transfer in Perth).

By Bus

From Glasgow by Bus to: **Edinburgh** (4/hour, 1.25-1.5 hours), **Oban** (3-6/day, 2.75-3 hours, some with transfer in Tyndrum), **Fort William** (buses #914, #915, and #916; 8/day, 3 hours), **Glencoe** (buses #914, #915, and #916; 8/day, 2.5 hours), **Inverness** (7/day, 3.5-4.5 hours, some transfer in Perth), **Portree** on the Isle of Skye (buses #915 and #916, 3/day, 6.5-7.5 hours), **Pitlochry** (3/day, 2.25 hours, transfer in Perth). Bus info: Tel. 0871-266-3333, www.citylink.co.uk.

By Plane

Glasgow International Airport: Located eight miles west of the city, this airport (code: GLA) has currency-exchange desks, a TI, Internet access, luggage storage, and ATMs (tel. 0844-481-5555, www.glasgowairport.com). Taxis connect downtown to the airport for about £20. Your hotel can likely arrange a private taxi service for £14. Bus #500 zips to central Glasgow (daily at least 4/hour 5:00-23:00, then hourly through the night, £6/one-way, £8.50/round-trip, 15-20 minutes to both train stations, 25 minutes to the bus station, catch at bus stop #1).

Prestwick Airport: A hub for Ryanair (as well as the US military, which refuels planes here), this airport (code: PIK) is about 30 miles southwest of the city center (tel. 0871-223-0700, ext. 1006, www.gpia.co.uk). The best connection is by train, which runs between the airport and Central Station (Mon-Sat 3/hour, 45 minutes, half-price with Ryanair ticket). Stagecoach buses link the airport with Buchanan Street Station (£10, daily 4/hour plus a few nighttime buses, 45-60 minutes, check schedules at www.travelinescotland.com). If you're wondering about the Elvis Presley Bar, this airport is said to be the only piece of Britain that Elvis ever set foot upon. (Elvis' manager, the Dutch-born Colonel Tom Parker, had a legal problem with British immigration.)

Route Tips for Drivers

From England's Lake District to Glasgow: From Keswick, take the A-66 for 18 miles to the M-6 and speed north nonstop (via Penrith and Carlisle), crossing Hadrian's Wall into Scotland. The road becomes the M-74 just north of Carlisle. To slip through Glasgow quickly, leave the M-74 at Junction 4 onto the M-73, following signs to *M-8/Glasgow*. Leave the M-73 at Junction 2, exiting onto the M-8. Stay on the M-8 west through Glasgow, exit at Junction 30, cross Erskine Bridge, and turn left on the A-82, following signs to *Crianlarich* and *Loch Lomond*. (For a scenic drive through Glasgow, take exit 17 off the M-8 and stay on the A-82 toward Dumbarton.)

GLASGOW

OBAN AND THE SOUTHERN HIGHLANDS

Oban • Islands of Mull and Iona
• Glencoe • Fort William

The area north of Glasgow offers a fun and easy dip into the southern part of the Scottish Highlands. Oban is a basket of Scottish traditions, with a handy pair of wind-bitten Hebrides islands (Mull and Iona) just a hop, skip, and jump away. Nearby, the evocative "Weeping Glen" of Glencoe aches with both history and natural beauty. Beyond that, Fort William anchors the southern end of the Caledonian Canal, offering a springboard to more Highlands scenery—this is where Britain's highest peak, Ben Nevis, keeps its head in the clouds, and where you'll find a valley made famous by a steam train carrying a young wizard named Harry.

Planning Your Time

Oban is a smart place to spend the night on a blitz tour of central Scotland; with more time to linger (and an interest in a day trip to the islands), spend two nights—Iona is worthwhile but adds a day to your trip. If you have a third night to spare, you can sleep in Iona and give yourself time to roam around Mull. Glencoe is worth considering as a very sleepy, rural overnight alternative to Oban, or if you have plenty of time and want a remote village experience on your way north.

Oban works well if you're coming from Glasgow, or even all the way from England's Lake District (for driving tips, see the end of this chapter). Assuming you're driving, here's an ambitious two-day plan for the Highlands.

Day 1

Morning   Drive up from the Lake District, or linger in Glasgow.

11:30	Depart Glasgow.
12:00	Rest stop on Loch Lomond, then joyride on.
13:00	Lunch in Inveraray.
16:00	Arrive in Oban, tour whisky distillery (last tour earlier off-season), and drop by the TI.
20:00	Dine in Oban.

Day 2

9:00	Leave Oban.
10:00	Visit Glencoe museum and the valley's visitors center.
12:00	Drive to Fort William and follow the Caledonian Canal to Inverness, stopping at Fort Augustus to see the locks and along Loch Ness to search for monsters.
16:00	Visit the Culloden Battlefield (closes earlier off-season) near Inverness.
17:00	Drive south.
20:00	Arrive in Edinburgh.

With More Time

While you'll see the Highlands on the above itinerary, you'll whiz past them in a misty blur. With more time, head north from Fort William to the Isle of Skye, spend a night or two there, head over to Inverness via Loch Ness, and consider a stop in Pitlochry.

Getting Around the Highlands

By Car: Drivers enjoy flexibility and plenty of tempting stopovers. Barring traffic, you'll make great time on good, mostly two-lane roads. Be careful, but don't be too timid about passing; otherwise, diesel fumes and large trucks might be your main memory of driving in Scotland. As you drive along Loch Ness, antsy locals may ride your bumper. For step-by-step instructions, read the "Route Tips for Drivers" at the end of this chapter.

By Public Transportation: Glasgow is the gateway to this region (so you'll most likely have to transfer there if coming from Edinburgh). The **train** zips from Glasgow to Fort William, Oban, and Kyle of Lochalsh in the west; and up to Stirling, Pitlochry, and Inverness in the east. For more remote destinations (such as Glencoe), the bus is better.

Most of the **buses** you'll need are operated by Scottish Citylink. Pay the driver in cash when you board, or buy tickets in advance at local TIs or online at www.citylink.co.uk (during busy times, it's smart to buy your ticket ahead of time to guarantee a seat on the bus). The nondescript town of Fort William serves as a hub for Highlands buses. Note that bus frequency is substantially reduced on Sundays and off-season—during these times, always carefully confirm schedules locally. Unless otherwise noted, I've listed bus information for summer weekdays.

These buses are particularly useful for connecting the sights in this book:

Buses **#976** and **#977** connect Glasgow with Oban (3-6/day, 2.75-3 hours, some with transfer in Tyndrum).

Bus **#913** runs one daily direct route from Edinburgh to this region—stopping at Glasgow, Stirling, and Glencoe on the way to Fort William (allow 4 hours from Edinburgh to Fort William; 3/day with change in Glasgow on buses #900 and #914, 5 hours).

Bus **#978** connects Edinburgh with Oban, stopping in Stirling, but not Glencoe (1/day direct, 4 hours; 6 more/day with changes in Glasgow and/or Tyndrum, 5-5.5 hours).

Bus **#914** goes from Glasgow to Fort William, stopping at Glencoe (1/day, 3 hours).

Buses **#915** and **#916** follow the same route (Glasgow-Glencoe-Fort William), then continue all the way up to Portree on the Isle of Skye (3/day, 6.75 hours for the full run).

Bus **#918** goes from Oban to Fort William, stopping en route at Ballachulish near Glencoe (3/day in summer, 2/day off-season, never on Sun; 1 hour to Ballachulish, 1.5 hours total to Fort William).

Bus **#919** connects Fort William with Inverness (5/day, 2 hours).

OBAN

Oban

Oban (pronounced "OH-bin") is called the "gateway to the isles." Equal parts functional and scenic, this busy little ferry-and-train terminal has no important sights, but makes up the difference in

character and a famous distillery. It's a low-key resort, with a winding promenade lined by gravel beaches, ice-cream stands, fish-and-chip joints, and a surprising diversity of good restaurants. When the rain clears, sun-starved Scots sit on benches along the Esplanade, leaning back to catch some rays. Wind, boats, gulls, layers of islands, and the promise of a wide-open Atlantic beyond give Oban a rugged charm.

Oban

1. Strathaven Terrace Accommodations
2. To Glenburnie House, The Barriemore & Kilchrenan House
3. The Rowantree Hotel
4. Backpackers Plus
5. Backpackers Plus Annexes (2)
6. SYHA Hostel
7. Jeremy Inglis' Hostel
8. Ee'usk & Piazza Restaurants
9. Coast Restaurant
10. Cuan Mòr Gastropub
11. Room 9 Restaurant
12. To Waypoint Bar & Grill (via Ferry)
13. Oban Fish & Chip Shop
14. The Oban Bay Fish & Chips; Skipinnish Ceilidh House
15. Shellfish Shack
16. The Kitchen Garden Deli & Café
17. Tesco Supermarket
18. Aulay's Bar
19. Great Western Hotel (Live Shows)
20. Cinema
21. Fancy That Shop (Internet)
22. West Coast Motors (Day Trips; Bag Storage)
23. Laundry
24. Bike Rental
25. Whisky Distillery
26. Oban War & Peace Museum

OBAN

TO ② & DUNLOLLIE CASTLE

CORRAN

ST. COLUMBA'S

OBAN BAY

BOATS TO MULL & IONA

FERRY TERMINAL

SOUTH PIER

TO KERREA FERRY

100 YARDS

100 METERS

IIII STAIRS

P PARKING

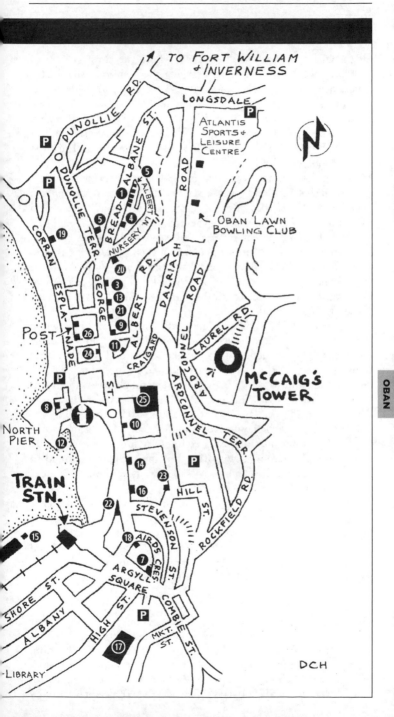

TO FORT WILLIAM
& INVERNESS

LONGSDALE

ATLANTIS
SPORTS &
LEISURE
CENTRE

OBAN LAWN
BOWLING CLUB

McCAIG'S
TOWER

DUNOLLIE RD.

ALBANE ST.

DUNOLLIE TERR.

CORRAN ESPLANADE

GEORGE ST.

NURSERY

ALBERT LN.

ALBERT RD.

DALRIACH RD.

ARDCONNEL ROAD

LAUREL RD.

ARDCONNEL TERR.

CRAIGARD

Post

North
Pier

TRAIN
STN.

STEVENSON ST.

HILL ST.

ROCKFIELD RD.

AIRDS CRES.

ARGYLL
SQUARE

SHORE ST.

ALBANY ST.

HIGH ST.

COMBIE ST.

MKT. ST.

LIBRARY

DCH

OBAN

1 · 4 · 5 · 3 · 13 · 21 · 9 · 11 · 20 · 26 · 24 · 19 · 8 · 12 · 25 · 10 · 14 · 23 · 16 · 22 · 18 · 7 · 15 · 17

Orientation to Oban

Oban, with about 10,000 people, is where the train system of Scotland meets the ferry system serving the Hebrides islands. It's always been on the way to something. As "gateway to the isles," its center is not a square or market, but its harbor.

Oban seems dominated by Caledonian-MacBrayne, Scotland's biggest ferry company. CalMac's 30 ships serve 24 destinations and transport over 4 million passengers a year. The city's port has long been a lifeline to the islands.

With the arrival of the train in 1880, Oban became the unofficial capital of Scotland's west coast and a destination for tourists. Caledonian Hotel, the original terminus hotel that once served those train travelers, dominates the harborfront.

Herring was the first big industry, then came tobacco (imported from the American colonies), then whisky. It's rare to find a distillery in the middle of a town, but Oban grew up around its distillery. With the success of its whisky, the town enjoyed an invigorating confidence, optimism, and, in 1811, a royal charter. Today the big industry is tourism.

A dozen boats still fish commercially (the fish market is across the harbor). The local tourist board, in an attempt to entice people to stay, is trying to rebrand the town as a seafood capital rather than "gateway to the isles." As the ocean's supply has become depleted, most local fish is farmed. There's still plenty of shellfish.

At the height of the Cold War, Oban played a critical role when the world's first two-way transatlantic telephone cable was laid from Gallanach Bay to Newfoundland in 1956—a milestone in global communication. This technology provided the White House and the Kremlin with the "hotline" that was crucial in helping to resolve the Cuban Missile Crisis without a nuclear conflagration.

Oban's business action, just a couple of streets deep, stretches along the harbor and its promenade. Everything in Oban is close together, and the town seems eager to please its many visitors. There's live music nightly in several bars and restaurants; wool and tweed are perpetually on sale; and posters announce a variety of day tours to Scotland's wild and wildlife-strewn western islands.

Tourist Information

Oban's TI, located at the North Pier, sells bus and ferry tickets and has a fine bookshop. Stop by to get brochures and information on everything from bike rental to golf courses to horseback riding to rainy-day activities and more. They can also book you a room for a £4 fee (flexible hours, generally July-Aug daily 9:00-19:00; April-June Mon-Sat 9:00-17:30, Sun 10:00-17:00; Sept-Oct daily

10:00-17:00; Nov-March Mon-Sat 10:00-17:00, Sun 11:00-15:00; 3 North Pier, tel. 01631/563-122, www.oban.org.uk).

Events and Activities: Black-and-gold signboards around town show "What's On." Fun low-key activities may include open-mic, disco, or quiz theme nights in pubs; Scottish folk shows; pipe-band concerts; coffee meetings; accordion concerts; and—if you're lucky—duck races. There's often free live entertainment upstairs in the Great Western Hotel on the Esplanade (most nights at 20:30 year-round; Scottish Night with bagpipes and sometimes dancers generally Wed and Fri; call for details, tel. 01631/563-101). On Wednesday nights, the Oban Pipe Band plays in the town square. And the city hosts Highland Games every August (www.oban games.com).

Helpful Hints

Internet Access: There's free Wi-Fi all over town. **Fancy That** is a souvenir shop on the main drag with seven high-speed Internet terminals and Wi-Fi in the back room (£1/20 minutes, daily 9:30-17:00, until 22:00 July-Aug, 108 George Street, tel. 01631/562-996). To surf for free, get online at the **library** just above the ferry terminal; you can just show up, but it's smart to call ahead to book a 30-minute time slot (Mon and Wed 10:00-13:00 & 14:00-19:00, Thu until 18:00, Fri until 17:00, closed Sat afternoon and all day Tue and Sun, 77 Albany Street, tel. 01631/571-444).

Bookstore: Waterstones, a huge bookstore overlooking the harborfront, offers maps and a fine collection of books on Scotland (daily, 12 George Street, tel. 0843/290-8529).

Baggage Storage: The train station has luggage lockers (£3-5 depending on bag size). **West Coast Motors**, which sells bus tickets, has a pricey left-luggage service (£1/hour per piece, unsecured in main office, Mon-Fri 9:00-13:00 & 14:00-17:00, Sat 9:00-14:00, closed Sun, July-Sept open during lunch, can be sporadically closed Oct-May, at Queens Park Place, www .westcoastmotors.co.uk).

Laundry: You'll find **Oban Quality Laundry** tucked a block behind the main drag on Stevenson Street (£7-10/load for same-day drop-off service, no self-service, Mon-Fri 9:00-17:00, Sat 9:00-13:00, closed Sun, tel. 01631/563-554).

Supermarket: Tesco is a five-minute walk from the train station (Mon-Sat 6:00-24:00, Sun 8:00-20:00, WC in front by registers, inexpensive cafeteria; walk through Argyll Square and look for entrance to large parking lot on right, Lochside Street).

Bike Rental: Nevis Cycles is on the main drag (£10/half-day, £25/day, includes helmets, can pick up in Oban and drop off in Fort William or Inverness for extra charge, daily 10:00-17:00, 87 George Street, tel. 01631/566-033).

Bus Station: The "station" is just a pullout, marked by a stubby clock tower, at the roundabout just in front of the train station.

Cinema: The Phoenix Cinema closed down for two years and then was saved by the community. It's now volunteer-run and booming (140 George Street, www.obanphoenix.com).

Characteristic Pub: Aulay's Bar, with decor that shows off Oban's maritime heritage, has two sides, each with a different personality. Having a drink here invariably comes with a good "blether" (conversation), and the gang is local (8 Airds Crescent, just around the corner from the train station and ferry terminal).

Sights in Oban

▲West Highland Malt Scotch Whisky Distillery Tours

The 200-year-old Oban Whisky Distillery produces more than 16,000 liters a week and exports much of that to the US. They offer serious and fragrant one-hour tours explaining the process from start to finish, with two smooth samples (in the tasting room at the end of the tour, say "yes" when the guide asks if anyone is a whisky drinker and you may get a third taste), a whisky glass (normally sells for £6.50), and a discount coupon for the shop. This is the handiest whisky tour you'll see, just a block off the harbor and better than anything in Edinburgh. The exhibition that precedes the tour gives a quick, whisky-centric history of Scotland. In high season, these popular tours (which are limited to 16 people every 20-30 minutes) fill up quickly. Call, go online, or stop by in advance to reserve your time slot.

Cost and Hours: £7.50; July-Sept Mon-Fri 9:30-19:30, Sat-Sun 9:30-17:00; Easter-June and Oct daily 9:30-17:00; March-Easter and Nov Mon-Fri 10:00-17:00, closed Sat-Sun; Dec and Feb Mon-Fri 12:30-16:00, closed Sat-Sun; closed Jan; last tour 1.25 hours before closing, Stafford Street, tel. 01631/572-004, www.discovering-distilleries.com. Connoisseurs can ask about the new "vertical tasting" (sampling whisky by age) held in their warehouse (£30, 2 hours, likely July-Sept, Mon-Fri at 16:00 only).

Oban War & Peace Museum

Opened in 1995 on the 50th anniversary of Victory in Europe Day, this museum covers more than war and peace. Photos show Oban through the years, and a 15-minute looped video gives a simple tour around the region. Volunteer staffers love to chat about the exhibit—or anything else on your mind (free, daily 10:00-16:00, longer hours in summer, Corran Esplanade, next to Regent Hotel on the promenade, www.obanmuseum.org.uk).

Skipinnish Ceilidh House

On most nights mid-June through mid-September, you can stroll into Skipinnish on the main drag for Highland music, song, and dancing. The owners—professional musicians Angus and Andrew—invest in talented musicians and put on a good show, featuring live bands, songs sung in Gaelic, Highland dancing, and great Scottish storytelling. For many, the best part is the chance to learn some *ceilidh* (KAY-lee) dancing. These group dances are a lot of fun—wallflowers and bad dancers are warmly welcomed, and the staff is happy to give you pointers.

Cost and Hours: £10 music session, pricier for concerts with visiting big-name *ceilidh* bands, music four nights/week mid-June–mid-Sept usually starting around 20:30, 2 hours, check website for off-season show schedule, 34 George Street, tel. 01631/569-599, www.skipinnishceilidhhouse.com.

McCaig's Tower

The unfinished "colosseum" on the hill overlooking town was an employ-the-workers-and-build-me-a-fine-memorial project undertaken by an Oban tycoon in 1900. While the structure itself is nothing to see up close, a 10-minute hike through a Victorian residential neighborhood leads you to a peaceful garden and a commanding view. McCaig died before completing the structure, so his complete vision for it remains a mystery.

Atlantis Leisure Centre

This industrial-type sports center is a good place to get some exercise on a rainy day or let the kids run wild for a few hours. It has a rock-climbing wall, tennis courts, two playgrounds, and an indoor swimming pool with a big water slide. The center's outdoor playground is free and open all the time; the indoor "soft play centre" for children under five costs £3.60 per hour, per child.

Cost and Hours: Pool only-£4/adult, £2/child, no rental towels or suits, lockers-£0.20; day pass for everything-£12/adult, £8/child; Mon-Fri 7:00-22:00, Sat-Sun 9:00-18:00; open-swim pool hours vary by season—call or check online for exact times; on the north end of Dalriach Road, tel. 01631/566-800, www.atlantis leisure.co.uk.

Oban Lawn Bowling Club

The club has welcomed visitors since 1869. This elegant green is the scene of a wonderfully British spectacle of old men tiptoeing wishfully after their balls. It's fun to watch, and—if there's no match scheduled and the weather's dry—anyone can rent shoes and balls and actually play.

Cost and Hours: £4/person; informal hours, but generally daily 10:00-16:00 & 17:00 to "however long the weather lasts"; lessons at 13:45; just south of sports center on Dalriach Road, tel. 01631/570-808, www.obanbowlingclub.com.

OBAN

Dunollie Castle and Museum

In a park just a mile up the coast, this spartan, stocky castle with 10-foot walls is a delightful stroll from the town center. The ruins offer a commanding, windy view of the harbor, a strategic spot back in the days when transport was mainly by water. For more than a thousand years, clan chiefs ruled this region from this ancestral home of Clan MacDougall, but the castle was abandoned in 1746. The adjacent house, which dates from 1745, shows off the MacDougall clan's family heritage—much of it naval; docents explain the charming if humble exhibits.

While the castle and museum are, frankly, not much, the local pride in the display and the walk from town make the visit fun. To get there, stroll out of town along the harborfront promenade. At the war memorial (where there are inviting sea-view benches), cross the street. A gate leads to a little lane, lined with historic and nature boards along the way to the castle (£4, free Sun; April-Nov Mon-Sat 11:00-16:00, Sun 13:00-16:00; closed Dec-March, tel. 01631/570-625).

Near Oban

Isle of Kerrera

Functioning like a giant breakwater, the Isle of Kerrera (KEH-reh-rah) makes Oban possible. Just offshore from Oban, this stark but very green island offers a quick, easy opportunity to get that romantic island experience. While it has no proper roads, it offers nice hikes, a ruined castle, and a few sheep farms. You may see the Kerrera ferry filled with sheep heading for Oban's livestock market.

Although Kerrera dominates Oban's sea view, you'll have to head two miles south of town (follow the coast road past the ferry terminal) to catch the boat to the middle of the island (ferry-£4.50 round-trip, bikes free, 5-minute trip; Easter-Sept first ferry Mon-Sat at 8:45, then daily 2/hour 10:30-12:30 & 14:00-17:00, last ferry at 18:00; Oct-Easter 5-6/day, last ferry at 17:50 but changes with demand; at Gallanach's dock; tel. 01631/563-665, if no answer contact Oban TI for info; www.kerrera-ferry.co.uk). For an easier approach from the center of Oban, you can ride the free shuttle ferry between Oban's North Pier and the Kerrera Marina. The tiny boat is designed for customers of the recommended Waypoint Bar & Grill (must show your receipt on the way back). It's fine to just drop in for a drink after an island stroll to get your receipt.

Sleeping on Kerrera: To spend the night on the island, your only option is the **$ Kerrera Bunkhouse,** a newly refurbished 18th-century stable that can sleep up to eight people in four compartments (£15/person, £100 for the entire bunkhouse, includes

OBAN

bedding but not towels, cheaper for 2 nights or more, open year-round but must book ahead, kitchen, tel. 01631/566-367, www.kerrerabunkhouse.co.uk, info@kerrerabunkhouse.co.uk, Martin and Aideen). They also run a tea garden that serves meals (April-Sept daily 10:30-16:30, closed Oct-March).

Isle of Seil

Enjoy a drive, a walk, some solitude, and the sea. Drive 12 miles south of Oban on the A-816 to the B-844 to the Isle of Seil (pronounced "seal"), connected to the mainland by a bridge (which, locals like to brag, "crosses the Atlantic"...well, maybe a small part of it).

Just over the bridge on the Isle of Seil is a pub called **Tigh-an-Truish** ("House of Trousers"). After a 1745 English law forbade the wearing of kilts on the mainland, Highlanders on the island used this pub to change from kilts to trousers before they made the crossing. The pub serves great meals and good seafood dishes to those either in kilts or pants (pub open daily April-Oct 11:00-23:00—food served 12:00-14:00 & 18:00-20:30, Nov-March shorter hours and soup/sandwiches only, darts anytime, tel. 01852/300-242).

Seven miles across the island, on a tiny second island and facing the open Atlantic, is **Easdale,** a historic, touristy, windy little slate-mining town—with a slate-town museum and an incredibly tacky, egomaniac's "Highland Arts" shop (shuttle ferry goes the 300 yards). An overpriced direct ferry runs from Easdale to Iona; but, at twice the cost of the Mull-Iona trip, the same time on the island, and very little time with a local guide, it's hardly worth it.

Tours from Oban

▲▲Nearby Islands

For the best day trip from Oban, tour the islands of Mull and Iona (offered daily Easter-Oct, described later)—or consider staying overnight on remote and beautiful Iona. With more time or other interests, consider one of many other options you'll see advertised.

Wildlife Tours

Those more interested in nature than church history will enjoy trips to the wildly scenic Isle of Staffa with Fingal's Cave (known for its basalt column formations—marking the Scottish end of the Giant's Causeway so famous in Northern Ireland). The journey to Treshnish Island brims with puffins, seals, and other sea critters. Several groups, including Sealife Adventures and SeaFari, run whale-watching tours that feature rare minke whales, basking sharks, bottlenose dolphins, and porpoises. Departures and options abound—check at the TI for information.

Open-Top Bus Tours

If there's good weather and you don't have a car, take a spin out of Oban for views of nearby castles and islands, plus a stop near McCaig's Tower with a narration by the driver (£8, £7 if pre-booked online, valid for 24 hours, ticket also valid on regular service buses, late May-late Sept daily at 11:00 and 14:00, no tours off-season, 2.5 hours, departs from rail station, tel. 01412/040-444, www.city-sightseeing.com).

Caledonian MacBrayne Day Tours

Choose from an array of ferry and boat tours from Oban to the islands (daily 8:30-18:00, purchase at ferry terminal or at www.calmac.co.uk, tel. 0631/562-244).

Sleeping in Oban

B&Bs on Strathaven Terrace

Oban's B&Bs offer a better value than its hotels. None of these B&Bs accept credit cards; all have free Wi-Fi. The following B&Bs line up on a quiet, flowery street that's nicely located two blocks off the harbor, three blocks from the center, and a 10-minute walk from the train station. By car, as you enter town, turn left after King's Knoll Hotel, and take your first right onto Breadalbane Street. ("Strathaven Terrace" is actually just the name for this row of houses on Breadalbane Street.) The alley behind the buildings has parking for all of these places.

$$ Sandvilla B&B rents five fine rooms with sleek contemporary decor (Db-£60-70, Tb-£83-90, at #4, tel. 01631/562-803, www.holidayoban.co.uk, sandvilla@holidayoban.co.uk, Joyce and Scott).

$$ Gramarvin Guest House has four fresh and cheery rooms (Db-£55-70, £65 in Aug, Tb-£82-105, at #5, tel. 01631/564-622, www.gramarvin.co.uk, mary@gramarvin.co.uk, Mary).

$$ Raniven Guest House has five simple, tastefully decorated rooms and gracious, fun-loving hosts (Sb-£30-35, Db-£55-60, price depends on season, at #1, tel. 01631/562-713, www.raniven.co.uk, info@raniven.co.uk, Moyra and Stuart).

$$ Tanglin B&B, with five Grandma's house-homey rooms, comes with lively, chatty hosts Liz and Jim Montgomery, who create an easygoing atmosphere (S-£28, Db-£54-56, family room available, at #3, tel. 01631/563-247, mobile 0774/8305-891, jim tanglin@aol.com).

Guesthouses and Small Hotels

These options are a step up from the B&Bs—in terms of both amenities and price. Glenburnie House, Kilchrenan House, and The Barriemore are along the Esplanade, which stretches north of town above a cobble beach (with beautiful bay views); they are a 5- to 10-minute walk from the center. The Rowantree is on the main drag in town.

$$$ Glenburnie House, a stately Victorian home, has an elegant breakfast room overlooking the bay. Its 12 spacious, comfortable, classy rooms feel like plush living rooms. There's a nice lounge and a tiny sunroom with a stuffed "hairy coo" head (Sb-£55, Db-£90-115, price depends on size and view, closed mid-Nov-March, free Wi-Fi, free parking, the Esplanade, tel. 01631/562-089, www.glenburnie.co.uk, stay@glenburnie.co.uk, Graeme).

$$$ Kilchrenan House, the turreted former retreat of a textile magnate, has 14 tastefully renovated, large rooms, most with bay views (Sb-£50, Db-£70-105, 2-night minimum, higher prices are for seaview rooms in June-Aug, lower prices are for back-facing rooms and Sept-May, stunning rooms #5, #9, and #15 are worth the few extra pounds, welcome drink of whisky or sherry, different "breakfast special" every day, closed Dec-Jan, a few houses past the cathedral on the Esplanade, tel. 01631/562-663, www .kilchrenanhouse.co.uk, info@kilchrenanhouse.co.uk, Colin and Frances).

$$$ The Rowantree Hotel is a group-friendly place with 24 renovated rooms reminiscent of a budget hotel in the US (complete with thin walls) and a central locale right on Oban's main drag (Sb-£60-90, Db-£100-160, includes breakfast, prices may be soft for walk-ins and off-season, easy parking, George Street, tel. 01631/562-954, www.rowantreehoteloban.co.uk).

OBAN

$$$ The Barriemore, at the very end of Oban's grand water-front Esplanade, comes with a nice patio, front sitting area, and well-appointed rooms. Some front-facing rooms have views; rooms in the modern addition in the back are cheaper (Sb-£65-75, Db-£90-110, Tb-£100-125, two ground-floor double mini suites with views-£130-165, less off-season, price depends on view, free Wi-Fi, the Esplanade, tel. 01631/566-356, www.barriemore-hotel .co.uk, reception@barriemore-hotel.co.uk, Sue and Jan).

Hostels

$ Backpackers Plus is the most central, laid-back, and fun, with a sprawling public living room, 48 beds, and a staff who is generous with travel tips (£17/bed, 6-12 bunks per room, includes breakfast, guest computer, free Wi-Fi, £4 laundry service for guests only, 10-minute walk from station, on Breadalbane Street, tel. 01631/567-189, www.backpackersplus.com, info@backpackersplus.com, Peter). Their bunkhouse across the street has several basic but cheerful private rooms that share a kitchen; a third property, at the top of the block, has seven private rooms, each with a bath (S-£17-23, Sb-£19-28, D-£46, Db-£54, T-£61-69, same contact info as hostel).

$ The HI-affiliated SYHA hostel, on the scenic waterfront Esplanade, is in a grand building with 98 beds and smashing views of the harbor and islands from the lounges and dining rooms. There are also some private rooms, including several that can usually be rented as twin rooms (£17.50-20/bed in 4- to 6-bed rooms with en-suite bathroom, bunk-bed Db-£46, Tb-£55-65, Qb-£75-88, price varies with demand, also has family rooms and 8-bed apartment with kitchen, £2/night more for nonmembers, breakfast-£4-6, dinner-£5.50-12, pay guest computer and Wi-Fi, great facilities, pay laundry, kitchen, tel. 01631/562-025, www.syha.org .uk, oban@syha.org.uk).

$ Jeremy Inglis' Hostel has 37 beds located two blocks from the TI and train station. This loosely run place feels more like a commune than a youth hostel...and it's cheap (£15/bed, S-£22, D-£30, cash only, includes linens, breakfast comes with Jeremy's homemade jam, free Wi-Fi, kitchen, no curfew, second floor at 21 Airds Crescent, tel. 01631/565-065, jeremyinglis@mctavishs .freeserve.co.uk).

Eating in Oban

Oban calls itself the "seafood capital of Scotland," and is passionate about good fish-and-chips. There are plenty of good fish places in town, but the two recommended fish-and-chips joints (listed at the end of this section) are the town favorites. Both have food to go and good seating inside.

Ee'usk (a phonetic rendering of *iasg,* Scottish Gaelic for "fish") is a popular, stylish, family-run place on the waterfront. It has a casual-chic atmosphere, a bright and glassy interior, sweeping views on three sides, and fish dishes favored by both natives and tourists. Reservations are recommended every day in summer and on weekends off-season (£9-12 lunches, £13-20 dinners, daily 12:00-15:00 & 17:45-21:30, North Pier, tel. 01631/565-666, www.eeusk.com, MacLeod family).

Piazza, next door and also run by the MacLeods, has similar decor but serves Italian cuisine and offers a more family-friendly ambience. They have some outdoor seats and big windows facing the sea (£8-12 pizzas and pastas, daily 12:00-15:00 & 17:30-21:00, smart to reserve ahead July-Aug, tel. 01631/563-628).

Coast proudly serves fresh local fish, meat, and veggies in a mod pine-and-candlelight atmosphere. As everything is prepared and presented with care by husband-and-wife team Richard and Nicola—who try to combine traditional Scottish elements in innovative new ways—come here only if you have time for a slow meal (£10-13 lunches, £13-18 dinners, £13 two-course and £16 three-course specials, open daily 12:00-14:00 & 17:30-21:00, closed Sun for lunch, 104 George Street, tel. 01631/569-900).

Cuan Mòr is a popular gastropub that combines traditional Scottish with modern flair—both in its tasty cuisine and in its furnishings, made entirely of wood, stone, and metal scavenged from the beaches of Scotland's west coast (£6 lunches, £9-13 main courses, food served daily 12:00-22:00, brewery in the back, 60 George Street, tel. 01631/565-078).

Room 9 seats just 24 diners in one tiny light-wood room, and has a select menu of homemade nouvelle-cuisine dishes. It's owned and run with care by chef Michael (dinner only, £13-16 meals, Mon-Sat 17:30-21:30, closed Sun, reservations smart Fri-Sat, 9 Craigard Road, tel. 01631/564-200, www.room9oban.co.uk).

Waypoint Bar & Grill, just across the bay from Oban, is a laid-back patio at the Kerrera Marina with a no-nonsense menu of grilled seafood. It's not fancy, but the food is fresh and inexpensive, and on a nice day the open-air waterside setting is unbeatable (£10-16 main courses, £10 large portion fish-and-chips, £25 seafood platter, June-Sept daily 12:00-21:00, closed Oct-May, reservations smart, tel. 07840/650-669, www.obanseafoodrestaurant.co.uk). A free-for-customers eight-minute ferry to the marina leaves from Oban's North Pier—look for the sign near the recommended Piazza restaurant (departs hourly at :10 past each hour).

Fish-and-Chip Joints: Oban Fish and Chip Shop, run by husband-and-wife team George and Lillian (with Lewis and Sammy working the fryer), serves praiseworthy haddock and

OBAN

mussels among other tasty options in a cheery blue cabana-like dining room. Consider venturing away from basic fish-and-chips into a world of more creative seafood dishes, all at a great price (£8 haddock-and-chips, £7-11 main courses, 116 George Street, tel. 01631/567-000 or 01631/569-828).

At **The Oban Bay Fish & Chips,** which is also family-run, Renato serves all things from the sea (plus an assortment of Scottish classics) battered and fried. Choose between the casual restaurant or take-away counter, where you can give fried haggis a try (£7-10 meals, slightly cheaper for take-away, "Fish Tea" for £8, daily 12:00-23:00, on the harborfront at 34 George Street, below Skipinnish, tel. 01631/565-855).

Lunch

The green **shellfish shack** at the ferry dock is the best spot to pick up a seafood sandwich or a snack. Get freshly caught and boiled seafood in Styrofoam cups to go; request a paper plate and bread to make a light meal (often free salmon samples, meal-size £3 salmon sandwiches, inexpensive coffee, picnic tables nearby, open daily from 10:00 until the boat unloads from Mull around 17:45).

The Kitchen Garden is fine for soup, salad, or sandwiches. It's a deli and gourmet-foods store with a charming café upstairs (£4 sandwiches to go, £5-8 dishes upstairs, Mon-Sat 9:00-17:30, Sun 10:00-16:30, closed Sun Jan-mid-Feb, 14 George Street, tel. 01631/566-332).

Oban Connections

By Train from Oban: Trains link Oban to the nearest transportation hub in **Glasgow** (3-4/day, just 1/day Sun in winter, 3 hours); to get to **Edinburgh,** you'll have to transfer in Glasgow (2/day, 4.25 hours). To reach **Fort William** (a transit hub for the Highlands), you'll take the same Glasgow-bound train, but transfer in Crianlarich—the direct bus is easier (see next). Oban's small train station has limited hours (ticket window open Mon-Sat 7:15-18:00, Sun 10:45-18:00, same hours apply to lockers, train info tel. 08457-484-950, www.nationalrail.co.uk).

By Bus: Bus #918 passes through Ballachulish—a half-mile from **Glencoe**—on its way to **Fort William** (3/day in summer, 2/day off-season, never on Sun; 1 hour to Ballachulish, 1.5 hours total to Fort William). Take this bus to Fort William, then transfer to bus #919 to reach **Inverness** (3.75 hours total, with a 20-minute layover in Fort William) or bus #915 or #916 to **Portree** on the Isle of Skye (2/day, 4.5-5 hours total). A different bus (#976 or #977) connects Oban with **Glasgow** (3-6/day, 2.75-3 hours, some with transfer in Tyndrum), from where you can easily connect by bus or train to **Edinburgh** (figure 4.5 hours total). Buses arrive and depart from a roundabout, marked by a stubby clock tower, just before the entrance to the train station (tel. 08712/663-333, www .citylink.co.uk).

By Boat: Ferries fan out from Oban to the southern Hebrides (see information on the islands of Iona and Mull, later). Caledonian MacBrayne Ferry info: Tel. 01631/566-688, free booking tel. 0800-066-5000, www.calmac.co.uk.

Between Glasgow and Oban

The drive from Glasgow (or Edinburgh) to Oban provides dreamy vistas and your first look at the dramatic landscapes of the Highlands. Drivers coming from the south can consider these stopovers, which are listed in order from Glasgow to Oban.

Loch Lomond

Within about an hour's drive of half the population of Scotland is the centerpiece of the country's leading national park, the scenic lake called Loch Lomond. It's a favorite retreat for Scots as well as foreign tourists. Leaving Glasgow on the A-82, you'll soon be driving along Loch Lomond. The first picnic turnout has the best lake views, benches, a park, and a playground. Twenty-four miles long and speckled with islands, Loch Lomond is second in size only to Loch Ness.

Loch Lomond is well-known mostly because of its easy proximity to Glasgow (about 15 miles away)—and also because its bonnie, bonnie banks inspired a beloved folk song: "Ye'll take the high road, and I'll take the low road, and I'll be in Scotland afore ye... For me and my true love will never meet again, on the bonnie, bonnie banks of Loch Lomond." As you'll be humming that all day, here's one interpretation of the song's poignant meaning: After the disastrous Scottish loss at the Battle of Culloden, the English brought the Jacobite ringleaders to London for a series of show trials. The Scottish were all executed, and their bodies transported back to Scotland by coaches along the "high road," while the wives, girlfriends, and families—who had walked to London for the trials—had to return along the commoners' "low road"—both ending up, at least in spirit, back in Scotland.

• *Halfway up the loch, at Tarbet, take the "tourist route" left onto the A-83, driving along Loch Long toward Inveraray.*

Rest-and-Be-Thankful Pass

As you climb into more rugged territory, be mindful that the roads connecting the Lowlands with the Highlands (like this one) were

OBAN

originally a military project designed to facilitate the English quelling of the Highland clans. A low-profile pullout on the A-83 just west of the A-82 offers a pleasant opportunity to stretch your legs and get your first taste of that rugged Scottish countryside. The colorful name comes from the 1880s, when second- and third-class coach passengers got out and pushed the coach and first-class passengers up the hill.

Inveraray

Nearly everybody stops at this lovely, seemingly made-for-tourists castle town on Loch Fyne. Park near the pier and browse the wide selection of restaurants and tourist shops.

Inveraray's **TI** sells bus and ferry tickets, has Internet access, and offers a free mini-guide and an exhibit about the Argyll region (daily June-Aug 9:00-17:30, Sept-Oct and April-May 10:00-17:00, Nov-March 10:00-16:00, Front Street, tel. 01499/302-063). Public WCs are at the end of the nearby pier.

The town's main "sight" is the **Inveraray Jail,** an overpriced, corny, but mildly educational former jail converted into a museum. This "living 19th-century prison" includes a courtroom where mannequins argue the fate of the accused. You'll have the opportunity to be locked up for a photo op by a playful guard (£9, daily April-Oct 9:30-18:00, Nov-March 10:00-17:00, last entry one hour before closing, Church Square, tel. 01499/302-381, www.inverary jail.co.uk).

You'll spot the dramatic **Inveraray Castle** (which you may recognize as Duneagle Castle from the PBS series *Downton Abbey*) on the right as you cross the bridge coming from Glasgow. This impressive-looking stronghold of one of the more notorious branches of the Campbell clan is striking from afar but dull inside; save your time for better castles elsewhere in the Highlands.

• *To continue on to Oban, leave Inveraray through a gate (at the Woolen Mill) to the A-819, and go through Glen Aray and along Loch Awe. The A-85 takes you into Oban.*

Islands of Mull and Iona

For the easiest one-day look at two of the dramatic and historic Hebrides (HEB-rid-eez) islands, take the Iona/Mull tour from Oban. (For a more in-depth look, head north to Skye—see next chapter.)

Here's the game plan: You'll take a ferry from Oban to Mull (45 minutes), ride a West Coast Motors tour bus across Mull (1.25 hours), then board a quick ferry from Mull to Iona. The

total round-trip travel time is
5.5 hours (all of it incredibly scenic), plus about two hours of free
time on Iona. Buy your strip of
six tickets—one for each leg—at
the West Coast Motors office in
Oban (£38, for Iona/Mull tour,
no tours Nov-March, book one
day ahead in July-Sept if possible, bus tickets can sell out

during busy summer weekends, office open daily 8:30-17:30, 1
Queens Park Place, a block from train station, tel. 01631/566-809
or 01631/563-221).

You'll leave in the morning from the Oban pier on the huge
Oban-Mull ferry run by Caledonian MacBrayne (boats depart
Sun-Fri at 9:50, Sat at 9:30, board at least 20 minutes before
departure; boats return daily around 17:45). As the schedule can
change slightly from year to year, confirm your departure time
carefully in Oban. The best inside seats on the ferry—with the
biggest windows—are in the sofa lounge on the uppermost deck
(level 4) at the back end of the boat. (Follow signs for the toilets,
and look for the big staircase to the top floor; this floor also has
its own small snack bar with hot drinks and £3 sandwiches.) On
board, if it's a clear day, ask a local or a crew member to point
out Ben Nevis, the tallest mountain in Great Britain. The ferry
has a fine cafeteria with select-your-own lunch bags (£4, includes
sandwich, chips, drink, and fruit) and a bookshop (though guidebooks are cheaper in Oban). Five minutes before landing on Mull,
you'll see the striking 13th-century Duart Castle on the left (www
.duartcastle.com).

Walk-on passengers disembark from deck 3, across from the
bookshop (port side). Upon arrival in Mull, find your tour company's bus for the entertaining and informative ride across the
Isle of Mull (bus may not have name on it; ask the drivers). The
right (driver's) side offers better sea views during the second half
of the journey to Fionnphort, while the left side has fine views of
Mull's rolling wilderness. The bus drivers spend the entire ride
chattering away about life on Mull, slowing to point out wildlife,
and sharing adages like, "If there's no flowers on the gorse, snog-
ging's gone out of fashion." They are hardworking local boys who
make historical trivia fascinating—or at least fun. Your destination is Mull's westernmost ferry terminal (Fionnphort), where
you'll board a small, rocking ferry for the brief ride to Iona.
Unless you stay overnight, you'll have only about two hours to
roam freely around the island before taking the ferry-bus-ferry
ride in reverse back to Oban.

Oban & the Southern Highlands

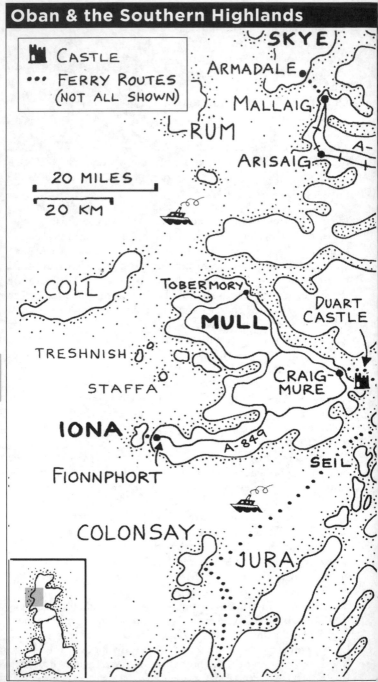

Castle

••• **Ferry Routes** (not all shown)

SKYE

ARMADALE

MALLAIG

RUM

ARISAIG

A-

20 MILES

20 KM

COLL

TOBERMORY

DUART CASTLE

MULL

TRESHNISH

STAFFA

CRAIG-MURE

IONA

A-849

FIONNPHORT

SEIL

COLONSAY

JURA

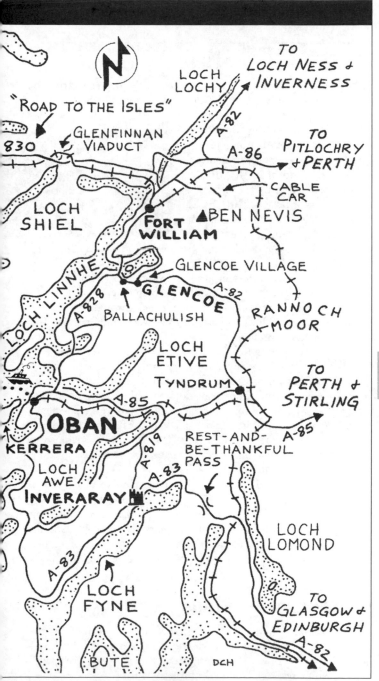

N

TO
LOCH NESS &
INVERNESS

LOCH
LOCHY

"ROAD TO THE ISLES"

GLENFINNAN
VIADUCT

830

A-82

A-86

TO
PITLOCHRY
& PERTH

LOCH
SHIEL

CABLE
CAR

FORT
WILLIAM

▲BEN NEVIS

LOCH LINNHE

GLENCOE VILLAGE

GLENCOE

A-82

A-828

BALLACHULISH

RANNOCH
MOOR

LOCH
ETIVE

TYNDRUM

TO
PERTH &
STIRLING

A-85

OBAN

A-85

KERRERA

A-819

REST-AND-
BE-THANKFUL
PASS

LOCH
AWE

A-83

INVERARAY

LOCH
LOMOND

A-83

TO
GLASGOW &
EDINBURGH

LOCH
FYNE

A-82

BUTE

DCH

Though this trip is spectacular when it's sunny, it's worthwhile in any weather.

Mull

The Isle of Mull, the second-largest in Scotland, has nearly 300 scenic miles of coastline and castles and a 3,169-foot-high mountain, one of Scotland's Munros. Called Ben More ("Big Mountain" in Gaelic), it was once much bigger. At 10,000 feet tall, it made up the entire island of Mull—until a volcano erupted. Things are calmer now, and, similarly, Mull has a noticeably laid-back population. My bus driver reported that there are no deaths from stress, and only a few from boredom.

With steep, fog-covered hillsides topped by cairns (piles of stones, sometimes indicating graves) and ancient stone circles, Mull has a gloomy, otherworldly charm. Bring plenty of rain protection and wear layers in case the sun peeks through the clouds. As my driver said, Mull is a place of cold, wet, windy winters and mild, wet, windy summers.

On the far side of Mull, the caravan of tour buses unloads at Fionnphort, a tiny ferry town. The ferry to the island of Iona takes about 200 walk-on passengers. Confirm the return time with your bus driver, then hustle to the dock to make the first trip over (otherwise, it's a 30-minute wait). There's a small ferry-passenger building/meager snack bar (and a pay WC). After the 10-minute ride, you wash ashore on sleepy Iona (free WC on this side), and the ferry mobs that crowded you on the boat seem to disappear up the main road and into Iona's back lanes.

The **About Mull Tours and Taxi** service can also get you around Mull (tel. 01681/700-507 or mobile 0788-777-4550, www.aboutmull.co.uk). They also do day tours of Mull (£35), focusing on local history and wildlife (half-day tours also available, shorter Mull tours can drop you off at Iona ferry dock at 15:00 for a quick Iona visit and pick you up at 18:00, minimum 2 people, must book ahead).

Iona

The tiny island of Iona, just 3 miles by 1.5 miles, is famous as the birthplace of Christianity in Scotland. You'll have about two hours here on your own before you retrace your steps (your driver will tell you which return ferry to take back to Mull).

History of Iona

St. Columba, an Irish scholar, soldier, priest, and founder of monasteries, got into a small war over the possession of an illegally copied psalm book. Victorious but sickened by the bloodshed, Columba left Ireland, vowing never to return. According to legend, the first bit of land out of sight of his homeland was Iona. He stopped here in 563 and established an abbey.

Columba's monastic community flourished, and Iona became the center of Celtic Christianity. Missionaries from Iona spread the gospel throughout Scotland and northern England, while scholarly monks established Iona as a center of art and learning. The *Book of Kells*—perhaps the finest piece of art from "Dark Ages" Europe—was probably made on Iona in the eighth century. The island was so important that it was the legendary burial place for ancient Scottish and even Scandinavian kings (including Shakespeare's Macbeth).

Slowly, the importance of Iona ebbed. Vikings massacred 68 monks in 806. Fearing more raids, the monks evacuated most of Iona's treasures to Ireland (including the *Book of Kells,* which is now in Dublin). Much later, with the Reformation, the abbey was abandoned, and most of its finely carved crosses were destroyed. In the 17th century, locals used the abbey only as a handy quarry for other building projects.

Iona's population peaked at about 500 in the 1830s. In the 1840s, a potato famine hit, and in the 1850s, a third of the islanders emigrated to Canada or Australia. By 1900, the population was down to 210, and today it's only around 100.

But in our generation, a new religious community has given the abbey fresh life. The Iona Community is an ecumenical gathering of men and women who seek new ways of living the Gospel in today's world, with a focus on worship, peace and justice issues, and reconciliation.

A pristine quality of the light and a thoughtful peace pervades the stark, (nearly) car-free island and its tiny community. With buoyant clouds bouncing playfully off distant bluffs, sparkling-white crescents of sand, and lone tourists camped thoughtfully atop huge rocks just looking out to sea, Iona is a place that's perfect for meditation. To experience Iona, it's important to get out and take a little hike; you can follow the "Welcome to Iona" walk outlined below. And you can easily climb a peak—nothing's higher than 300 feet above the sea.

Staying Longer on Iona: For a chance to really experience peaceful, idyllic Iona, consider spending a night or two. Scots bring their kids and stay on this tiny island for a week. If you want to overnight in Iona, don't buy your tickets at the bus-tour office in Oban—they require a same-day return. Instead, buy each leg of the ferry-bus-ferry (and return) trip separately. Get your Oban-Mull ferry ticket in the Oban ferry office (one-way for walk-on passengers-£5.40, round-trip-£9, ticket good for 5 days). Once you arrive in Mull (Craignure), follow the crowds to the tour buses and buy a ticket directly from the driver (£14 round-trip). When you arrive at the ferry terminal (Fionnphort), walk into the small trailer ferry office to buy a ticket to Iona (£2.50 each way). If it's closed, just buy your ticket from the ferry worker at the dock (cash or credit/debit cards accepted; leaving Iona, do the same as there's no ferry office).

If you want to spend more time on Iona (about four hours) and return to Oban the same day, you have another option. Take the first boat of the day, usually around 7:45, then connect at Mull to bus #496, which takes you to Fionnphort and the Iona ferry (no tour narration, buy each leg separately as described earlier). The benefit of taking the tour—besides the helpful commentary—is the guarantee of a seat each way. Ask at the bus tour office for details.

Orientation to Iona

The village, Baile Mòr, has shops, a restaurant/pub, enough beds, and no bank (get cash back with a purchase at the grocery store). The only taxi on Iona is **Iona Taxi** (tel. 07810-325-990, www.ionataxi.co.uk). Up the road from the ferry dock is a little **Spar** grocery (Mon-Sat 9:00-17:15, Sun 12:00-16:00, shorter hours and closed Sun Oct-April, free island maps). Iona's official website (www.isle-of-iona.net) has good information about the island.

Self-Guided Walk

Welcome to Iona

With a couple of hours, I recommend this basic route, which includes the nunnery ruins, abbey/chapel, a hilltop overview, and a pretty beach.

From the ferry dock, head directly up the single paved road that passes through the village and up a small hill to visit the **Nunnery Ruins**, one of Britain's best-preserved medieval nunneries (free). Turn right on North Road to reach the chapel and abbey.

St. Oran's Chapel, in the graveyard of the **Iona Abbey**, is the oldest church building on the island. Inside the chapel you'll

find several grave slabs carved in the distinctive Iona School style, which was developed by local stone-carvers in the 14th century. Look for the depictions of medieval warrior aristocrats. Many more of these carved graves have been moved to the abbey, where you can see them in its cloisters and old infirmary. It's free to see the graveyard and chapel; the abbey itself has an admission fee, but it's worth the cost just to sit in the stillness of its lovely, peaceful interior courtyard (£7.10, not covered by bus tour ticket, includes audioguide and 30-minute guided tour, £5 guidebook, daily April-Sept 9:30-17:30, Oct-March 9:30-16:30, tel. 01681/700-512, www.historic-scotland.gov.uk). While the present abbey, nunnery, and graveyard go back to the 13th century, much of what you'll see was rebuilt in the 20th century.

Across from the abbey is the **Iona Community's welcome center** (free WCs), which runs the abbey with Historic Scotland and hosts modern-day pilgrims who come here to experience the birthplace of Scottish Christianity. (If you're staying longer, you could attend a worship service at the abbey—check the schedule here; tel. 01681/700-404, www.iona.org.uk.) Its gift shop is packed with books on the island's important role in Christian history.

After you leave the abbey, turn right and continue on North Road. A 10-minute walk brings you to the footpath for **Dun I,** a steep but short climb with good views of the abbey looking back toward Mull.

From Dun I, walk another 20-25 minutes to the end of the paved road, where you'll arrive at a gate leading through a sheep- and cow-strewn pasture to Iona's pristine white-sand **North Beach**. Dip your toes in the Atlantic and ponder what this Caribbean-like alcove is doing in Scotland. Be sure to allow at least 40 minutes to return to the ferry dock.

With Extra Time: The **Heritage Centre**, on your left past the nunnery ruins, is small but well done, with displays on local and natural history and a tiny tearoom (£2.50, Mon-Sat 10:30-16:15, closed Sun and Nov-mid-April).

Sleeping and Eating on Iona

(area code: 01681)
In addition to the options listed below, there are many B&Bs, apartments, and a hostel on the island (see www.isle-of-iona.net/accommodation).

SOUTHERN HIGHLANDS

$$$ Argyll Hotel, built in 1867, proudly overlooks the waterfront, with 16 cottage-like rooms and pleasingly creaky hallways lined with bookshelves (Sb-£63-68, D-£72-79, Db-£93-99, larger Db-£136-144, cheaper off-season, extra bed for kids-£15, reserve far in advance for July-Aug, free Wi-Fi, comfortable lounge and sunroom, tel. 01681/700-334, www.argyllhoteliona.co.uk, reception @argyllhoteliona.co.uk). Its white-linen dining room is open to the public for lunch (12:30-14:00, tea served until 16:00) and dinner (£12-20 main courses, 18:30-20:00). Both the hotel and restaurant are closed from November through mid-March.

$$$ St. Columba Hotel, situated in the middle of a peaceful garden with picnic tables, has 27 institutional rooms and spacious lodge-like common spaces (Sb-£70-83, Db-£120-140, huge view Db-£180, front rooms have sea views but windows are small, discounts for stays of 4 or more nights, extra bed for kids-£15, free guest computer, closed Nov-March, next door to abbey on road up from dock, tel. 01681/700-304, www.stcolumba-hotel.co.uk, info@stcolumba-hotel.co.uk). Their fine 21-table restaurant, overlooking the water, is open to the public for lunch (£5-10, daily 12:00-14:30), tea (14:00-17:00), and dinner (£10-13, 18:30-20:00). Even if you're not staying here, you can stop by to use the Internet (£0.50/15 minutes).

$$ Calva B&B, near the abbey, has three spacious rooms (Db-£65, second house on left past the abbey, look for sign in window and gnomes on porch, tel. 01681/700-340; friendly Janetta, Ken, and Jack the bearded collie).

Glencoe

This valley is the essence of the wild, powerful, and stark beauty of the Highlands. Along with its scenery, Glencoe offers a good dose of bloody clan history: In 1692, British Redcoats (led by a local Campbell commander) came to the valley, and were sheltered and fed for 12 days by the MacDonalds—whose leader had been late in swearing an oath to the British monarch. Then, the morning of February 13, the soldiers were ordered to rise up early and kill their sleeping hosts, violating the rules of Highland hospitality and earning the valley the name "The Weeping Glen." It's fitting that such an epic, dramatic incident should be set in this equally epic, dramatic valley, where the cliffsides seem to weep (with running streams) when it rains.

Orientation to Glencoe

The valley of Glencoe is just off the main A-828/A-82 road between Oban and points north (such as Fort William and Inverness). If you're coming from the north, the signage can be tricky—at the roundabout south of Fort William, follow signs to *Crianlarich* and *A-82*. The most appealing town here is the one-street Glencoe village, while the slightly larger and more modern town of Ballachulish (a half-mile away) has more services. Though not quite quaint, the very sleepy village of Glencoe is worth a stop for its folk museum and its status as the gateway to the valley. The town's hub of activity is its grocery store (ATM, daily June-Aug 7:30-21:00, Sept-May 8:00-20:00).

Tourist Information

Your best source of information (especially for walks and hikes) is the **Glencoe Visitors Centre,** described later. The nearest **TI** is well-signed in Ballachulish (daily Easter-Sept 9:00-17:00, Oct-Easter 10:00-16:00, bus timetables, free phone to call area B&Bs, café, shop, tel. 01855/811-866, www.glencoetourism.co.uk). For more information on the area, see www.discoverglencoe.com.

Sights in Glencoe

Glencoe Village

Glencoe village is just a line of houses sitting beneath the brooding mountains.

Glencoe and North Lorn Folk Museum

Two tiny, thatched-roof, early-18th-century croft houses are jammed with local history, creating a huggable museum filled with humble exhibits gleaned from the town's old closets and attics. When one house was being re-thatched, its owner found a cache of 200-year-old swords and pistols hidden there from the British Redcoats after the disastrous battle of Culloden. Be sure to look for the museum's little door that leads out back, where you'll find exhibits on the Glencoe Massacre, native slate, farm tools, and more.

Cost and Hours: £3, call ahead for hours—generally Easter-Oct Mon-Sat 10:00-16:30, last admission at 16:00, closed Sun and off-season, tel. 01855/811-664, www.glencoemuseum.com.

In Glencoe Valley
▲▲Driving Through Glencoe Valley

If you have a car, spend an hour or so following the A-82 through the valley, past the Glencoe Visitors Centre (see next listing), into the desolate moor beyond, and back again. You'll enjoy grand views, dramatic craggy hills, and, if you're lucky, a chance to hear a bagpiper in the wind—roadside Highland buskers (most often seen on good-weather summer weekends). If you play the recorder (and no other tourists are there), ask to finger a tune while the piper does the hard work. At the end of the valley you hit the vast Rannoch Moor—500 bleak square miles with barely enough decent land to graze a sheep.

Glencoe Visitors Centre

This modern facility, a mile up the A-82 past Glencoe village (off to the right) into the dramatic valley, is designed to resemble a *clachan*, or traditional Highlands settlement. The information desk inside the shop at the ranger desk is your single best resource for advice (and maps or guidebooks) about local walks and hikes, some of which are described next. At the back of the complex you'll find a viewpoint with a handy 3-D model of the hills for orientation. There's also a pricey £6.50 exhibition about the surrounding landscape, the region's history, mountaineering, and conservation. It's worth the time to watch the more-interesting-than-it-sounds video on geology and the 14-minute film on the Glencoe Massacre, which thoughtfully traces the events leading up to the tragedy rather than simply recycling romanticized legends.

Cost and Hours: Free; April-Oct daily 9:30-17:30; Nov-March Thu-Sun 10:00-16:00, closed Mon-Wed; last entry 45 minutes before closing, free parking, WCs, café, tel. 01855/811-307, www.glencoe-nts.org.uk.

Walks

For a steep one-mile hike, climb the Devil's Staircase (trailhead just off the A-82, 8 miles east of Glencoe). For a three-hour hike, ask at the visitors center about the Lost Valley of the MacDonalds (trailhead just off the A-82, 3 miles east of Glencoe). For an easy 40-minute walk above Glencoe, head to the mansion on the hill (over the bridge, turn left, fine loch views, well-signed). This mansion was built in 1894 by Canadian Pacific Railway magnate Lord Strathcona for his Canadian wife. She was homesick for the Rockies, so he had the grounds landscaped to represent the lakes, trees, and mountains of her home country. It didn't work, and they eventually returned to Canada. The house originally had 365 windows, to allow a different view each day.

Glencoe's Burial Island and Island of Discussion

In the loch just outside Glencoe (near Ballachulish), notice the burial island—where the souls of those who "take the high road" are piped home. (Ask a local about "Ye'll take the high road, and I'll take the low road.") The next island was the Island of Discussion—where those in dispute went until they found agreement.

Sleeping in Glencoe

(area code: 01855)

Glencoe is an extremely low-key place to spend the night between Oban or Glasgow and the northern destinations. These places are accustomed to one-nighters just passing through, but some people stay here for several days to enjoy a variety of hikes. The following B&Bs are along the main road through the middle of the village, and all are cash-only.

$$ Inchconnal B&B is a cute, renovated house with a bonnie wee potted garden out front, renting two bright rooms with views—one cottage-style, the other woodsy (Db-£50-54, tel. 01855/811-958, www.inchconnal.com, enquiries@inchconnal.com, warm Caroline MacDonald).

$$ Tulachgorm B&B has one comfortable room with a private bathroom in a modern house with fine mountain views (D-£50, tel. 01855/811-391, mellow Ann Blake and friendly border collie Jo).

$$ Grianan B&B, across from the grocery store, comes with a homey feeling and two large rooms sharing a bath (D-£46-48, great for families, also rents self-catering cottages, tel. 01855/811-322, donaldyoung@hotmail.co.uk, Jane).

$$ Morven Cottage offers two rooms with free Wi-Fi, a breakfast room overlooking the gardens, owners with plenty of character, and a son who was an extra in a Harry Potter movie (Db-£50, can accommodate double/twin/family, dogs welcome, tel. 01855/811-544, www.morvenbnb.com, Freddie and Bob).

$$ Ghlasdrum B&B, next to the police station and set back from A-82, has four large rooms, a cozy dining room with a fireplace, and the nicest bathrooms (Sb-£35, Db-£55, tel. 01855/811-593, Maureen@ken110.orangehome.co.uk, Maureen, Ken, and shih tzu Daisy).

Outside of Town: **$$$ Clachaig Inn,** which runs three popular pubs on site, also rents 23 rooms, all with private bath (Db-£100-104, tel. 01855/811-252, 3 miles from Glencoe, www.clachaig.com). It works well for hikers who want a comfy mountain inn, or Harry Potter fans who want a glimpse of where part of the movie was filmed. Nothing remains from the movie, but that doesn't seem to matter to die-hard fans. For directions to the inn, see "Eating in Glencoe," next.

Eating in Glencoe

The choices around Glencoe are slim—this isn't the place for fine dining. But four options offer decent food a short walk or drive away. For evening fun, take a walk or ask your B&B host where to find music and dancing.

In Glencoe: The only real restaurant is **The Glencoe Gathering & Inn,** with lovely dining areas and a large outdoor deck. Choose between the quirky, fun pub, specializing in seafood with a Scottish twist, or the fancier restaurant (£8-15 main courses, food served daily 12:00-22:00, at junction of A-82 and Glencoe village, tel. 01855/811-245).

The **Glencoe Café**, also in the village, is just right for soups and sandwiches, and Justine's homemade baked goods—especially the carrot loaf—are irresistible (£4 soups, £8.50 soup and *panini* lunch combo, daily 9:30-17:00, last order at 16:15, free Wi-Fi).

Near Glencoe: **Clachaig Inn,** set in a stunning valley, serves food all day long in three pubs to a clientele that's half locals and half tourists. This unpretentious and very popular social hub features billiards, live music, pub grub, and over 300 whiskies and 15 hand-pulled ales (£5-13 main courses, open daily for lunch and dinner, music Sat from 21:00, tel. 01855/811-252). Drive to the end of Glencoe village, cross the bridge, and follow the little single-track road for three miles, past campgrounds and hostels, until you reach the inn on the right.

In Ballachulish: **Laroch Bar & Bistro,** in the next village over from Glencoe (toward Oban), has a nice patio and is family-friendly (£6-9 pub grub, food served daily 18:00-21:00, Sat-Sun also open for lunch 12:00-14:30, tel. 01855/811-274). Drive into Ballachulish village, and you'll see it on the left.

Glencoe Connections

Unfortunately, buses don't actually drive down the main road through Glencoe village. Some buses (most notably those going between Glasgow and Fort William) stop near Glencoe village at a place called **"Glencoe Crossroads"**—a short walk into the village center. Other buses (such as those between Oban and Fort William) stop at the nearby town of **Ballachulish,** which is just a half-mile away (or a £3 taxi ride). Tell the bus driver where you're going ("Glencoe village") and ask to be let off as close to there as possible.

From **Glencoe Crossroads,** you can catch bus #914, #915, or #916 (8/day) to **Fort William** (30 minutes) or **Glasgow** (2.5 hours).

From **Ballachulish,** you can take bus #918 (3/day in summer, 2/day off-season, never on Sun) to **Fort William** (30 minutes) or **Oban** (1 hour). Bus info: Tel. 08712/663-333, www.citylink.co.uk.

To reach **Inverness** or **Portree** on the Isle of Skye, transfer in Fort William. To reach **Edinburgh,** transfer in Glasgow.

Fort William

Laying claim to the title of "outdoor capital of the UK," Fort William is well-positioned between Oban, Inverness, and the Isle of Skye. This crossroads town is a transportation hub and has a pleasant-enough, shop-studded, pedestrianized main drag, but few charms of its own. Most visitors just pass through...and should. But while you're here, consider buying lunch and stopping by the TI to get your questions answered.

Tourist Information: The TI is on the car-free main drag (July-Sept Mon-Sat 9:30-18:30, Sun 9:30-17:00; Easter-June Mon-Sat 9:00-17:00, Sun 10:00-17:00; shorter hours off-season; Internet access £1/20 minutes, free public WCs up the street next to parking lot; follow signs to short-term parking, £1/2 hours, 15 High Street, tel. 01397/701-801).

Sights in Fort William

West Highland Museum

This humble-but-well-presented museum is Fort William's only real sight. It features exhibits on local history, wildlife, dress, Jacobite memorabilia, and more.

Cost and Hours: Free, guidebook-£1, Mon-Sat 10:00-17:00, Nov-Dec and March until 16:00, closed Sun and Jan-Feb, on Cameron Square, tel. 01397/702-169, www.westhighlandmuseum .org.uk.

Near Fort William

The appealing options described below lie just outside of town.

Ben Nevis

From Fort William, take a peek at Britain's highest peak, Ben Nevis (4,406 feet). Thousands walk to its summit each year. On a clear day, you can admire it from a distance. Scotland's only mountain cable cars—at the **Nevis Range Mountain Experience**—can take you to a not-very-lofty 2,150-foot perch on the slopes of Aonach Mor for a closer look (£11.50, daily July-Aug 9:30-18:00, Sept-June 10:00-17:00, 15-minute ride, shuts down in high winds and mid-Nov-mid-Dec—call ahead, signposted on the A-82 north of Fort William, tel. 01397/705-825, www.nevisrange.co.uk). They also have high-wire obstacle courses (£24.50, under age 17-£16.75, sessions run throughout the day, call for more information).

Toward the Isle of Skye:
The Road to the Isles and the Jacobite Steam Train

The magical steam train that scenically transports Harry Potter to the wizarding school of Hogwarts runs along a real-life train line. The West Highland Railway Line chugs 42 miles from Fort William west to the ferry port at Mallaig. Along the way, it passes the iconic **Glenfinnan Viaduct,** with 416 yards of raised track over 21 supporting arches. This route is also graced with plenty of loch-and-mountain views and, near the end, passes along a beautiful stretch of coast with some fine sandy beaches. While many people take the Jacobite Steam Train to enjoy this stretch of Scotland, it can be more rewarding to drive the same route—especially if you're headed for the Isle of Skye.

By Train: The **Jacobite Steam Train** (they don't actually call it the "Hogwarts Express") offers a small taste of the Harry Potter experience...but many who take this trip for that reason alone are disappointed. Although one of the steam engines and some of the coaches were used in the films, don't expect a Harry Potter theme ride. However, you can expect beautiful scenery. Along the way, the train stops for 20 minutes at Glenfinnan Station (just after the Glenfinnan Viaduct), and then gives you way too much time (1.75 hours) to poke around the dull port town of Mallaig before heading back to Fort William (one-way—£28 adults, £17 kids; round-trip—£33 adults, £19 kids; £3.25 booking fee, more for first class, tickets must be purchased in advance—see details next, 1/day Mon-Fri mid-May-Oct, 2/day Mon-Fri early June-Aug, also 1/day Sat-Sun late-June-late-Sept, departs Fort William at 10:15 and returns at 16:00, afternoon service in summer departs Fort William at 14:30 and returns at 20:24, about a 2-hour ride each way, WCs on board, tel. 0844/850-4680 or 0844/850-4682, www.westcoastrailways.co.uk).

Note: Trains leave Fort William from the main train station, but you must book ahead online or by phone—you cannot buy tickets for this train at the Fort William or Mallaig train-station ticket offices. There may be a limited amount of seats available each day on a first-come, first-served basis (cash only, buy from conductor), but in summer, trips are often sold out.

The 84-mile round-trip from Fort William takes the better part of a day to show you the same scenery twice. Modern "Sprinter" trains follow the same line—consider taking the steam train one-way to Mallaig, then speeding back on a regular train to avoid the long Mallaig layover and slow return (£11.40 one-way between Fort William and Mallaig, 1.5 hours, 2-4/day, book at least two days ahead July-Aug, tel. 08457-550-033, www.scotrail .co.uk). Note that you can use this train to reach the Isle of Skye: Take the train to Mallaig, walk onto the ferry to Armadale (on Skye), then catch a bus in Armadale to your destination on Skye (tel. 08712/663-333, www.citylink.co.uk).

There are lockers for storing luggage at the Fort William train station (£4-5/24 hours, station open Mon-Sat 7:20-22:10, Sun 11:30-22:10).

By Car: While the train is time-consuming and expensive, driving the same **"Road to the Isles"** route (A-830)—ideally on your way to Skye—can be a fun way to see the same famous scenery more affordably and efficiently. The key here is to be sure you leave enough time to make it to Mallaig before the Skye ferry departs—get timing advice from the Fort William TI. I'd allow at least 1 hour and 20 minutes to get from Fort William to the ferry landing in Mallaig (if you keep moving, with no stops en route)—and note that vehicles are required to arrive 30 minutes before the boat departs. As you leave Fort William on the A-830, a sign on the left tells you what time the next ferry will depart Mallaig.

Sleeping in Fort William

(area code: 01397)
These two B&Bs are on Union Road, a five-minute walk up the hill above the main pedestrian street that runs through the heart of town. Each place has three rooms, one of which has a private bathroom in the hall.

$$ Glenmorven Guest House is a friendly, flower-bedecked, family-run place at the end of the road. The hospitality, special extras, and views of Loch Linnhe are worth the walk (Db-£65-70, free pick-up from train or bus station with advance notice, laundry service, welcome whisky, Fort William, tel. 01397/703-236, www .glenmorven.co.uk, glenmorven@yahoo.com, Anne and Colin Jamieson).

$$ Gowan Brae B&B ("Hill of the Big Daisy") has three antique-filled rooms with loch or garden views in a hobbit-cute house (Db-£70 in high season, £60 off-season, free Wi-Fi, tel. 01397/704-399, www.gowanbrae.co.uk, gowan_brae@btinternet .com, Jim and Ann Clark).

Eating in Fort William

All three places listed below are on the main walking street, near the start of town; the first two serve only lunch.

Hot Roast Company sells beef, turkey, ham, or pork sandwiches, topped with some tasty extras, along with soup, salad, and coleslaw (£3 take-away, a bit more for sit-down service, Mon-Sat 9:30-15:30, sandwiches from 11:00, closed Sun, free Wi-Fi, 127 High Street, tel. 01397/700-606).

Café 115 features good food and modern bistro decor (£4-8 meals, £6 fish-and-chips, daily 10:00-17:00, mid-July-Aug until 21:30, 115 High Street, tel. 01397/702-500).

The Grog & Gruel serves real ales, good pub grub, and Tex-Mex and Cajun dishes, with unusual meals such as vegetarian haggis with Drambuie sauce, boar burgers, and venison chili (£5-12 meals, food served daily 12:00-23:30, Sun in winter 17:00-23:30, free Wi-Fi, 66 High Street, tel. 01397/705-078, www.grogand gruel.co.uk). Their upstairs restaurant features the same menu (daily 17:00-23:30).

Fort William Connections

Fort William is a major transit hub for the Highlands, so you'll likely change buses here at some point during your trip.

From Fort William by Bus to: Glencoe (all Glasgow-bound buses—#914, #915, and #916; 8/day, 30 minutes), **Ballachulish** near Glencoe (Oban-bound bus #918, 3/day in summer, 2/day off-season, never on Sun, 30 minutes), **Oban** (bus #918, 3/day in summer, 2/day off-season, never on Sun, 1.5 hours), **Portree** on the Isle of Skye (buses #915 and #916, 3/day, 3.5 hours), **Inverness** (Citylink bus #919 or Stagecoach bus #19, 10/day, 2 hours), **Glasgow** (buses #914, #915, and #916; 8/day, 3 hours), **Edinburgh** (bus #913, 1/day direct, 4 hours; more with transfer in Glasgow on buses #900 and #914/915, 5 hours). Bus info: Tel. 0871-266-3333, www.citylink.co.uk or www.stagecoachbus.com.

Route Tips for Drivers

From Oban to Glencoe and Fort William: From Oban, follow the coastal A-828 toward Fort William. After about 20 miles, you'll see the photogenic Castle Stalker marooned on a lonely island. At North Ballachulish, you'll reach a bridge spanning Loch Leven; rather than crossing the bridge, turn off and follow the A-82 into the Glencoe Valley for about 15 minutes. After exploring the valley, make a U-turn and return through Glencoe. To continue on to Fort William, backtrack to the bridge at North Ballachulish (great view from bridge) and cross it, following the A-82 north. (For a scenic shortcut directly back to Glasgow or Edinburgh, head north only as far as Glencoe, and then cut to Glasgow or Edinburgh on the A-82 via Rannoch Moor and Tyndrum.)

From Fort William to Loch Ness and Inverness: Follow the Caledonian Canal north along the A-82, which goes through Fort Augustus (and its worthwhile Caledonian Canal Heritage Centre) and then follows the north side of Loch Ness on its way to Inverness. Along the way, the A-82 passes Urquhart Castle and two Loch Ness Monster exhibits in Drumnadrochit. These attractions are described in the Inverness and the Northern Highlands chapter.

From Fort William to the Isle of Skye: You have two options for this journey: Head west on the A-830 (the Road to the Isles), then catch the ferry from Mallaig to Armadale on the Isle of Skye; or head north on the A-82 to Invergarry, and turn left (west) on the A-87, which you'll follow (past Eilean Donan Castle) to Kyle of Lochalsh and the Skye Bridge to the island. Consider using one route one way, and the other on the return trip—for example, follow the "Road to the Isles" from Fort William to Mallaig, and take the ferry to Skye; later, leaving Skye, take the A-87 east from the Skye Bridge past Eilean Donan Castle to Loch Ness and Inverness.

ISLE OF SKYE

*The Trotternish Peninsula • More Sights
on the Isle of Skye • Portree • Kyleakin*

The rugged, remote-feeling Isle of Skye has a reputation for unpredictable weather ("Skye" means "cloudy" in Old Norse, and locals call it "The Misty Isle"). But it also offers some of Scotland's best scenery, and it rarely fails to charm its many visitors. Narrow, twisty roads wind around Skye in the shadows of craggy, black, bald mountains.

Skye seems to have more sheep than people; 200 years ago, many human residents were forced to move off the island to make room for more livestock during the Highland Clearances. The people who remain are some of the most ardently Gaelic Scots in Scotland. The island's Sleat Peninsula is home to a rustic but important Gaelic college. Half of all native island residents speak Gaelic (which they pronounce "gallic") as their first language. A generation ago, it was illegal to teach Gaelic in schools; today, Skye offers its residents the opportunity to enroll in Gaelic-only education, from primary school to college.

Set up camp in one of the island's home-base towns, Portree or Kyleakin. Then dive into Skye's attractions. Drive around the appealing Trotternish Peninsula, enjoying stark vistas of jagged rock formations with the mysterious Outer Hebrides looming on the horizon. Explore a gaggle of old-fashioned stone homes, learn about Skye's ancient farming lifestyles, and pay homage at the grave of a brave woman who rescued a bonnie prince. Climb the dramatic Cuillin Hills, and drive to a lighthouse at the end of the world. Visit a pair of castles—the familial thought-provoking Dunvegan, and nearby but not on Skye, the photo-perfect Eilean Donan.

Planning Your Time

With a week in Scotland, Skye merits two nights, with a full day to hit its highlights (Trotternish Peninsula, Dunvegan Castle, Cuillin Hills, Talisker Distillery). Mountaineers need extra time for hiking and hillwalking. Because it takes time to reach, Skye (the northernmost destination in this book) is skippable if you only have a few days in Scotland—instead, focus on Edinburgh and the more accessible Highlands sights near Oban.

Skye fits neatly into a Highlands itinerary between Oban/Glencoe and Loch Ness/Inverness. To avoid seeing the same scenery twice, it works well to drive the "Road to the Isles" from Fort William to Mallaig, then take the ferry to Skye; later, leave Skye via the Skye Bridge and follow the A-87 east toward Loch Ness and Inverness, stopping at Eilean Donan Castle en route.

Getting to the Isle of Skye

By Car: Your easiest bet is the slick, free **Skye Bridge** that crosses from Kyle of Lochalsh on the mainland to Kyleakin on Skye.

The island can also be reached from the mainland via a pair of **car ferry** crossings. The major ferry line connects the mainland town of Mallaig (west of Fort William along the "Road to the Isles" and the Harry Potter steam-train line) to Armadale on Skye (£23.50/car, £4.50/passenger, late March-late Oct 8/day each way, 4-6/day on Sun, late Oct-late March very limited Sat-Sun connections, check-in closes 30 minutes before sailing, can be canceled in rough weather, 30-minute trip, operated by Caledonian MacBrayne, www.calmac.co.uk). A tiny, six-car, proudly local "turntable" ferry crosses the short gap between the mainland Glenelg and Skye's Kylerhea (£14/car with up to 4 passengers, £20 round-trip, roughly Easter-Oct daily every 20 minutes 10:00-18:00, June-Aug until 19:00, no need to book ahead, no boats off-season, Skye Ferry, www.skyeferry.com).

By Public Transportation: Skye is connected to the outside world by a series of Scottish Citylink **buses** (www.citylink.co.uk), which use Portree as their Skye hub. Rates listed are rough estimates for one-way travel. From Portree, buses connect to **Inverness** (£30, bus #917, 3-4/day, 3.25 hours), **Glasgow** (£40, buses #915 and #916, 3/day, 6.5-7.5 hours, also stops at **Fort William** and **Glencoe**), and **Edinburgh** (£50, 4/day, 7.5-8 hours, transfer in Inverness or Glasgow).

There are also some more complicated connections possible for the determined: Take the train from Edinburgh, Glasgow, or Inverness to Fort William; transfer to the steam train to Mallaig; take the ferry across to Armadale; and catch a bus to Portree. Alternatively, you can take the train from Edinburgh or Glasgow

ISLE OF SKYE

Isle of Skye

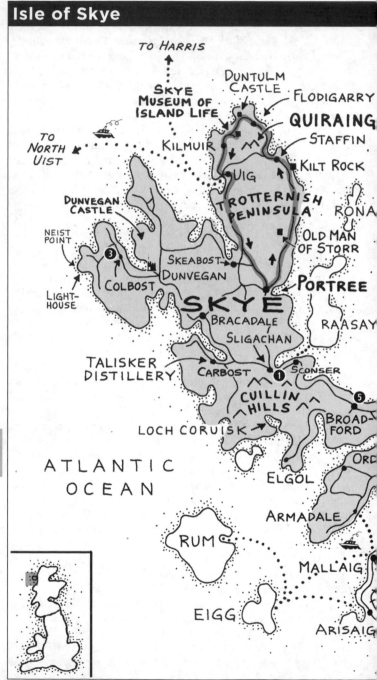

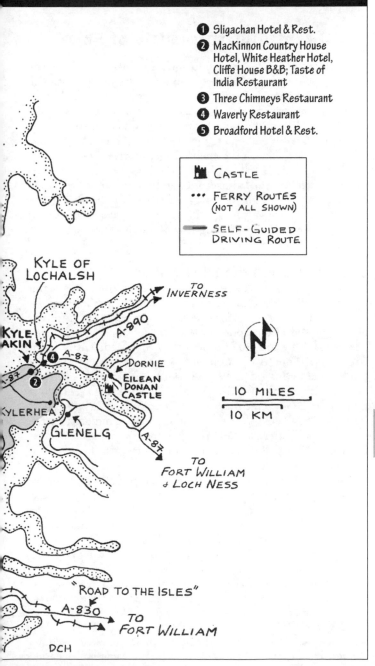

1. Sligachan Hotel & Rest.
2. MacKinnon Country House Hotel, White Heather Hotel, Cliffe House B&B; Taste of India Restaurant
3. Three Chimneys Restaurant
4. Waverly Restaurant
5. Broadford Hotel & Rest.

Castle

Ferry Routes (not all shown)

Self-Guided Driving Route

KYLE OF LOCHALSH

TO INVERNESS

A-890

KYLE-AKIN

A-87

DORNIE

EILEAN DONAN CASTLE

KYLERHEA

GLENELG

A-87

TO FORT WILLIAM & LOCH NESS

10 MILES

10 KM

"ROAD TO THE ISLES"

A-830

TO FORT WILLIAM

DCH

ISLE OF SKYE

to Inverness, take the train to Kyle of Lochalsh, then take the bus to Portree.

Orientation to the Isle of Skye

The Isle of Skye is big (over 600 square miles), with lots of ins and outs—but you're never more than five miles from the sea. The island is punctuated by peninsulas and inlets (called "sea lochs"). Skye is covered with hills, but the most striking are the mountain-like Cuillin Hills in the south-central part of the island.

There are only about 11,000 people on the entire island; roughly a quarter live in the main village, Portree. Other popula-tion centers include Kyleakin (near the bridge connecting Skye with the mainland) and Broadford (a tidy string of houses on the road between Portree and the bridge, with the biggest and handiest grocery store and gas station on the island, open daily 9:00-22:00). A few of the villages—including Broadford and Dunvegan—have **TIs**, but the most useful one is in Portree.

Getting Around the Isle of Skye

By Car: Once on Skye, you'll need a car to enjoy the island. (Even if you're doing the rest of your trip by public transpor-tation, a car rental is worthwhile here to bypass the frustrating public-transportation options.) If you're driving, a good map is a must (look for a 1:130,000 map that covers the entire island with enough detail to point out side roads and attractions; Philip's and Ordnance Survey are good). You'll be surprised how long it takes to traverse this "small" island. Here are driving-time estimates for some likely trips: Kyleakin and Skye Bridge to Portree—45 minutes; Portree to Dunvegan—30 minutes; Portree to the tip of Trotternish Peninsula and back again—1.5-2 hours; Portree to Armadale—1 hour; Uig (on Trotternish Peninsula) to Dunvegan—45 minutes.

By Bus: Skye is frustrating by bus, especially on Sundays, when virtually no local buses run (except for a few long-distance buses to the ferry dock and mainland destinations). Portree is the hub for bus traffic. Most Skye buses are operated by Stagecoach. The company is experimenting by adding a new hop-on, hop-off bus service (#60); this open-top motor coach, which operates only in summer, stops in Sligachan, Dunvegan Castle, and the Trotternish Peninsula (www.stagecoachbus.com/highlands, time-table info from Traveline, tel. 0871-200-2233, www.traveline.org .uk). If you'll be using buses a lot, consider a Skye Dayrider ticket (£8/day, includes Kyle of Lochalsh) or the Skye North Island Megarider (£31/7 days, covers the northern half of Skye, including Portree, Dunvegan, and the Trotternish Peninsula; no Megarider for southern half of the island). You can buy either of these tickets from any driver.

From Portree, you can go around the **Trotternish Peninsula** (#57, Mon-Sat 4-5/day in each direction—clockwise and counter-clockwise; none on Sun), and to **Dunvegan** (#56, 5/day Mon-Fri, 3/day Sat, none on Sun, 40 minutes, goes right to the castle, catch a bus that leaves no later than 12:45 to have enough time at the castle). To bus it from Portree to **Kyleakin**, you'll need to travel on Scottish Citylink (#917, 4/day, 55 minutes).

By Tour: If you're without a car, consider taking a tour. Several operations on the island take visitors to hard-to-reach spots on a half-day or full-day tour. Some are more educational, while others are loose and informal. Look for brochures around the island, or ask locals for tips. **Kathleen MacAskil** with Skye Tours gives small-group tours by car or minibus (£22.50/person, 4 hours, minimum 4 people, tel. 01470/582-306, www.skyctours .co.uk, kathleenmacaskil@aol.com).

The Trotternish Peninsula

This inviting peninsula north of Portree is packed with windswept castaway scenery, unique geological formations, and some offbeat sights. In good weather, a spin around Trotternish is the single best Skye activity (and you'll still have time to visit Dunvegan Castle or the Cuillin Hills later on).

Self-Guided Driving Tour

Peninsula Loop

The following loop tour starts and ends in Portree, circling the peninsula counterclockwise. If you did it without stopping, you'd make it back to Portree within two hours—but it deserves the better part of a day. Note that from Portree to Uig, you'll be driving on a paved single-track road; use the occasional "passing places" to pull over and allow faster cars to go by.

The Drive Begins

Begin in the island's main town, Portree. (If you're heading up from Kyleakin, you'll enjoy some grand views of the Cuillin Hills on your way up—especially around the crossroads of Sligachan.)

• *Head north of Portree on the A-855, following signs for* Staffin. *About three miles out of town, you'll begin to enjoy some impressive views of the Trotternish Ridge. As you pass the small loch on your right, straight*

ISLE OF SKYE

ahead is the distinctive feature called the...

Old Man of Storr: This 160-foot-tall tapered slab of basalt stands proudly apart from the rest of the Storr. The unusual landscape of the Trotternish Peninsula is due to massive landslides (the largest in Britain). This block slid down the cliff about 6,500 years ago and landed on its end, where it was slowly whittled by weather into a pinnacle. The lochs on your right have been linked together to spin the turbines at a nearby hydroelectric plant that once provided all of Skye's electricity.

• *After passing the Old Man, enjoy the scenery on your right, overlooking...*

Nearby Islands and the Mainland: Some of Skye's most appealing scenery isn't the island itself, but the surrounding terrain. In the distance, craggy mountains recede into the horizon. The long island in the foreground, a bit to the north, is called Rona. This military-owned island, and the channel behind it, were used to develop and test one of Margaret Thatcher's pet projects, the Sting Ray remote-control torpedo.

• *After about five miles, keep an eye out on the right for a large parking lot near a wee loch. Park and walk to the viewpoint to see...*

Kilt Rock: So named because of its resemblance to a Scotsman's tartan kilt, this 200-foot-tall sea cliff has a layer of volcanic rock with vertical lava columns that look like pleats (known as columnar jointing), sitting atop a layer of horizontal sedimentary rock.

• *After continuing through the village of Staffin (whose name means "the pinnacle place"), you'll begin to see interesting rock formations high on the hill to your left. When you get to the crossroads, head left toward the Quiraing (a rock formation). This crossroads is a handy pit stop—there's a public WC in the Staffin Community Hall (in the same building as the licensed grocer, on your left as you pass through).*

Now twist your way up the road to the...

Quiraing: As you drive up, notice (on your left) a couple of modern cemeteries high in the hills, far above the village. It seems like a strange spot to bury the dead, in the middle of nowhere. But it's logical since the earth here is less valuable for development, and since it's not clay, like down by the water, it also provides better drainage.

You'll enjoy fine views on the right of the jagged, dramatic northern end of the Trotternish Ridge, called the Quiraing—rated ▲▲. More landslides caused the dramatic scenery in this area, and each rock formation has a name, such as "The Needle" or "The Prison." As you approach the summit of this road, you'll reach a parking area on the left. This marks a popular trailhead for hik-

ing out to get a closer look at the formations. If you've got the time, energy, and weather for a sturdy 30-minute uphill hike, here's your chance. You can either follow the trail along the base of the rock formations, or hike up to the top of the plateau and follow it to the end (both paths are faintly visible from the parking area). Once up top, your reward is a view of the secluded green plateau called "The Table," another landslide block, which isn't visible from the road.

• *You could continue on this road all the way to Uig, at the other end of the peninsula, but it's worth backtracking, then turning left onto the main road (A-855), to see the...*

Tip of Trotternish: A few miles north, you'll pass a hotel called **Flodigarry,** with a cottage on the premises that was once home to Bonnie Prince Charlie's rescuer, Flora MacDonald (her story is explained later; the cottage is now part of the hotel and not open to the public).

Soon after, at the top of the ridge at the tip of the peninsula, you'll see the remains of an old **fort**—not from the Middle Ages or the days of Bonnie Prince Charlie, but from World War II, when the Atlantic was monitored for U-boats from this position.

Farther down the road, you'll pass (on the right) the crumbling remains of another fort, this one much older: **Duntulm Castle,** which was the first stronghold on Skye of the influential MacDonald clan. The castle was abandoned around 1730 for Armadale Castle on the southern end of Skye; according to legend, the family left after a nursemaid accidentally dropped the infant heir out a window onto the rocks below. In the distance beyond, you can see the **Outer Hebrides**—the most rugged, remote, and Gaelic part of Scotland. (Skye, a bit closer to the mainland, belongs to the Inner Hebrides.)

• *A mile after the castle, you'll come to a place called Kilmuir. Watch for the turn-off on the left to the excellent...*

Skye Museum of Island Life: This fine little stand of seven thatched stone huts, organized into a family-run museum and worth ▲▲, explains how a typical Skye family lived a century and

ISLE OF SKYE

a half ago (£2.50, Easter-Oct Mon-Sat 9:30-17:00, closed Sun and Nov-Easter, tel. 01470/552-206, www.skyemuseum.co.uk). Though there are ample posted explanations, the £1.25 guidebook is worthwhile.

The three huts closest to the sea are original (more than 200 years old). Most interesting is the one called The Old Croft House, which was the residence of the Graham family until 1957. Inside you'll find three rooms: kitchen (with peat-burning fire) on the right, parents' bedroom in the middle, and a bedroom for the 12 kids on the left. Nearby, The Old Barn displays farm implements, and the Ceilidh House contains some dense but very informative displays about crofting (the traditional tenant-farmer lifestyle on Skye—explained later), Gaelic, and other topics.

The four other huts were reconstructed here from elsewhere on the island, and now house exhibits about weaving and the village smithy (which was actually a gathering place). As you explore, admire the smart architecture of these humble but deceptively well-planned structures. Rocks hanging from the roof keep the thatch from blowing away, and the streamlined shape of the structure embedded in the ground encourages strong winds to deflect around the hut rather than hit it head-on.

• *After touring the museum, drive out to the very end of the small road that leads past the parking lot, to a lonesome cemetery. The tallest Celtic cross at the far end of the cemetery (you can enter the gate to reach it) is the...*

Monument to Flora MacDonald: This local heroine supposedly rescued beloved Scottish hero Bonnie Prince Charlie at his darkest hour. After his loss at Culloden, and with a hefty price on his head, Charlie retreated to the Outer Hebrides. But the Hanover

dynasty, which controlled the islands, was closing in. Flora MacDonald rescued the prince, disguised him as her Irish maid, Betty Burke, and sailed him to safety on Skye. (Charlie pulled off the ruse thanks to his soft, feminine features—hence the nickname "Bonnie," which means "beautiful.") The flight inspired a popular Scottish folk song: "Speed bonnie boat like a bird on the wing, / Onward, the sailors cry. / Carry the lad that's born to be king / Over the sea to Skye."

ISLE OF SKYE

• *Return to the main road and proceed about six miles around the peninsula. On the right, notice the big depression.*

The Missing Loch: This was once a large loch, but it was drained in the mid-20th century to create more grazing land for sheep. If you look closely, you may see a scattering of stones in the middle of the field. Once a little island, this is the site of a former monastery...now left as high, dry, and forgotten as the loch. Beyond the missing loch is Prince Charlie's Point, where the bonnie prince supposedly came ashore on Skye with Flora MacDonald.

• *Soon after the loch, you'll drop down over the town of...*

Uig: Pronounced "OO-eeg," this village is the departure point for ferries to the Outer Hebrides (North Uist and Harris islands, 2-3/day). It's otherwise unremarkable, but does have a café with good sandwiches (follow *Uig Pier* signs into town—look for a white building with blue *Café* sign, next to ferry terminal at entrance to town).

• *Continue past Uig, climbing the hill across the bay. Near the top is a large parking strip on the right. Pull over here and look back to Uig for a lesson about Skye's traditional farming system.*

Crofting: You'll hear a lot about crofts during your time on Skye. Traditionally, arable land on the island was divided into plots. If you look across  to the hills above Uig, you can see strips of demarcated land running up from the water—these are crofts. Crofts were generally owned by landlords (mostly English aristocrats or Scottish clan chiefs, and later the Scottish government) and rented to tenant farmers. The crofters lived and worked under very difficult conditions, and were lucky if they could produce enough potatoes, corn, and livestock to feed their families. Rights to farm the croft were passed down from father to son over generations, but always under the auspices of a wealthy landlord.

ISLE OF SKYE

Finally, in 1976, new legislation kicked off a process of privatization called "decrofting." Suddenly crofters could have their land decrofted, then buy it for an affordable price (£130 per quarter-hectare, or about £8,000 for one of the crofts you see here). Many decroftees would quickly turn around and sell their old family home for a huge profit, but hang on to most of their land and build a new house at the other end. In the crofts you see here, notice that some have a house at the top of a strip of land and another house at the bottom. Many crofts (like most of these) are no longer cultivated, but that should change, as crofters are now legally required to farm their land...or lose it. In many cases, families who have other jobs still hang on to their traditional croft, which they use to grow produce for themselves or to supplement their income.

• *Our tour is finished. From here, you can continue along the main road south toward Portree (and possibly continue from there on to the Cuillin Hills). Or take the shortcut road just after Kensaleyre (B-8036), and head west on the A-850 to Dunvegan and its castle. Both options are described later.*

More Sights on the Isle of Skye

▲▲Cuillin Hills

These dramatic, rocky "hills" (which look more like mountains to me) stretch along the southern coast of the island, dominating Skye's landscape. More craggy and alpine than anything else you'll see in Scotland, the Cuillin seem to rise directly from the deep. You'll see them from just about anywhere on the southern two-thirds of the island, but no roads actually take you through the heart of the Cuillin—that's reserved for hikers and climbers, who love this area. To get the best views with a car, consider these options:

Near Sligachan: The road from the Skye Bridge to Portree is the easiest way to appreciate the Cuillin (you'll almost certainly drive along here at some point during your visit). These mountains are all that's left of a long-vanished volcano. As you approach, you'll clearly see that there are three separate ranges (from right to left): red, gray, and black. The steep and challenging Black Cuillin is the most popular for serious climbers; the granite Red Cuillin ridge is more rounded.

The crossroads of Sligachan, with an old triple-arched bridge and a landmark hotel, is nestled at the foothills of the Cuillin, and is a popular launch pad for mountain fun. The 2,500-foot-tall cone-shaped hill looming over Sligachan, named Glamaig ("Greedy Lady"), is the site of an annual 4.5-mile race in July: Speed hikers begin at the door of the Sligachan Hotel, race to the summit, run around a bagpiper, and scramble back down to the hotel. The record: 44 minutes (30 minutes up, 13 minutes down, 1 minute dancing a jig up top).

Elgol: For the best view of the Cuillin, locals swear by the drive from Broadford (on the Portree-Kyleakin road) to Elgol, at the tip of a small peninsula that faces the Black Cuillin head-on. While it's just 12 miles as the crow flies from Sligachan, give it a half-hour each way to drive (mostly on single-track roads) into Elgol from Broadford. To get an even better Cuillin experience, take a boat excursion from Elgol into Loch Coruisk, a "sea loch" (fjord) surrounded by the Cuillin (April-Oct, various companies do the trip several times a day, fewer on Sun and off-season, generally 3 hours round-trip including 1.5 hours free time on the shore of the loch, figure £15-22 round-trip).

▲Dunvegan Castle

Perched on a rock overlooking a sea loch, this ancestral castle is a strange and intriguing artifact of Scotland's antiquated,

nearly extinct clan system. Dunvegan Castle is the residence of the MacLeod (pronounced "McCloud") clan—along with the MacDonalds, one of Skye's preeminent clans. Worth ▲▲▲ to people named MacLeod, the castle offers an interesting look at aristocratic life and is a good way to pass the time on a rainy day. The owners claim it's the oldest continuously inhabited castle in Scotland.

Cost and Hours: £9.50, April-mid-Oct daily 10:00-17:30, last entry 30 minutes before closing, mid-Oct-March Mon-Fri open by appointment only, no interior photos, café, tel. 01470/521-206, www.dunvegancastle.com.

Getting There: It's near the small town of Dunvegan in the northwestern part of the island, well-signposted from the A-850. As you approach Dunvegan on the A-850, the two flat-topped plateaus you'll see are nicknamed "MacLeod's Tables."

You can also get to the castle by bus from Portree (#56, 5/day Mon-Fri, 3/day Sat, none on Sun; leave Portree no later than 12:45 to have time to tour the castle).

Background: In Gaelic, *clann* means "children," and the clan system was the traditional Scottish way of passing along power—similar to England's dukes, barons, and counts. Each clan traces its roots to an ancestral castle, like Dunvegan. The MacLeods (or, as they prefer, "MacLeod of MacLeod") eventually fell on hard times. Having run out of male heirs in 1935, Dame Flora MacLeod of MacLeod became the 28th clan chief. Her grandson, John MacLeod of MacLeod, became the 29th chief after her death in 1976. With their castle looking rough around the edges and their leaky roof in need of fixing, John MacL of MacL threatened to sell the Black Cuillin ridge of hills (which technically belonged to him) for £10 million to pay for a new roof. The deal outraged locals, but it wasn't concluded prior to the chief's passing in early 2007. The current clan chief, Hugh Magnus MacLeod of MacLeod, is a film producer who divides his time between London and the castle, where his noble efforts are aimed at preserving Dunvegan (roof included) for future generations.

➜ **Self-Guided Tour:** Unlike medieval castles, the interior feels lived in; you'll notice the MacLeods proudly display their heritage—old photographs and portraits of former chiefs—like any family decorating the walls of their home. You'll wander through halls, the dining room, and the library, and peer down into the dungeon's deep pit. Pick up the laminated flier in each room to discover some of the history. In the **Drawing Room,** look for the tattered silk remains of the Fairy Flag, a mysterious swatch with about a dozen different legends attached to it (most say that it was a gift from a fairy, and somehow it's related to the Crusades). It's said that the clan chief can invoke the power of the flag three times, in the clan's darkest moments. It's worked twice before on the battlefield—which means there's just one use left.

The most interesting historical tidbits are in the **North Room,** which was built in 1360 as the original Great Hall. The family's coat of arms in the middle of the carpet has a confused-looking bull and the clan motto, "Hold Fast"—recalling an incident where a MacLeod saved a man from being gored by a bull when he grabbed its horns and forced it to stop. (Notice the book in the display case along the wall. It's opened to a different coat of arms claiming MacLeod heritage—this one with lions instead of a bull.) Also in the room, find the Dunvegan Cup and the Horn of Rory Mor. Traditionally, this horn would be filled with nearly a half-gallon of claret (Bordeaux wine), which a potential heir had to drink without stopping (or falling) to prove himself fit for the role. (The late chief, John MacLeod of MacLeod, bragged that he did it in less than two minutes...but you have to wonder if Dame Flora chug-a-lugged.) Other artifacts in the North Room include bagpipes and several relics related to Bonnie Prince Charlie (including a lock of his hair and his vest). Look for a portrait of Flora MacDonald and some items that belonged to her.

At the end of the tour, you can wander out onto the **terrace** (overlooking a sea loch) and, in the cellar, watch a **video** about the clan. Between the castle and the parking lot are five acres of enjoyable **gardens** to stroll through while pondering the fading clan system. You can also take a **boat ride** on Loch Dunvegan to visit a seal colony on a nearby island (£6, boats run mid-April-Sept only, 10:00-17:00, last trip around 16:30, 25 minutes, tel. 01470/521-500).

The flaunting of inherited wealth and influence in some English castles rubs me the wrong way. But here, seeing the rough edges of a Scottish clan chief's castle, I had the opposite feeling: sympathy and compassion for a proud way of life that's slipping into the sunset of history. You have to admire the way they "hold fast" to this antiquated system (in the same way the Gaelic tongue is kept on life support). Paying admission here feels more like donating to charity than padding the pockets of a wealthy family. In fact, watered-down McClouds and McDonalds from America, eager to reconnect with their Scottish roots, help keep the Scottish clan system alive.

▲Neist Point and Lighthouse

To get a truly edge-of-the-world feeling, consider an adventure on the back lanes of the Duirinish Peninsula, west of Dunvegan.

This trip is best for hardy drivers looking to explore the most remote corner of Skye and undertake a strenuous hike to a lighthouse. (The lighthouse itself is a letdown, so do this only if you believe a journey is its own reward.) Although it looks close on the map, give this trip 30 minutes each way from Dunvegan, plus 30 minutes or more for the lighthouse hike.

The owner of this private property has signs on his padlocked gate stating that you enter at your own risk—which many walkers happily do. (It's laughably easy to walk around the unintimidating "wall.") From here you can enjoy sheep and cliff views, but you can't see the lighthouse itself unless you do the sturdy 30-minute hike (with a steep uphill return). After hiking around the cliff, the lighthouse springs into view, with the Outer Hebrides beyond.

Getting There: Head west from Dunvegan, following signs for *Glendale*. You'll cross a moor, then twist around the Dunvegan sea loch, before heading overland and passing through rugged, desolate hamlets that seem like the setting for a BBC sitcom about backwater Britain. After passing through Glendale, carefully track *Neist Point* signs until you reach an end-of-the-road parking lot.

Eating: It's efficient and fun to combine this trek with lunch or dinner at the pricey, recommended **Three Chimneys Restaurant,** on the road to Neist Point at Colbost (reservations essential).

▲Talisker Distillery

Opened in 1830, Talisker is a Skye institution (and the only distillery on the island). If you've tried only mainland whisky, island whisky is worth a dram to appreciate the differences. Island whisky is known for having a strong smoky flavor, due to the amount of peat smoke used during the malting of the barley. The Isle of Islay has the smokiest, and Talisker workers describe theirs as "medium smoky," which may be easier for non-connoisseurs to take. Talisker produces single-malt whisky only, so it's a favorite with whisky purists: On summer days, this tiny distillery swarms with visitors from all over the world.

Cost and Hours: £7 for a 45-minute tour, a wee dram, and a £3 voucher toward a bottle, £25 tasting tour offered on selected weekdays—call ahead; April-Oct Mon-Sat 9:30-17:00, closed Sun except in June-Aug when it's open 11:00-17:00, last tour one hour before closing; Nov-March Mon-Fri 10:00-16:30, tours at 10:30, 12:00, 14:00, and 15:30, closed Sat-Sun, call ahead; no photos or mobile phones, down a tiny road in Carbost village, tel. 01478/614-308, www.discovering-distilleries.com.

Skye Bridge

Connecting Kyleakin on Skye with Kyle of Lochalsh on the mainland, the Skye Bridge severely damaged B&B business in the towns it connects. Environmentalists worry about the bridge disrupting the habitat for otters—keep an eye out for these furry native residents. But it's been a boon for Skye tourism—making a quick visit to the island possible without having to wait for a ferry.

The bridge, which was Europe's most expensive toll bridge per foot when it opened in 1995, has stirred up a remarkable amount of controversy among island-dwellers. Here's the Skye natives' take on things: A generation ago, Lowlanders (city folk) began selling their urban homes and buying cheap property on Skye. Natives had grown to enjoy the slow-paced lifestyle that came with living life according to the whim of the ferry, but these new transplants found their commute into civilization too frustrating by boat. They demanded a new bridge be built. Finally a deal was struck to privately fund the bridge, but the toll wasn't established before construction began. So when the bridge opened—and the ferry line it replaced closed—locals were shocked to be charged upward of £5 per car each way to go to the mainland. A few years ago, the bridge was bought by the Scottish Executive, the fare was abolished, and the Skye natives were appeased...for now.

▲▲Near the Isle of Skye: Eilean Donan Castle

This postcard castle, watching over a sea loch from its island perch, is conveniently and scenically situated on the road between the Isle of Skye and Loch Ness. Famous from such films as Sean Connery's *Highlander* (1986) and the James Bond movie *The World Is Not Enough* (1999), Eilean Donan (EYE-lan DOHN-an) might be Scotland's most photogenic countryside castle (chances are good it's on that Scotland calendar you bought during your trip).

Though it looks ancient, the castle is actually less than a century old. The original castle on this site (dating from 800 years ago) was destroyed in battle in 1719, then rebuilt between 1912 and 1932 by the MacRae family as their residence.

Even if you're not going inside, the castle warrants a five-minute photo stop. But the interior—with cozy rooms—is worth a peek if you have time. Walk across the bridge and into the castle complex, and make your way into the big, blocky keep. First you'll see the claustrophobic, vaulted Billeting Room (where soldiers had their barracks), then head upstairs to the inviting Banqueting Room. Docents posted in these rooms can tell you more. Another flight of stairs takes you to the circa-1930 bedrooms. Downstairs is the cute kitchen exhibit, with mannequins preparing a meal (read the recipes posted throughout). Finally, you'll head through a few more assorted exhibits to the exit.

Cost and Hours: £6.50, good £3.50 guidebook; daily July-Aug 9:00-18:00, March-June & Sept-Oct 10:00-18:00; generally closed Nov-Feb but may be open a few times a week—call ahead, last entry one hour before closing; café, tel. 01599/555-202, www.eileandonancastle.com.

Getting There: It's not actually on the Isle of Skye, but it's quite close, in the mainland town of Dornie. Follow the A-87 about 15 minutes east of Skye Bridge, through Kyle of Lochalsh and toward Loch Ness and Inverness. The castle is on the right side of this road, just after a long bridge.

Portree

Skye's main attraction is its natural beauty, not its villages. But of the villages, the best home base is Portree (say poor-TREE fast, comes from Port Righ, literally, "Royal Port"). This village (with less than 3,000 people, too small to be con-

sidered a "town") is Skye's largest settlement and the hub of activity and transportation.

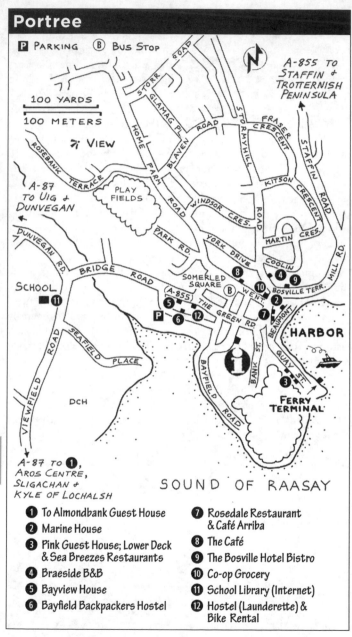

Portree

Ⓟ PARKING   Ⓑ BUS STOP

100 YARDS
100 METERS

7i VIEW

A-855 TO STAFFIN & TROTTERNISH PENINSULA

A-87 TO UIG & DUNVEGAN

PLAY FIELDS

SCHOOL

SOMERLED SQUARE

A-87 TO ①, AROS CENTRE, SLIGACHAN & KYLE OF LOCHALSH

HARBOR

FERRY TERMINAL

SOUND OF RAASAY

ISLE OF SKYE

① To Almondbank Guest House
② Marine House
③ Pink Guest House; Lower Deck & Sea Breezes Restaurants
④ Braeside B&B
⑤ Bayview House
⑥ Bayfield Backpackers Hostel
⑦ Rosedale Restaurant & Café Arriba
⑧ The Café
⑨ The Bosville Hotel Bistro
⑩ Co-op Grocery
⑪ School Library (Internet)
⑫ Hostel (Launderette) & Bike Rental

Orientation to Portree

This functional village has a small harbor and, on the hill above it, a tidy main square (from which buses fan out across the island and to the mainland). Surrounding the central square are just a few streets. Homes, shops, and B&Bs line the roads to other settlements on the island.

Tourist Information

Portree's helpful TI is a block off the main square. They can help you sort through bus schedules, give you maps, and book you a room for a £4 fee (Mon-Sat 9:00-18:00, closes at 17:00 off-season; Sun 10:00-16:00; Bayfield Road, just south of Bridge Road, tel. 01478/612-992 or 0845-225-5121). Public WCs are across the street and down a block, across from the hostel.

Helpful Hints

Internet Access: The **TI** has two terminals in the back (£1/20 minutes), and the big **Aros Centre** outside of town has several computers as well (£2/hour, see listing under "Sights in Portree," later). You can get online at the **library** in Portree High School (free, picture ID required, Mon-Fri 9:15-17:00, Tue and Thu until 20:00, Sat 10:00-16:00, closed Sun, Viewfield Road, tel. 01478/614-823).

Laundry: The **Independent Hostel,** just off the main square, has a self-service launderette down below (about £4 self-service, £8 full-service, usually 11:00-21:00, last load starts at 20:00, The Green/A-855, tel. 01478/613-737).

Supermarket: A **Co-op** is on Bank Street (daily 7:00-23:00).

Bike Rental: Island Cycles rents bikes in the middle of town, also just off the main square (£8.50/half-day, £15/24 hours, Mon-Sat 9:00-17:00, closed Sun, The Green/A-855, tel. 01478/613-121).

Car Rental: M2 Motors will pick you up at your B&B or the bus station (£45-55/day, half-day available, Dunvegan Road, tel. 01478/613-344). Other places to rent a car are outside of town, on the road toward Dunvegan. The **MacRae Dealership** is a 10-minute walk from downtown Portree (£46-52/day, Mon-Fri 9:00-17:00, Sat 9:00-12:00, no pick-up Sun, call at least a week in advance in summer, tel. 01478/612-554); farther along the same road are **Jansvans** (£57/day, Mon-Sat 8:00-17:30, closed Sun, tel. 01478/612-087) and **Portree Coachworks** (£48/day, Mon-Fri 8:30-17:30, Sat 9:00-13:00, no pick-up Sun, book in advance, tel. 01478/612-688).

Parking: As you enter town, a free parking lot is off to the right—

look for the sign. You can also pay to park in the main town square or in front of the TI.

Sights in Portree

Harbor

Portree has some shops to peruse, but the best activity is to simply wander along the colorful harbor, where boat captains offer £18 1.5-hour excursions out to the sea-eagle nests and around the bay (ask at TI).

Aros Centre

This visitors center and cinema, a mile outside of town on the road to Kyleakin and Skye Bridge, overlooks the sea loch. It offers a humble but earnest exhibit run by the Royal Society for the Protection of Birds (RSPB) about the island's wildlife (mainly its birds; ask if there's still a heron nest in the trees at the far end of the parking lot). Enjoy the 20-minute movie with spectacular aerial photos of otherwise-hard-to-reach parts of Skye, and chat with the ranger. The exhibit also describes the local sea eagles. These raptors were hunted to extinction on Skye but have been reintroduced to the ecosystem from Scandinavia. A live webcam shows their nests nearby—or, if there are no active nests, a "greatest hits" video of past fledglings.

Cost and Hours: £4.75, Easter-Oct daily 9:00-17:00, last entry 30 minutes before closing, closed Nov-Easter, café, gift shop, a mile south of town center on Viewfield Road, tel. 01478/613-649, www.aros.co.uk.

Sleeping in Portree

(area code: 01478)

$$$ Almondbank Guest House, on the road into town from Kyleakin, works well for drivers and has great views of the loch from the public areas. It has four tidy, homey rooms (two with sea views for no extra charge) and is run by friendly Effie Nicolson (Sb-£68, Db-£85, free Wi-Fi, Viewfield Road, tel. 01478/612-696, j.n.almondbank@btconnect.com).

$$ Marine House, run by sweet Skye native Fiona Stephenson, has three simple, homey rooms (two with a private bathroom down the hall) and fabulous views of the harbor (S-£25-30, D-£66-70, Db-£70-72, cash only, 2 Beaumont Crescent, tel. 01478/611-557, stephensonfiona@yahoo.com).

$$ At Pink Guest House, energetic Robbie and Fiona rent 11 bright, spacious rooms (8 with sea views) on the harbor. The rates include a full Scottish breakfast and the hosts' youthful enthusiasm (Db-£70, sea-view Db-£80, large family rooms, free Wi-Fi,

Sleep Code

(£1 = about $1.60, country code: 44)

S = Single, **D** = Double/Twin, **T** = Triple, **Q** = Quad, **b** = bathroom, **s** = shower only. Unless otherwise noted, credit cards are accepted at hotels and hostels—but not B&Bs—and breakfast is included.

To help you sort easily through these listings, I've divided the accommodations into three categories based on the price for a standard double room with bath (during high season):

$$$ Higher Priced—Most rooms £75 or more.
 $$ Moderately Priced—Most rooms between £50-75.
  $ Lower Priced—Most rooms £50 or less.

Prices can change without notice; verify the hotel's current rates online or by email.

Quay Street, tel. 01478/612-263, www.pinkguesthouse.co.uk, info@pinkguesthouse.co.uk).

$$ Braeside B&B has three comfortable rooms at the top of town, up from the Bosville Hotel (Db-£70, Tb-£90, £5 cheaper without breakfast, cash only, steep stairs, Stormyhill, tel. 01478/612-613, www.braesideportree.co.uk, mail@braesideportree .co.uk, Ruth).

$$ Bayview House has seven small and basic rooms, well-located on the main road just below the square (Db-£50-60, no breakfast, free Wi-Fi, Bridge Road, tel. 01478/613-340, www.bay viewhouse.co.uk, info@bayviewhouse.co.uk, Murdo and Alison). If there's no answer, walk down the stairs to Bayfield Backpackers, described next.

Hostel: **$ Bayfield Backpackers**—run by Murdo and Alison from the Bayview House (see listing above)—is a modern-feeling, institutional, cinderblock-and-metal hostel with 24 beds in 4- to 8-bed rooms (£16-17/bunk, pay Wi-Fi, kitchen, tel. 01478/612-231, www.skyehostel.co.uk, info@skyehostel.co.uk).

Sleeping near Portree, in Sligachan

$$$ Sligachan Hotel, a compound of related sleeping and eating options, is a local institution and a haven for hikers. It's been in the Campbell family since 1913. The hotel's 21 renovated rooms are comfortable, if a bit simple for the price, while the nearby campground and bunkhouse offer a budget alternative. The setting—surrounded by the mighty Cuillin Hills—is remarkably scenic (May-Sept: Db-£135, superior Db-£155; April and Oct: Db-£110, superior Db-£135; March: Db-£95, superior Db-£115;

closed Nov-Feb, campground-£6/person, bunkhouse-£20/person in 4- to 6-bed rooms, pay guest computer in pub, free Wi-Fi for hotel guests, on the A-87 between Kyleakin and Portree in Sligachan, hotel and campground tel. 01478/650-204, bunkhouse tel. 01478/650-458, www.sligachan.co.uk, reservations@sligachan .co.uk).

Eating in Portree

Note that Portree's few eateries tend to close early (21:00 or 22:00), and during busy times, lines begin to form soon after 19:00. Eating early works best here.

On the Waterfront: A pair of good eateries vie for your attention along Portree's little harbor. **Lower Deck** feels like a salty sailor's restaurant, decorated with the names of local ships (£6-10 lunches, £10-14 dinners, daily 12:00-14:30 & 18:00-21:30, closed Nov-March, tel. 01478/613-611). **Sea Breezes,** with a more contemporary flair, serves tasty cuisine with an emphasis on seafood (£8-12 lunches, £12-20 dinners, £18 two-course early-bird specials 17:00-18:00, open daily June-Aug 12:30-14:00 & 17:00-21:30, shorter hours generally in April-May and Sept-Oct, closed Nov-March, reserve ahead for dinner, tel. 01478/612-016, www .seabreezes-skye.co.uk).

Rosedale Restaurant, with just a dozen tables and stunning views of the harbor, is the place for fresh, local seafood. Willie and Fiona work the front of the house while son-in-law Robert creates delicious, local dishes featuring all things shellfish (£7-13 lunches, £12-20 dinners, £60 seafood platter for two, daily 12:00-14:00 & 17:30-21:00, reservations smart, tel. 01478/613-214, www .portreerestaurant.co.uk).

Elsewhere in Portree: **Café Arriba** tries hard to offer eclectic flavors in this small Scottish town. With an ambitious menu that includes local specialties, Mexican, Italian, and more, this youthful, colorful, easygoing eatery's hit-or-miss cuisine is worth trying. Drop in to see what's on the blackboard menu today (£4-9 meals, lots of vegetarian options, daily 8:00-18:00, Quay Brae, tel. 01478/611-830).

The Café, a few steps off the main square, is a busy, popular hometown diner serving good crank-'em-out food to an appreciative local crowd. The homemade ice-cream stand in the front is a nice way to finish your meal (£9-10 lunches and burgers, £10-15 dinners, also does take-away, daily 8:30-15:30 & 17:30-21:00, Wentworth Street, tel. 01478/612-553).

The Bosville Hotel Bistro offers a popular selection of inexpensive, casual dishes (£7-9 lunch sandwiches, £10-16 lunches, £11-22 dinners, daily 12:00-14:00 & 17:30-21:00, until 21:30 in

June-Aug). Their 19 rooms are expensive, but worth considering (Db-£128-165, tel. 01478/612-846, www.bosvillehotel.co.uk).

Eating Elsewhere on the Isle of Skye

In Sligachan

Sligachan Hotel (described earlier) has a lovely dining room and a microbrew pub serving up mountaineer-pleasing grub. Its setting is extremely scenic, nestled in the Cuillin Hills (traditional dinners in restaurant, served nightly 18:30-21:00; pub grub—£7-11, served until 21:30; pub closed Oct-Feb, on the A-87 between Kyleakin and Portree in Sligachan, tel. 01478/650-204).

In Colbost, near Dunvegan

Three Chimneys Restaurant is your big-splurge-on-a-small-island meal. The high-quality Scottish cuisine, using local ingredients, earns rave reviews. Its 16 tables fill an old three-chimney croft house, with a stone-and-timbers decor that artfully melds old and new. It's cozy, classy, and candlelit, but not stuffy. Because of its remote location—and the fact that it's almost always booked up—reservations are absolutely essential, ideally several weeks if not months ahead, although it's worth calling in case of last-minute cancellations (lunch: £28.50 for two courses, £37 for three courses; dinner: £60 for three courses, £90 for seven-course "showcase menu"; dinner served nightly from 18:15, last booking at 21:45, lunch mid-March-Oct Mon-Sat 12:15-13:45, no lunch Sun or Nov-mid-March, closed for 3 weeks in Jan, tel. 01470/511-258, www.threechimneys.co.uk, Eddie and Shirley Spear). They also rent six swanky, pricey suites next door (Db-£295-415, less off-season).

Getting There: It's in the village of Colbost, about a 10- to 15-minute drive west of Dunvegan on the Duirinish Peninsula (that's about 45 minutes each way from Portree). To get there, first head for Dunvegan, then follow signs toward Glendale. This single-track road twists you through the countryside, over a moor, and past several dozen sheep before passing through Colbost. You can combine this with a visit to the Neist Point Lighthouse (described earlier), which is at the end of the same road.

Kyleakin

Kyleakin (kih-LAH-kin), the last town in Skye before the bridge, used to be a big tourist hub...until the bridge connecting it to the

mainland made it much easier for people to get to Portree and other areas deeper in the island. Today this unassuming little village, with a ruined castle (Castle Moil), a cluster of lonesome fishing boats, and a forgotten ferry slip, still works well as a home base.

If you want to pick up information on the island before you drive all the way to Portree, stop by the tiny **TI** in Broadford, about 15 minutes farther up the road from Kyleakin, where the friendly "one 'ell of a Callum" helps travelers sort out options (April-Oct Mon-Sat 9:30-17:00—until 18:00 July-Aug, Sun 10:00-16:00, closed Nov-March, maps and hiking books, in Co-op parking lot, WCs across street next to church; no phone or email in Kyleakin office, but questions answered by Visit Scotland at tel. 0845-225-5121, info@visit scotland.com).

Helpful Hints

Internet Access: If you're desperate, **Saucy Mary's** store/bar has a laptop and printer available for visitors to use (Main Street, tel. 01599/534-845).

Laundry: **Saucy Mary's** offers laundry service (£12 wash/dry); there is also a launderette in Broadford, next to the Co-op supermarket (daily 6:00-20:00, shorter hours in winter).

Supermarkets: A **Co-op** is across the bridge in Kyle of Lochalsh (daily 7:00-23:00, Bridge Road, tel. 01599/530-190), and another is up the road in Broadford (daily 9:00-22:00, Main Street, tel. 01471/820-420).

Car Rental: You can rent a car for the day from **Skye Car Hire** (about £45/day, daily 9:00-17:00, in Kyle of Lochalsh, free delivery within 5 miles, tel. 01599/534-323, www.skyecarhire .co.uk).

Taxi: For taxi services or local tours, contact **Kyle Taxi** (also in Kyle of Lochalsh, same phone number as Skye Car Hire, www.lochalsh.net/taxi).

Sleeping in Kyleakin

(area code: 01599)

$$$ MacKinnon Country House Hotel is my favorite country-side home base on Skye. It sits quietly in the middle of five acres of gardens just off the bustling Skye Bridge and boasts of famous visitors such as Queen Elizabeth II and Winston Churchill. Ian and Carol Smith Tongs have lovingly restored this old 1912 country home with Edwardian antiques and 18 clan-themed rooms, an inviting overstuffed-sofa lounge, and a restaurant with garden views in nearly every direction (Sb-£50-55, Db-£110-150 depending on room size and amenities, 10 percent discount when you mention this book in 2014, about 20 percent cheaper Oct-Easter, room fridges, free Wi-Fi; 10-minute walk from Kyleakin, at the turnoff for the bridge; tel. 01599/534-180, www.mackinnonhotel.co.uk, info@mackinnonhotel.co.uk). Ian also serves a delicious dinner to guests and non guests alike (see "Eating in Kyleakin," later). Moss, the border collie, will try to take you for a walk.

$$$ White Heather Hotel, run by friendly and helpful Gillian and Craig Glenwright, has nine small but nicely decorated rooms with woody pine bathrooms, across from the waterfront and the castle ruins (Sb-£52, Db-£76, family rooms, cheaper for stays longer than 2 nights, free guest computer and Wi-Fi, lounges, washer and dryer available, closed late Oct-Feb, The Harbour, tel. 01599/534-577, www.whiteheatherhotel.co.uk, info@whiteheatherhotel.co.uk).

$$$ Cliffe House B&B rents three rooms in a white house perched at the very edge of the water. All of the rooms, including the breakfast room, enjoy wonderful views over the strait and the bridge (Db-£70-80, cash only, closed Dec-Jan, tel. 01599/534-019, www.cliffehousebedandbreakfast.co.uk, info@cliffehousebedandbreakfast.co.uk, Ian and Mary Sikorski).

Eating in and near Kyleakin

Locals like the **Taste of India,** just past the roundabout outside Kyleakin on the A-87 toward Broadford (£8-13 main courses, also does take-away, daily 17:00-23:00, tel. 01599/534-134). For a nice dinner, head up to the recommended **MacKinnon Country House Hotel** (£15-20 main courses, nightly 19:00-20:30, just outside Kyleakin at roundabout, tel. 01599/534-180). Little Kyleakin also has a few pubs; ask your B&B host for advice.

In Kyle of Lochalsh: If you can get reservations, eat fresh Scottish cuisine at the **Waverly Restaurant,** a tiny six-table place with locally sourced food, across the bridge from Kyleakin in Kyle

ISLE OF SKYE

of Lochalsh (£13-20 main courses, £12.75 two-course dinner special 17:30-19:00, open Fri-Tue 17:30-21:30, closed Wed-Thu, reservations essential, Main Street, across from Kyle Hotel and up the stairs, tel. 01599/534-337, www.waverleykyle.co.uk, Dutch chef/owner Ank).

In Broadford: Up the road in Broadford are more eateries, including the renovated **Broadford Hotel,** overlooking the bay (£9-17 main courses, Torrin Road at junction with Elgol, tel. 01471/822-204). It was here that a secret elixir—supposedly once concocted for Bonnie Prince Charlie—was re-created by hotelier James Ross after finding the recipe in his father's belongings. Now known as Drambuie, the popular liqueur, which caught on in the 19th century, is made with Scottish whisky, honey, and spices. With its wide variety of Drambuie drinks, the Broadford is the place to try it.

INVERNESS AND THE NORTHERN HIGHLANDS

Inverness • Loch Ness • Culloden Battlefield
• Clava Cairns

Filled with more natural and historical mystique than people, the northern Highlands are where Scottish dreams are set. Legends of Bonnie Prince Charlie linger around crumbling castles as tunes played by pipers in kilts swirl around tourists. Explore the locks and lochs of the Caledonian Canal while the Loch Ness monster plays hide-and-seek. Hear the music of the Highlands in Inverness and the echo of muskets at Culloden, where the English drove Bonnie Prince Charlie into exile and conquered his Jacobite supporters.

I've focused my coverage on the handy hub of Inverness, with several day-trip options into the surrounding countryside. For Highlands sights to the south and west, see the Oban and the Southern Highlands chapter; for the Isle of Skye off Scotland's west coast, see the previous chapter.

Planning Your Time

Though it has little in the way of sights, Inverness does have a workaday charm and is a handy spot to spend a night or two en route to other Highland destinations. One night here gives you time to take a quick tour of nearby attractions. With two nights, you can find a full day's worth of sightseeing nearby.

Note that Loch Ness is on the way toward Oban or the Isle of Skye. If you're heading to one of those places, it makes sense to see Loch Ness en route, rather than as a side trip from Inverness.

Getting Around the Highlands

With a car, the day trips around Inverness are easy. Without a car, you can get to Inverness by train (better from Edinburgh or

Pitlochry) or by bus (better from Skye, Oban, and Glencoe), then side-trip to Loch Ness, Culloden, and other nearby attractions by public bus or with a package tour.

Inverness

The only city in the north of Scotland, Inverness is pleasantly situated on the River Ness at the base of a castle (now a court-house, not a tourist attraction). Inverness' charm is its normalcy—it's a nice, mid-size Scottish city that gives you a palatable taste of the "urban" Highlands, and is well-located for enjoying the surrounding country-side sights. Check out the bustling, pedestrian down-town or meander the picnic-friendly riverside paths—best at sunset, when the light hits the castle and couples hold hands while strolling along the water and over the many footbridges.

Orientation to Inverness

Inverness, with about 60,000 people, is the fastest-growing city in Scotland. Marked by its castle, Inverness clusters along the River Ness. Where the main road crosses the river at Ness Bridge, you'll find the TI; within a few blocks (away from the river) are the train and bus stations and an appealing pedestrian shopping zone. The best B&Bs huddle atop a gentle hill  behind the castle (a 10-minute uphill walk, or a £5 taxi ride, from the city center).

Tourist Information

At the centrally located TI, you can pick up activity and day-trip brochures, the self-guided *Historic Trail* walking-tour leaf-let, a map of the trail from Culloden to Clava Cairns, and the *What's On* weekly events sheet for the latest theater, music, and film showings (all free). The office also has a bulletin board with timely local event information, books rooms for a £4 fee, and offers tours (open July-mid-Sept Mon-Sat 9:00-18:30, Sun 9:30-18:00; mid-Sept-June Mon-Sat 9:00-18:00, Sun 9:30-18:00; Internet access, free WCs up behind TI, Castle Wynd, tel. 01463/252-401).

Helpful Hints

Festivals and Events: In mid-June, the city fills up for the **RockNess Music Festival** (www.rockness.co.uk), and there's a **marathon** the last week of September or first week of October (www.lochnessmarathon.com); book ahead for these times. For a real Highland treat, catch a **shinty match** (a combination of field hockey, hurling, and American football—but without pads). Inverness Shinty Club plays at Bought Park, along Ness Walk (the TI or your B&B can tell you if there are any matches on, or check www.spanglefish .com/invernessshintyclub).

Internet Access: You can get online at the **TI** (£1/20 minutes), or for free at the Neoclassical **library** behind the bus station (30-minute limit, Mon-Tue and Fri 9:00-18:30, Wed 10:00-18:30, Thu 9:00-20:00, Sat 9:00-17:00, closed Sun, computers shut down 15 minutes before closing, photo ID required, tel. 01463/236-463). **New City Launderette,** listed below, also has Internet access (£1/20 minutes).

Baggage Storage: The train station has lockers (£3-5/24 hours, open Mon-Sat 6:45-19:45, Sun 10:45-18:15), and the bus station offers daily baggage storage (£4/bag, daily 8:45-17:30).

Laundry: New City Launderette is just across the Ness Bridge from the TI (£5-6 for self-service, about £10 for same-day full-service, price calculated by weight, Internet access, Mon-Sat 8:00-18:00, until 20:00 Mon-Fri June-Oct, Sun 10:00-16:00 year-round, last load one hour before closing, 17 Young Street, tel. 01463/242-507). **Thirty Degrees Laundry** on Church Street is another option (£8 full-service only, drop off first thing in the morning for same-day service, Mon-Sat 8:30-17:30, closed Sun, 84 Church Street, tel. 01463/710-380).

Supermarkets: The **Co-operative** (Mon-Sat 7:00-22:00, Sun 7:00-20:00, 59 Church Street) and **Marks & Spencer** (described in "Eating in Inverness," later) are handy for picnics.

Charity Shops: Inverness is home to several pop-up charity shops. Occupying vacant rental spaces, these are staffed by volunteers who are happy to talk about their philanthropy. You can pick up a memorable knickknack, adjust your wardrobe for the weather, and learn about local causes.

Inverness

1. Craigside Lodge B&B
2. Eildon Guesthouse
3. Dionard Guest House
4. Ardconnel House & Crown Hotel Guest House
5. Ryeford Guest House
6. Heathmount Hotel & Restaurant
7. Inverness Palace Hotel & Spa
8. Premier Inn Inverness Centre River Ness
9. Mercure Inverness & The Joy of Taste Restaurant
10. Waterside Inverness
11. Inverness Student Hotel & Bazpackers Hostel
12. Café 1; Pockets Snooker & Pool Bar
13. Number 27 Restaurant
14. La Tortilla Asesina Rest.
15. Hootananny Café/Bar
16. Rocpool Restaurant
17. The Mustard Seed
18. The Kitchen
19. Rajah Indian Restaurant
20. Leakey's Bookshop & Café
21. The Gellions Pub
22. Marks & Spencer (Groceries)
23. Co-op Supermarket
24. Library (Internet)
25. Launderettes (2)

INVERNESS

Tours in Inverness

Walking Tours

Happy Tours

Cameron—a.k.a. "the man in the kilt"—at Happy Tours offers history walks by day, and "Crime and Punishment" tours by night. These one-hour walks are cheeky, and peppered with his political opinions—a fun mix of history, local gossip, Scottish culture, and comedy. Cameron also offers other tours, guides bike tours to

Loch Ness, and rents bikes for £15 per day (tours-£6/person; history tour daily April-Sept at 11:00, 13:00, and 15:00; Crime and Punishment at 19:00 and 20:30; tours leave from steps of TI, just show up, tel. 07828/154-683, www.happy-tours.biz).

Excursions from Inverness

While thin on sights of its own, Inverness is a great home base for day trips. The biggest attraction is Loch Ness, a 20-minute drive southwest. Tickets are available at the TI, and tours depart from somewhere nearby. It's smart to book ahead, especially in peak season.

Jacobite Tours

This outfit runs a variety of tours, from a one-hour basic boat ride to a 6.5-hour extravaganza. Most tours run daily (£13-40, tours fill up in summer—book in advance). Their 3.5-hour "Sensation" tour includes a guided bus tour with live narration, a half-hour cruise of Loch Ness with recorded commentary, and an hour apiece at Urquhart Castle and the better of the two Loch Ness exhibits (£30, includes admissions to both sights, departs at 10:30 from Bank Street, near the TI; ticket/info counter in bus station open daily 9:00-16:00, tel. 01463/233-999, www.jacobite.co.uk).

Highland Experience Tours

Choose from several daylong tours, including one that focuses on the Isle of Skye, with stops along Loch Ness and at scenic Eilean Donan Castle. You'll get a few hours on Skye; unfortunately, it only takes you as far as the Sleat Peninsula at the island's southern end, rather than to the more scenic Trotternish Peninsula (£45, departs from Bridge Street outside the TI at 9:30, returns at 19:30; mid-May-Sept runs daily, mid-April-mid-May and most of Oct runs several days a week, no tours late-Oct-mid-April, reservations recommended, tel. 01463/719-222, www.highlandexperience.com). For more on the Isle of Skye, see the previous chapter.

More Options

Several companies host daily excursions to whisky distilleries, the Orkney Islands, and the nearby bay for dolphin-watching (ask at TI). Skip the City Sightseeing hop-on, hop-off bus tour (whose main objective is connecting you with Jacobite—their sister company—cruise docks).

Self-Guided Walk

Humble Inverness has meager conventional sights, but its fun history and quirky charm become clear as you take this short self-guided walk.

• *Start at the clock tower and TI.*

Clock Tower and TI: Notice the Scottish language on signs all around you. While nobody speaks Gaelic as a first language and few Scottish people speak it at all, the old Celtic Scottish language symbolizes the strength of the local culture. The recommended Gellions Bar (across from the TI and described later, in "Nightlife in Inverness") flies two Scottish flags.

The steeple towering 130 feet above you is all that remains of a tollbooth building erected in 1791. This is the highest spire in town, and for generations was a collection point for local taxes. Here, four streets—Church, Castle, Bridge, and High—come together, integrating God, defense, and trade—everything necessary for a fine city. This is naturally the center of Inverness.

About 800 years ago, a castle was built on the bluff overhead and the town of Inverness coalesced right about here. In 1854 the train arrived, injecting energy from Edinburgh and Glasgow, and the Victorian boom hit. Before the Industrial Age the economy was based on cottage industries. Artisans who made things also sold them. With the Industrial Age came wholesalers, distributors, mass production, and affluence. The cityscape is neo-Gothic—over-the-top and fanciful, like the City Hall, built in 1882. With the Victorian Age also came tourism.

Look across the street at the Bible quotes chiseled into the wall. A city leader, tired of his council members being drunkards, edited these Bible verses for maximum impact, especially the bottom two.

Inverness Castle is just up the hill—with some of the best views of Inverness looking west and south. Today the building holds a courthouse without a lot of action. In the last 30 years, there have been only two murders to prosecute. Locals like to say "no guns, no problems." While hunters can own a gun, gun ownership in Scotland is complicated and tightly regulated.

By the way, every day and night in peak season, from this spot, Cameron ("the man in the kilt" who gave me the material for this walk) gives entertaining hour-long guided walks (see "Tours in Inverness," earlier).

• *Walk a few steps uphill to the Scottish hamburger restaurant that caught on big-time in the USA.*

Mercat Cross and Old Town Center: Standing in front of the City Hall is a well-worn mercat cross, which designated the market in centuries past. This is where the townspeople gathered to hear important proclamations, share news, watch hangings, gossip, and so on. The scant remains of a prehistoric stone at the base of the cross are what's left of Inverness' "Stone of Destiny." According to tradition, whenever someone moved away from Inverness, they'd take a tiny bit of home with them in the form of a chip of this stone—so it's been chipped and pecked almost to oblivion.

A yellow Caledonian building faces McDonald's at the base of High Street. (Caledonia was the ancient name of Scotland.) It was built in 1847, complete with Corinthian columns and a Greek-style pediment, as the leading bank in town, back when banks were designed to hold the money of the rich and powerful...and intimidate working blokes. A few doors up High Street from here is the Victorian Gothic Royal Tartan Warehouse, with Queen Victoria's august coat of arms, indicating that the royal family shopped here. Notice how nicely pedestrianized High Street welcomes people and seagulls...but not cars.

Church Street to the Church: The street art at the start of Church Street is *Earthquake*, a reminder of the quake that hit Inverness in 1816. According to the statues, the town's motto is "Open Heartedness, Insight, and Perseverance."

Stroll down Church Street. Look up above the modern store-fronts to see Old World facades. Union Street (first corner on the right)—stately, symmetrical, and neo-Classical—was the best street in the Highlands when it was built in the 19th century. Its buildings had indoor toilets. That was big news.

Midway down the next block of Church Street (on the right), an alley marked by an ugly white canopy leads to the Victorian Market. Explore this gallery of shops under an iron-and-glass domed roof dating from 1876. (If this entrance is closed, there are other entrances around the block.)

Continuing down Church Street, on the next corner you come to Hootananny, famous locally for its live music (pop in to see what's on tonight). Next door is Abertarff, the oldest house in Inverness. It was the talk of the town in 1593 for its "turnpike" (spiral staircase) connecting the floors.

The lane on the left leads to the "Bouncy Bridge" (where we'll finish this walk). Opposite that lane (on the right) is the Dunbar Hospital, with four-foot-thick walls. In 1668, Alexander Dunbar was a wealthy landowner who built this as a poor folks' home. You can almost read the auld script in his coat of arms above the door.

Walk through the iron gate and churchyard (ignoring the church on left and focusing on the one on the right). Looking at the WWI and WWII memorials on the church's wall, it's clear which war hit Britain harder. While no one famous is buried here, many tombstones go back to the 1700s. Being careful not to step on a rabbit, head for the bluff overlooking the river.

Old High Church: There are a lot of churches in Inverness (46 Protestant, two Catholic, and two Gaelic-language) but, these days, most are used for other purposes. This one, dating from the 11th century, is the most historic (but is generally closed). It was built on what was likely the site of a pagan holy ground. Early Christians called upon St. Michael to take the fire out of pagan spirits, so it only made sense that the first Christians would build their church here and dedicate the spot as St. Michael's Mount.

In the sixth century the Irish evangelist monk St. Columba brought Christianity to northern England, the Scottish Lowlands (at Iona), and the Scottish Highlands (in Inverness). He stood here amongst the pagans and preached to King Brude and the Picts.

Study the bell tower from the 1600s. The small door to nowhere (about one floor up) indicates that back before the castle offered protection, this tower was the place of last refuge for townsfolk under attack. They'd gather inside and pull up the ladder. The church became a prison for Jacobites after the Battle of Culloden, and executions were carried out in the churchyard.

Every night at 20:00, the bell in the tower rings 100 times. It has rung like this since 1730 to remind townsfolk that it's dangerous to be out after dinner.

• *From here you can circle back to the lane leading to the "Bouncy Bridge" and then hike out onto the bridge, or you can just survey the countryside from this bluff.*

River Ness: "Inverness" means the area around the river. "Ness" means river. So River Ness means "River River." Emptying out of Loch Ness and flowing seven miles to the sea (a mile from here), this is the shortest river in the country. While it's shallow (you can almost walk across it), there are plenty of fish in it. A 64-pound salmon was recently pulled out of the river right here. In the 19th century, Inverness was smaller, and across the river stretched nothing but open fields. Then, with the Victorian boom, the suspension footbridge (a.k.a. "Bouncy Bridge") was built in 1881 to connect new construction across the river with the town.

• *Your tour is over and you are now free to enjoy the bridge.*

Sights in Inverness

Inverness Museum and Art Gallery

This free, likable town museum is worth poking around on a rainy day to get a taste of Inverness and the Highlands. The ground-floor exhibits on geology and archaeology peel back the layers of Highland history: Bronze and Iron ages, Picts (including some carved stones), Scots, Vikings, and Normans. Upstairs you'll find the "social history" exhibit (everything from Scottish nationalism to hunting and fishing) and temporary art exhibits.

Cost and Hours: Free; April-Oct Tue-Sat 10:00-17:00, closed Sun-Mon; Nov-March Thu-Sat 10:00-17:00, closed Sun-Wed; cheap café, in the modern building behind the TI on the way up to the castle, tel. 01463/237-114, http://inverness.highland.museum.

Inverness Castle

Inverness' biggest nonsight has nice views from its front lawn, but the building itself isn't worth visiting. A wooden fortress that stood on this spot was replaced by a stone structure in the 15th century. In 1715, that castle was made Fort George to assert English control over the area. In 1745, it was destroyed by Bonnie Prince Charlie's Jacobite army and remained a ruin until the 1830s, when the present castle was built. The statue (from 1899) outside depicts Flora MacDonald, who helped Bonnie Prince Charlie escape from the English. Today the castle is used as a courthouse, and when trials are in session, loutish-looking men hang out here, waiting for their bewigged barristers to arrive.

River Walks

As with most European cities, where there's a river, there's a walk. Inverness, with both the River Ness and the Caledonian Canal, does not disappoint. Consider an early-morning stroll along the Ness Bank to capture the castle at sunrise, or a post-dinner jaunt to Bought Park for a local shinty match (see "Helpful Hints—Festivals and Events," earlier). From the Ness Bridge, the Caledonian Canal is also less than a 15-minute walk (follow Tomnahurich Street, which turns into Glenurquhart Road; it's a straight shot to the canal—when you see the gates for the Commonwealth War Graves you're two minutes away). Where Tomnahurich Bridge crosses the canal you'll find paths on either bank, allowing you to walk along the Great Glen Way until you're ready to turn around. On your way back to town, instead of retracing the route, turn right on Bought Drive (or Bought Road—your choice) and circle around Queens Park to connect with the Ness Bank back into the city.

Nightlife in Inverness

Scottish Folk Music

While you're likely to find traditional folk music sessions in pubs and hotel bars anywhere in town, two places are well established as the music pubs. **The Gellions** has live folk and Scottish music nightly. Just across the street from the TI, it has local ales on tap and brags it's the oldest bar in town (14 Bridge Street, tel. 01463/233-648, www.gellions.co.uk). **Hootananny** is an energetic place with several floors of live rock, blues, or folk music, and drinking fun nightly. Upstairs is the Mad Hatter's nightclub (Thu-Sun only), complete with a "chill-out room" (bar open 18:00-24:00, music begins at 21:30, 67 Church Street, tel. 01463/233-651, www.hootananny.co.uk). They also serve dinner; see their listing in "Eating in Inverness," later.

Pockets Snooker & Pool Bar

If you'd rather just shoot some pool, try this modern sports bar, a local hangout with free darts, pool, and snooker (snooker and pool-£4/hour, nightly until 24:00, across from the Castle at #67 Castle Street).

Sleeping in Inverness

B&Bs on and near Ardconnel Street and Old Edinburgh Road

These B&Bs are popular; book ahead for June through August (and during the marathon in late September or early October), and be aware that some require a two-night minimum during busy

Sleep Code

(£1 = about $1.60, country code: 44, area code: 01463)
S = Single, **D** = Double/Twin, **T** = Triple, **Q** = Quad, **b** = bathroom, **s** = shower only. Unless otherwise noted, you can assume credit cards are accepted at hotels and hostels—but not B&Bs—and breakfast is included.

To help you sort easily through these listings, I've divided the accommodations into three categories based on the price for a standard double room with bath (during high season):

$$$ Higher Priced—Most rooms £75 or more.
$$ Moderately Priced—Most rooms between £45-75.
$ Lower Priced—Most rooms £45 or less.

Prices can change without notice; verify the hotel's current rates online or by email. For the best prices, always book direct.

times. The rooms are all a 10-minute walk from the train station and town center. To get to the B&Bs, either catch a taxi (£5) or walk: From the train and bus stations, go left on Academy Street. At the first stoplight (the second if you're coming from the bus station), veer right onto Inglis Street in the pedestrian zone. Go up the Market Brae steps. At the top, turn right onto Ardconnel Street toward the B&Bs and hostels.

$$ Craigside Lodge B&B has five large, comfortable, cheery rooms with a tasteful modern flair mirroring the energy of the hosts. Guests share an inviting sunroom and a cozy lounge with a great city view (Sb-£40-45, Db-£70-75, prices depend on season, free Wi-Fi, just above Castle Street at 4 Gordon Terrace, tel. 01463/231-576, www.craigsideguesthouse.co.uk, enquiries@craigsideguesthouse.co.uk, Ewan and Amy).

$$ Eildon Guesthouse, set on a quiet corner, offers six tranquil rooms with spacious baths at an excellent value. The cute-as-a-button 1890s countryside brick home exudes warmth and serenity from the moment you open the gate (Sb-£30-35, Db-£60-70, Tb-£90-105, family rooms available, in-room fridges, free Wi-Fi, parking, 29 Old Edinburgh Road, tel. 01463/231-969, eildonguesthouse@yahoo.co.uk, www.eildonguesthouse.co.uk, Jacqueline).

$$ Dionard Guest House, just up Old Edinburgh Road from Ardconnel Street, has cheerful common spaces and six pleasant rooms, including two on the ground floor (Sb-£50, Db-£67-85 depending on size, no single-occupancy rate during high season, in-room fridges, free Wi-Fi, 39 Old Edinburgh Road, tel.

INVERNESS

01463/233-557, www.dionardguesthouse.co.uk, enquiries@dionard
guesthouse.co.uk, Brian and Doris).

$$ Ardconnel House offers a nice, large guest lounge and
a warm welcome, along with six spacious and comfortable rooms
(Sb-£45, Db-£75, family room-£95, family deals but no children
under 10, slightly cheaper off-season or for 2 or more nights, free
Wi-Fi, 21 Ardconnel Street, tel. 01463/240-455, www.ardconnel
-inverness.co.uk, ardconnel@gmail.com, John and Elizabeth).

$$ Crown Hotel Guest House has six clean, bright rooms
and an enjoyable breakfast room (Sb-£35, Db-£60, family room-
£80-100, lounge, 19 Ardconnel Street, tel. 01463/231-135, www
.crownhotel-inverness.co.uk, reservations@crownhotel-inverness
.co.uk, friendly Catriona—pronounced "Katrina"—Barbour).

$$ Ryeford Guest House is a decent value, with six flow-
ery rooms and plenty of teddy bears (Sb-£45, Db-£70, Tb-£105,
family deals, vegetarian breakfast available, small twin room #1
in back has fine garden view, free Wi-Fi in front lounge, above
Market Brae steps, go left on Ardconnel Terrace to #21, tel. 01463/
242-871, www.scotland-inverness.co.uk/ryeford, joananderson
@uwclub.net, Joan and George Anderson).

Hotels

The following hotels may have rooms when my recommended
B&Bs are full.

$$$ Heathmount Hotel's understated facade hides a chic
retreat for comfort-seeking travelers. Its eight uniquely decorated
elegant rooms come with free Wi-Fi, parking, and fancy extras
(Sb-£79-95, Db-£95-140, Kingsmill Road, tel. 01463/235-877,
info@heathounthotel.com, www.heathmounthotel.com). Their
restaurant is also recommended; see "Eating in Inverness."

$$$ Inverness Palace Hotel & Spa, a Best Western, is a
fancy splurge with a pool, a gym, and 88 overpriced rooms. It's
located right on the River Ness, across from the castle (Db-£209-
229, but you can almost always get a much better rate—even half-
price—if you book a package deal on their website, £89 last-minute
rooms, prices especially soft on weekends, river/castle view rooms
about £40 more than rest, breakfast extra, elevator, free Wi-Fi,
free parking, 8 Ness Walk, tel. 01463/223-243, www.inverness
palacehotel.co.uk, palace@miltonhotels.com).

$$$ Premier Inn Inverness Centre River Ness, along the
River Ness, offers 99 predictable rooms, all with private bath.
What the hotel lacks in charm and glitz it makes up for in affordable rates and location (Db-£60-120, £29 rooms not uncommon
if booked online well in advance; Wi-Fi free for 30 minutes, then
£3/day; 19-21 Huntly Street, tel. 01463/246-490, www.premierinn
.com).

$$$ **Mercure Inverness,** across the river from the Premier Inn, has 106 rooms, a gym, pool, and spa, and feels less commercial than other chain hotels (Db-£125-175, much cheaper rates if booked in advance online, free Wi-Fi, parking-£2/night; entrance is at Church Street, tel. 0844/815-9006, sales.mercureinverness @jupiterhotels.co.uk, www.mercureinverness.co.uk).

$$$ **Waterside Inverness,** in a nice location along the River Ness, has 35 crisp, recently updated rooms and a riverview restaurant (Sb-£75, Db-£140, superior Db-£170, Qb-£190, call or check website for deals as low as Db-£79, 19 Ness Bank, tel. 01463/233-065, www.thewatersideinverness.co.uk, info@thewaterside inverness.co.uk).

Hostels on Culduthel Road

For inexpensive dorm beds near the center and the recommended Castle Street restaurants, consider these friendly side-by-side hostels, geared toward younger travelers. They're about a 12-minute walk from the train station.

$ **Inverness Student Hotel** has 57 beds in nine rooms and a cozy, inviting, laid-back lounge with a bay window overlooking the River Ness. The knowledgeable, friendly staff welcomes any traveler over 18. Dorms come in some interesting shapes, and each bunk has its own playful name (£17-18 beds in 6- to 10-bed rooms, price depends on season, breakfast-£2, free tea and coffee, cheap guest computer, free Wi-Fi, full-service laundry for £3.50, kitchen, 8 Culduthel Road, tel. 01463/236-556, www.inverness studenthotel.com, info@invernessstudenthotel.com).

$ **Bazpackers Hostel,** a stone's throw from the castle, has a quieter, more private feel and 20 beds in basic 4- to 6-bed dorms (beds-£17, D-£44, cheaper Oct-May, linens provided, reception open 7:30-23:00 but available 24 hours, no curfew, pay guest computer, free Wi-Fi, £4 laundry service, 4 Culduthel Road, tel. 01463/717-663, www.bazpackershostel.co.uk). They also rent a small apartment nearby (£70-80, sleeps up to 4).

Eating in Inverness

You'll find a lot of traditional Highland fare—game, fish, lamb, and beef. Reservations are smart at most of these places, especially on summer weekends.

Near the B&Bs, on or near Castle Street

The first three eateries line Castle Street, facing the back of the castle.

Café 1 serves up high-quality modern Scottish and international cuisine with trendy, chic bistro flair. This popular place fills up on weekends, so it's smart to call ahead (£12-20 main courses, lunch and early-bird dinner specials 17:30-18:45, open Mon-Fri 12:00-14:00 & 17:30-21:30, Sat 12:00-15:30 & 18:00-21:30, closed Sun, 75 Castle Street, tel. 01463/226-200).

Number 27 has a straightforward, crowd-pleasing menu that offers something for everyone—burgers, pastas, and more. The food is surprisingly elegant for this price range (£9-13 main courses, £8 two-course lunch Mon-Fri; open daily 12:00-21:00, generous portions, local ales on tap, noisy bar up front not separated from restaurant in back, 27 Castle Street, tel. 01463/241-999).

La Tortilla Asesina has Spanish tapas, including spicy king prawns (the house specialty). It's an appealing and vivacious dining option that feels like Spain (£3-7 cold and hot tapas—three make a meal, cheap tapas combo-specials; April-Sept daily 12:00-22:00; Oct-March daily 12:00-21:00; 99 Castle Street, tel. 01463/709-809).

The recommended **Heathmount Hotel** serves good food in their quiet dining room (£6-9 lunches, £11-19 dinners, Mon-Fri 12:00-14:30 & 17:00-22:00, Sat-Sun 12:30-21:30, 5-minute walk down Argyle Street to Kingsmills Road, tel. 01463/235-877).

In the Town Center

Hootananny mixes an energetic pub and live music with Scottish staples like lamb stovies (stew) and cullen skink (fish chowder). It's got a great join-in-the-fun vibe at night (£4-8 dishes, food served Mon-Sat 12:00-15:00 & 17:00-21:30, no food on Sun; see "Nightlife in Inverness," earlier).

Rocpool Restaurant is a hit with locals and good for a splurge. Owner/chef Steven Devlin serves creative modern European food in a sleek—and often crowded—chocolate/pistachio dining room. Reserve ahead or be sorry (£15 lunch specials, £17 early-bird special before 18:45 Mon-Fri, £13-21 dinners; open Mon-Sat 12:00-14:30 & 17:45-22:00, closed Sun; across Ness Bridge from TI at 1 Ness Walk, tel. 01463/717-274, www.rocpoolrestaurant.com).

The Mustard Seed serves Scottish food with a modern twist in an old church with a river view. It's pricey, but worth considering for a nice lively-at-lunch, mellow-at-dinner meal. Ask for a seat on the balcony if the weather is cooperating. Reservations are essential on weekends (£7 lunch specials, £12 early-bird specials 17:30-19:00, £15-20 meals, daily 12:00-15:00 & 17:30-22:00, on the corner of Bank and Fraser Streets, 16 Fraser Street, tel. 01463/220-220, www.mustardseedrestaurant.co.uk).

The Kitchen is the sister restaurant of The Mustard Seed. Equally good and popular, they serve fantastic homemade comfort food—pizza, pasta, and burgers—in an ultra-modern townhouse (daily 12:00-22:00, similar specials, directly across the river at 15

Huntly Street, tel. 01463/259-119, www.kitchenrestaurant.co.uk).

Rajah Indian Restaurant provides a tasty break from meat and potatoes, with vegetarian options served in a classy red-velvet, white-linen atmosphere (£8-14 meals, 10 percent less for takeout, Mon-Sat 12:00-23:00, Sun 15:00-23:00, last dine-in order 30 minutes before closing, just off Church Street at 2 Post Office Avenue, tel. 01463/237-190).

The Joy of Taste serves up European cuisine along with altruism—a portion of their profits goes to charity, and volunteers (including local teachers and newspaper reporters) donate their time to fill shifts. The menu changes with the fancy of the chef, but usually includes staples such as steak, seafood, and slow-cooked shoulder of lamb (£5-7 lunch salads and sandwiches, £13/£16 early evening specials 17:30-18:45, £13-18 main dishes; open Mon-Sat 12:00-15:00 & 17:30-21:30, also open Sun late July-Sept; 25 Church Street, tel. 01463/241-459, www.thejoyoftaste.co.uk).

Leakey's Bookshop and Café, located in a converted church built in 1649, has the best lunch deal in town. Browse through stacks of musty old books and vintage maps, warm up by the wood-burning stove, and climb the spiral staircase to the loft for hearty homemade soups, sandwiches, and sweets (£3-4 light lunches, limited menu, Mon-Sat 10:00-16:30, bookstore stays open until 17:30, closed Sun, in Greyfriar's Hall on Church Street, tel. 01463/239-947, Charles Leakey).

Picnic: The **Marks & Spencer** food hall is best (you can't miss it—on the main pedestrian mall, near the Market Brae steps at the corner of the big Eastgate Shopping Centre; plastic utensils at the registers, Mon-Sat 8:00-18:00, Thu until 20:00, Sun 11:00-17:00, tel. 01463/224-844).

Inverness Connections

From Inverness by Train to: Pitlochry (every 1-2 hours, 1.5 hours), **Stirling** (every 1-2 hours, 2.75-3 hours, some transfer in Perth), **Kyle of Lochalsh** near Isle of Skye (4/day, 2.5 hours), **Edinburgh** (every 1-2 hours, 3.5-4 hours, some with change in Perth), **Glasgow** (11/day, 3 hours, 4 direct, the rest change in Perth). ScotRail does a great sleeper service to **London** (generally £140-190 for first class/single private compartment or £100-150 for standard class/twin shared compartment with breakfast, not available Sat night, www.firstscotrail.com). Consider dropping your car in Inverness and riding to London by train. Train info: tel. 0845-748-4950, www.nationalrail.co.uk.

By Bus: To reach most destinations in western Scotland, you'll first head for **Fort William** (10/day, 2 hours). To reach **Portree** on the Isle of Skye, you can either take the direct bus (3-4/

day, 3.25 hours), or transfer in Fort William. These buses are run by Scottish Citylink; for schedules, see www.citylink.co.uk. You can buy tickets in advance by calling Citylink at tel. 0871-266-3333 or stopping by the Inverness bus station (daily 8:45-17:30, £0.50 extra for credit cards, daily baggage storage-£4/bag, 2 blocks from train station on Margaret Street, tel. 01463/233-371). For bus travel to England, check National Express (www.nationalexpress.com) or Megabus (http://uk.megabus.com).

Route Tips for Drivers

Inverness to Edinburgh (150 miles, 3 hours minimum): Leaving Inverness, follow signs to the A-9 (south, toward Perth). If you haven't seen the Culloden Battlefield yet (described later), it's an easy detour: Just as you leave Inverness, head four miles east off the A-9 on the B-9006. Back on the A-9, it's a wonderfully speedy, scenic highway (A-9, M-90, A-90) all the way to Edinburgh. If you have time, consider stopping en route in Pitlochry (just off the A-9; see the Between Inverness and Edinburgh chapter).

To Oban, Glencoe, or Isle of Skye: See the "Route Tips for Drivers" at the end of the Oban and the Southern Highlands chapter.

Sights near Inverness

Inverness puts you in the heart of the Highlands, within easy striking distance of a gaggle of famous and worthwhile sights: Squint across Loch Ness looking for Nessie—or, if you're a skeptic, just appreciate the majesty of Britain's largest body of water (by volume). (I'm thankful the loch is in Scotland, where property laws make it extremely difficult to buy or build along its banks, and not in California.) Commune with the Scottish soul at the historic Culloden Battlefield, where Scottish, English, and world history reached a turning point. Ponder three mysterious Neolithic cairns, which remind visitors that Scotland's history goes back even before Braveheart. And enjoy a homey country castle at Cawdor.

Loch Ness

I'll admit it: I had my zoom lens out and my eyes on the water. The local tourist industry thrives on the legend of the Loch Ness Monster. It's a thrilling thought, and there have been several

Inverness & the Northern Highlands

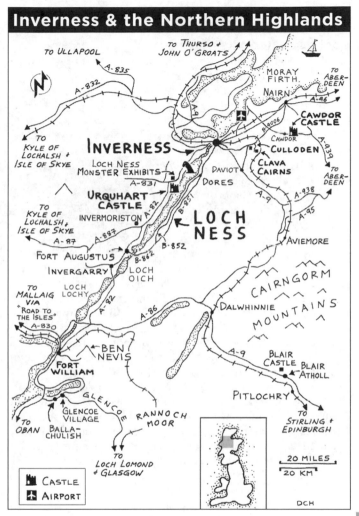

seemingly reliable "sightings" (by monks, police officers, and sonar images). But even if you ignore the monster stories, the loch is impressive: 23 miles long, less than a mile wide, the third-deepest in Europe (754 feet), and containing more water than in all the freshwater bodies of England and Wales combined.

Getting There: The Loch Ness sights are a quick drive southwest of Inverness. Various buses go from Inverness to Urquhart Castle and Drumnadrochit in about 35-40 minutes (buses #19, #19a, and #919, 8/day, fewer on Sun, figure £14 round-trip to Urquhart, confirm routes at Inverness bus station or TI).

Sights on Loch Ness

Loch Ness Monster Exhibits

In July of 1933, a couple swore that they saw a giant sea monster shimmy across the road in front of their car by Loch Ness. Within days, ancient legends about giant monsters in the lake (dating as far back as the sixth century) were revived—and suddenly everyone was spotting "Nessie" poke its head above the waters of Loch Ness. Further sightings and photographic "evidence" have bolstered the claim that there's something mysterious living in this unthinkably deep and murky lake. (Most sightings take place in the deepest part of the loch, near Urquhart Castle.) Most witnesses describe a waterbound dinosaur (resembling the real, but extinct, plesiosaur). Others cling to the slightly more plausible theory of a gigantic eel. And skeptics figure the sightings can be explained by a combination of reflections, boat wakes, and mass hysteria. The most famous photo of the beast (dubbed the "Surgeon's Photo") was later discredited—the "monster's" head was actually attached to a toy submarine. But that hasn't stopped various cryptozoologists from seeking photographic, sonar, and other proof.

And that suits the thriving local tourist industry just fine. The Nessie commercialization is so tacky that there are two different monster exhibits within 100 yards of each other, both in the town of Drumnadrochit. Each has a tour-bus parking lot and more square footage devoted to their kitschy shops than to the exhibits. The overpriced exhibitions are actually quite interesting—even though they're tourist traps, they'll appease that small part of you that knows the *real* reason you wanted to see Loch Ness.

▲Loch Ness Centre & Exhibition

This exhibit—the better option of the two—is headed by a naturalist who has spent many years researching lake ecology and scientific phenomena. With a 30-minute series of video bits and special effects, this exhibit explains the geological and historical environment that bred the monster story, as well as the various searches that have been conducted. Refreshingly, it retains an air of healthy skepticism instead of breathless monster-chasing. It also has some artifacts related to the search, such as a hippo-foot ashtray used to fake monster footprints and the *Viperfish*—a harpoon-equipped submarine used in a 1969 Nessie search.

Cost and Hours: £7, daily Easter-June and Sept-Oct 9:30-17:00, July-Aug 9:30-18:00, Nov-Easter 10:00-15:30, in the big

The Caledonian Canal

Two hundred million years ago two tectonic plates collided, creating the landmass we know as Scotland and leaving a crevice of thin lakes slashing right across the country. Called the Great Glen Fault, this diagonal slash across Scotland from Inverness to Oban is easily visible on any map.

Two hundred years ago, British engineer Thomas Telford connected the lakes with a series of canals so ships could avoid the long trip around the north of the country. The Caledonian Canal runs 62 miles from Scotland's east to west coasts, and 22 miles of it is man-made. Telford's great feat of engineering took 19 years to complete, opening in 1822 at a cost of one million pounds. But the timing was bad, and the canal was a disaster commercially. Napoleon's defeat in 1815 meant that ships could sail the seas more freely. And by the time the canal opened, commercial ships were generally too big for its 15-foot depths. Just a couple decades after the Caledonian Canal opened, the arrival of the train made the canal almost useless...except for Romantic Age tourism. From the time of Queen Victoria (who cruised the canal in 1873), the canal has been a popular tourist attraction. To this day the canal is a hit with vacationers, recreational boaters, and lock-keepers who compete for the best-kept lock.

The scenic drive from Inverness along the canal is entertaining, with Urquhart Castle (Nessie centers), Fort Augustus (five locks), and Fort William (under Ben Nevis, Neptune's

Staircase). You'll follow Telford's work—20 miles of canals and locks between three lakes, raising ships from sea level to 51 feet (Ness), 93 feet (Lochy), and 106 feet (Oich).

While "Neptune's Staircase," a series of eight locks near Fort William, has been cleverly named to sound intriguing, the best lock stop is midway, at Fort Augustus, where the canal hits the south end of Loch Ness. In Fort Augustus, the **Caledonian Canal Visitor Centre,** three locks above the main road, gives a good rundown on Telford's work (see page 229). Stroll past several shops and eateries to the top of the locks for a fine view.

Seven miles north in the town of Invermoriston is another Telford structure worthy of a quick detour—a stone bridge, dating from 1805, which spans the Morriston Falls as part of the original road. Look for a small parking lot just before the junction at A-82 and A-887, on your right as you drive from Fort Augustus. Carefully cross the A-82 and walk three minutes back the way you came. The bridge, which took eight years to build and is still in use today, is on your right.

stone mansion right on the main road to Inverness, tel. 01456/450-573, www.lochness.com.

Nessieland Castle Monster Centre

The other exhibit (up a side road closer to the town center, affiliated with a hotel) is less serious. It's basically a tacky high-school-quality photo report and a 30-minute *We Believe in the Loch Ness Monster* movie, which features credible-sounding locals explaining what they saw and a review of modern Nessie searches. (The most convincing reason for locals to believe: Look at the hordes of tourists around you.) It also has small exhibits on the area's history and on other "monsters" and hoaxes around the world.

Cost and Hours: £6, daily May-Sept 9:00-19:00, Oct-April 9:00-17:00, tel. 01456/450-342, www.loch-ness-monster-nessieland.com.

▲Urquhart Castle

The ruins at Urquhart (UR-kurt), just up the loch from the Nessie exhibits, are gloriously situated with a view of virtually the entire lake.

Cost and Hours: £8, guidebook-£4, daily April-Sept 9:30-18:00, Oct 9:30-17:00, Nov-March 9:30-16:30, last entry 45 minutes before closing, café, tel. 01456/450-551, www.historic-scotland.gov.uk.

Visiting the Castle: Its visitors center has a tiny exhibit with interesting castle artifacts and a good eight-minute film taking

you on a sweep through a thousand years of tumultuous history—from St. Columba's visit to the castle's final destruction in 1692. The castle itself, while dramatically situated and fun to climb through, is a relatively empty shell. After its English owners blew it up to keep the Jacobites from taking it, the largest medieval castle in Scotland (and the most important in the Highlands) wasn't considered worth rebuilding or defending, and was abandoned. Well-placed, descriptive signs help you piece together this once mighty fortress. As you walk toward the ruins, take a close look at the trebuchet (a working replica of one of the most destructive weapons of English King Edward I), and ponder how this giant slingshot helped Edward grab almost every castle in the country away from the native Scots.

NORTHERN HIGHLANDS

Fort Augustus

Perhaps the most idyllic stop along the Caledonian Canal is the little lochside town of Fort Augustus. It was founded in the 1700s—before there was a canal here—as part of a series of garrisons and military roads built by the English to quell the Highland clansmen, even as the Stuarts kept trying to take the throne in London. Before then, there were no developed roads in the Highlands—and without roads, it's hard to keep indigenous people down.

From 1725 to 1733 the English built 250 miles of hard roads and 40 bridges to open up the region; Fort Augustus was a central Highlands garrison at the southern tip of Loch Ness, designed to awe clansmen. It was named for William Augustus, Duke of Cumberland—notorious for his role in destroying the clan way of life in the Highlands. (When there's no media and no photographs to get in the way, ethnic cleansing has little effect on one's reputation.)

Fort Augustus makes for a delightful stop if you're driving through the area. Parking is easy. There are plenty of B&Bs, charming eateries, and an inviting park along the town's four lochs. You can still see the capstans, surviving from the days when the locks were cranked open by hand.

The fine little **Caledonian Canal Visitor Centre** nicely tells the story of the canal's construction (free, daily Easter-Oct 10:00-17:30, closed Nov-Easter, tel. 01320/366-493).

You can eat reasonably at eateries along the canal. If picnicking, pick up good sandwiches at the MacVean Supermarket. Their restaurant out back has peaceful tables overlooking the river (not the canal), where you can eat your grocery store purchases for just a few pence more than the grocery price.

Culloden Battlefield

Jacobite troops under Bonnie Prince Charlie were defeated at Culloden (kuh-LAW-dehn) by supporters of the Hanover dynasty (King George II's family) in 1746. This last major land battle fought on British soil spelled the end of Jacobite resistance and the beginning of the clan chiefs' fall from power. Wandering the desolate, solemn battlefield, you sense that something terrible occurred here. Locals still bring white roses and speak of "the '45" (as Bonnie Prince Charlie's entire campaign is called) as if it just happened. The battlefield at Culloden and its high-tech visitors center together are worth ▲▲▲.

NORTHERN HIGHLANDS

Orientation to Culloden

Cost and Hours: £10.50, daily April-May and Sept-Oct 9:00-17:30, June-Aug 9:00-18:00, Nov-Dec and Feb-March 10:00-16:00, closed Jan, last entry 30 minutes before closing.

Information: £5 guidebook, café, tel. 0844-493-2159, www.nts.org.uk/culloden.

Tours: Tours with live **guides** are included with your admission. Check for a schedule—there are generally 3-4/day, focusing on various aspects of the battle. **Audioguides** are free, with good information tied by GPS to important sites on the battlefield (pick up before 17:00 at the end of the indoor exhibit and return by 17:15; earlier off-season).

Getting There: It's a 15-minute **drive** east of Inverness. Follow signs to *Aberdeen,* then *Culloden Moor,* and the B-9006 takes you right there (well-signed on the right-hand side). Parking is £2. Public **buses** leave from Inverness' Queensgate Street and drop you off in front of the entrance (£3.60 round-trip ticket, bus #2B, roughly hourly, 40 minutes, ask at the TI for route/schedule updates and confirm that bus is going all the way to the battlefield).

Length of This Tour: Allow 2-2.5 hours.

Background

The Battle of Culloden (April 16, 1746) marks the end of the power of the Scottish Highland clans and the start of years of repression of Scottish culture by the English. It was the culmination of a year's worth of battles, known collectively as "the '45." At the center of it all was the charismatic, enigmatic Bonnie Prince Charlie (1720-1788).

Charles Edward Stuart, from his first breath, was raised with a single purpose—to restore his family to the British throne. His grandfather was King James II, deposed in 1688 by Parliament for his tyranny and pro-Catholic bias. In 1745, young Charlie crossed the Channel from exile in France to retake the throne for the Stuarts. He landed on the west coast of Scotland and rallied support for the "Jacobite" cause (from the Latin for "James"). Though Charles was not Scottish-born, he was the rightful heir directly down the line from Mary, Queen of Scots—and so many Scots joined the Stuart family's rebellion out of resentment at being ruled by a foreign king (English royalty of German descent).

Bagpipes droned, and "Bonnie" (beautiful) Charlie led an army of 2,000 tartan-wearing, Gaelic-speaking Highlanders across Scotland, seizing Edinburgh. They picked up other supporters of the Stuarts from the Lowlands and from England. Now 6,000 strong, they marched south toward London, and King George II made plans to flee the country. But anticipated support for the Jacobites failed to materialize in the numbers they were hoping for (both in England and from France). The Jacobites had so far been victorious in their battles against the Hanoverian government forces, but the odds now turned against them. Charles retreated to the Scottish Highlands, where many of his men knew the terrain and might gain an advantage when outnumbered. The English government troops followed closely on his heels.

Against the advice of his best military strategist, Charles' army faced the Hanoverian forces at Culloden Moor on flat, barren terrain that was unsuited to the Highlanders' guerrilla tactics. The Scots—many of them brandishing only broadswords and spears—were mowed down by English cannons and horsemen. In less than an hour, the government forces routed the Jacobite army, but that was just the start. They spent the next weeks methodically hunting down ringleaders and sympathizers (and many others in the Highlands who had nothing to do with the battle), ruthlessly killing, imprisoning, and banishing thousands.

Charles fled with a £30,000 price on his head. He escaped to the Isle of Skye, hidden by a woman named Flora MacDonald (her grave is on the Isle of Skye, and her statue is outside Inverness Castle). Flora dressed Charles in women's clothes and passed him off as her maid. Later, Flora was arrested and thrown in the Tower of London before being released and treated like a celebrity.

Charles escaped to France. He spent the rest of his life wandering Europe trying to drum up support to retake the throne. He drifted through short-lived romantic affairs and alcohol, and died in obscurity, without an heir, in Rome.

Though usually depicted as a battle of the Scottish versus the English, in truth Culloden was a civil war between two opposing dynasties: Stuart (Charlie) and Hanover (George). In fact, about one-fifth of the government's troops were Scottish, and several redcoat deserters fought along with the Jacobites. However, as the history has faded into lore, the battle has come to be remembered as a Scottish-versus-English standoff—or, in the parlance of the Scots, the Highlanders versus the Strangers.

The Battle of Culloden was the end of 60 years of Jacobite rebellions, the last major battle fought on British soil, and the final stand of the Highlanders. From then on, clan chiefs were deposed; kilts, tartans, and bagpipes became illegal paraphernalia; and farmers were cleared off their ancestral land, replaced by more-profitable sheep. Scottish culture would never recover from the events of the campaign called "the '45."

Self-Guided Tour

Culloden's visitors center, opened in 2008, is a state-of-the-art £10 million facility. The ribbon was cut by two young local men, each descended from soldiers who fought in the battle (one from either side). On the way up to the door, look under your feet at the memorial stones for fallen soldiers and clans, mostly purchased by their American and Canadian descendants. Your tour takes you through two sections: the exhibit and the actual battlefield.

The Exhibit

The initial part of the exhibit provides you with some background. As you pass the ticket desk, note the **family tree** of Bonnie Prince Charlie ("Prince Charles Edward") and George II, who were essentially distant cousins. Next you'll come across the first of the exhibit's shadowy-figure **touchscreens,** which connect you with historical figures who give you details from both the Hanoverian and Jacobite perspectives. A **map** here shows the other power struggles happening in and around Europe, putting this fight for political control of Britain in a wider context. This battle was no small regional skirmish, but rather a key part of a larger struggle between Britain and its neighbors, primarily France, for control over trade and colonial power. In the display case are **medals** from the early 1700s, made by both sides as propaganda.

Your path through this building is cleverly designed to echo the course of the Jacobite army. Your short march gets under way as Charlie sails from France to Scotland, then finagles the support of Highland clan chiefs. As he heads south with his army to take London, you, too, are walking south. Along the way, maps show the movement of troops, and wall panels cover the build-up to the attack, as seen from both sides. Note the clever division of information: To the left and in red is the story of the "government" (a.k.a. Hanoverians/Whigs/English, led by the Duke of Cumberland); to the right, in blue, is the Jacobites' perspective (Prince Charlie and his Highlander/French supporters).

But you, like Charlie, don't make it to London—in the dark room at the end, you can hear Jacobite commanders arguing over whether to retreat back to Scotland. Pessimistic about their chances of receiving more French support, they decide to U-turn, and so do you. Heading back up north, you'll get some insight into some of the strategizing that went on behind the scenes.

By the time you reach the end of the hall, it's the night before the battle. Round another bend into a dark passage, and listen to the voices of the anxious troops. While the English slept soundly in their tents (recovering from celebrating the Duke's 25th birthday), the scrappy and exhausted Jacobite Highlanders struggled through the night to reach the battlefield (abandoning their plan of a surprise attack at Nairn and instead retreating back toward Inverness).

At last the two sides meet. As you wait outside the theater for the next showing, study the chart depicting how the forces were arranged on the battlefield. Once inside the theater, you'll soon be surrounded by the views and sounds of a windswept moor. An impressive four-minute **360° movie** projects the re-enacted battle with you right in the center of the action (the violence is realistic; young kids should probably sit this one out). If it hasn't hit you already, the movie drives home how truly outmatched the Jacobites were, and what a hopeless and tragic day it was for them.

Leave the movie, then enter the last room. Here you'll find **period weapons,** including ammunition and artifacts found on the battlefield, as well as **historical depictions** of the battle. You'll also find a section describing the detective work required to piece together the story from historical evidence. On the far end is a huge map, with narration explaining the combat you've just experienced while giving you a bird's-eye view of the field through which you're about to roam.

The Battlefield

Collect your free **audioguide** and go outside. From the back wall of the visitors center, survey the battlefield. In the foreground is a cottage used as a makeshift hospital during the conflict (it's decorated as it would have been then). To the east (south of the River Nairn) is the site that Lord George Murray originally chose for the action. In the end, he failed to convince Prince Charlie of its superiority, and the battle was held here—with disastrous consequences. Although not far from Culloden, the River Nairn site was miles away tactically, and things might have turned out differently for the Jacobites had the battle taken place there instead.

Head left, down to the battlefield. Your GPS guide knows where you are, and the attendant will give you directions on where to start. As you walk along the path, stop each time you hear the "ping" sound (if you keep going, you'll confuse the satellite). The basic audioguide has 10 stops—including the Jacobite front line, the Hanoverian front line, and more—and takes a minimum of 30 minutes, which is enough for most people. At the third stop, you have the option of detouring along a larger loop (6 extra stops— figure another 30 minutes minimum) before rejoining the basic route. Each stop has additional information on everything from the Brown Bess musket to who was standing on what front line— how long this part of the tour takes depends on how much you want to hear. Notice how uneven and boggy the ground is in parts, and imagine trying to run across this hummocky terrain with all your gear, toward almost-certain death.

As you pass by the **mass graves,** marked by small headstones, realize that entire clans fought, died, and were buried together. (The fallen were identified by the clan badge on their caps.) The Mackintosh grave alone was 77 yards long.

When you've finished your walking tour, re-enter the hall, return your audioguide, then catch the last part of the exhibit, which covers the aftermath of the battle. As you leave the building, hang a left to see the wall of **protruding bricks,** each representing a soldier who died. The handful of Hanoverian casualties are on the left (about 50); the rest of the long wall's raised bricks represent the multitude of dead Jacobites (about 1,500).

If you're having trouble grasping the significance of this battle, play a game of "What if?" If Bonnie Prince Charlie had persevered on this campaign and taken the throne, he likely wouldn't have plunged Britain into the Seven Years' War with France (his ally). And increased taxes on either side of that war led directly to the French and American revolutions. So if the Jacobites had won...the American colonies might still be part of the British Empire today.

Clava Cairns

Scotland is littered with reminders of prehistoric peoples—especially along the coast of the Moray Firth—but the Clava Cairns are among the best-preserved, most interesting, and easiest to reach. You'll find them nestled in the spooky countryside just beyond Culloden Battlefield. These "Balnauran of Clava" are Neolithic burial chambers dating from 3,000 to 4,000 years ago. Although they appear to be just some giant piles  of rocks in a sparsely forested clearing, they warrant a closer look to appreciate the prehistoric logic behind them. (The site is well-explained by informative plaques.) There are three structures: a central "ring cairn" with an open space in the center but no access to it, flanked by two "passage cairns," which were once covered. The entrance shaft in each passage cairn lines up with the setting sun at the winter solstice. Each cairn is surrounded by a stone circle, injecting this site with even more mystery.

Cost and Hours: Free, always open.

Getting There: Just after passing Culloden Battlefield on the B-9006 (coming from Inverness), signs on the right point to *Clava Cairns*. Follow this twisty road to the free parking lot by the stones. You can also walk from Culloden Battlefield (the Inverness

TI has maps as well as information on the Cairns; about 3 miles round-trip). Skip the cairns if you don't have a car or if the weather is bad.

Cawdor Castle

Homey and intimate, this castle is still the residence of the Dowager (read: widow) Countess of Cawdor, a local aristocratic

branch of the Campbell family. The castle's claim to fame is its connection to Shakespeare's *Macbeth*, in which the three witches correctly predict that the protagonist will be granted the title "Thane of Cawdor." The castle is not used as a setting in the play —which takes place in Inverness, 300 years before this castle was built—but Shakespeare's dozen or so references to "Cawdor" are enough for the marketing machine to kick in. Today, virtually nothing tangibly ties Cawdor to the Bard or to the real-life Macbeth. But even if you ignore the Shakespeare lore, the castle is worth a visit.

Cost and Hours: £9.75, good £5 guidebook explains the family and the rooms, May-Sept daily 10:00-17:30, last entry at 17:00, gardens open until 18:00, closed Oct-April, tel. 01667/404-401, www.cawdorcastle.com.

Getting There: It's on the B-9090, just off the A-96, about 15 miles east of Inverness (6 miles beyond Culloden and the Clava Cairns). Public transportation no longer goes to Cawdor Church, making it difficult to visit without a car.

Visiting the Castle: The chatty, friendly docents (including Jean at the front desk, who can say "welcome" and "mind your head" in 60 different languages) give the castle an air of intimacy—most are residents of the neighboring village of Cawdor and act as though they're old friends with the Dowager Countess (many probably are). Entertaining posted explanations—written by the countess' late husband, the sixth Earl of Cawdor—bring the castle to life and make you wish you'd known the old chap. While many of today's castles are still residences for the aristocracy, Cawdor feels even more lived-in than the norm—you can imagine the Dowager Countess stretching out in front of the fireplace with a good book. Notice her geraniums in every room.

Stops on the tour include a tapestry-laden bedroom and a "tartan passage" speckled with modern paintings. In another bedroom (just before the stairs back down) is a tiny pencil sketch by Salvador Dalí. Inside the base of the tower, near the end of the tour, is the castle's proud symbol: a holly tree dating from 1372. According to the beloved legend, a donkey leaned against this tree to mark the spot where the castle was to be built—which it was, around the tree. (The tree is no longer alive, but its withered trunk is still propped up in the same position. No word on the donkey.)

The **gardens,** included with the ticket, are also worth exploring, with some 18th-century linden trees, a hedge maze (not open to the public), and several surprising species (including sequoia and redwood). In May and June, the laburnum arbors drip with yellow blossoms.

The nine-hole **golf course** on the castle grounds is bigger than pitch-and-putt and plenty of fun even for non-golfers (£12.50/person; golf shack staff generally include clubs and balls without an extra rental fee).

Nearby: The close but remote-feeling **village of Cawdor**—with a few houses, a village shop, and a tavern—is also worth a look if you've got time to kill.

BETWEEN INVERNESS AND EDINBURGH

Pitlochry • Stirling

 To break up the trip between Inverness and Edinburgh (3 hours by car, 3.5 hours by train), consider stopping over at one of these two worthwhile destinations. The town of Pitlochry, right on the train route, mixes whisky and hillwalking with a dash of countryside charm. Farther south, the historic city of Stirling boasts an impressive castle, a monument to a Scottish hero (William "Braveheart" Wallace), and one of the country's most important battle sites (Bannockburn).

Planning Your Time

Visiting both Pitlochry and Stirling on a one-day drive from Inverness to Edinburgh is doable but busy (especially since part of Pitlochry's allure is slowing down to taste the whisky).

Pleasant Pitlochry is well-located, a quick detour off the main A-9 highway from Inverness to Edinburgh (via Perth) or an easy stop for train travelers. The town deserves an overnight for whisky-lovers, or for those who really want to relax in small-town Scotland. Though many find the town of Pitlochry appealing, it lacks the rugged Highlands scenery and easy access to other major sights found in Oban and Glencoe.

Stirling, off the busy A-9/M-9 motorway between Perth and Edinburgh, is well worth a sightseeing stop, especially for historians and romantics interested in Scottish history. (If skipping Stirling, notice that you can take the M-90 due south over the Firth of Forth to connect Perth and Edinburgh.) Stirling also works well as a stop-off between Edinburgh and points west (such as Glasgow or Oban)—just take the northern M-9/A-80 route instead of the more direct M-8.

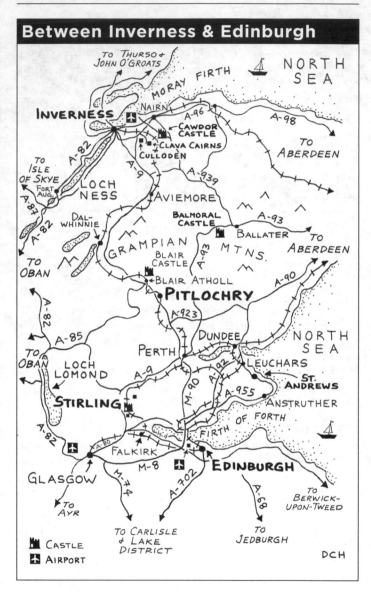

Between Inverness & Edinburgh

TO THURSO &
JOHN O'GROATS

MORAY FIRTH

NORTH SEA

INVERNESS

NAIRN

A-96

A-98

CAWDOR CASTLE

TO ABERDEEN

A-82

A-9

CLAVA CAIRNS

CULLODEN

A-939

TO ISLE OF SKYE

FORT AUG.

LOCH NESS

AVIEMORE

A-87

A-82

DAL-WHINNIE

BALMORAL CASTLE

A-93

BALLATER

TO ABERDEEN

TO OBAN

GRAMPIAN

A-93

MTNS.

BLAIR CASTLE

BLAIR ATHOLL

PITLOCHRY

A-90

A-923

A-82

DUNDEE

NORTH SEA

A-85

PERTH

LEUCHARS

TO OBAN

LOCH LOMOND

A-9

A-92

A-90

ST. ANDREWS

A-955

ANSTRUTHER

STIRLING

FIRTH OF FORTH

A-82

A-80

FALKIRK

M-8

EDINBURGH

A-702

A-68

GLASGOW

M-74

TO AYR

TO BERWICK-UPON-TWEED

TO CARLISLE & LAKE DISTRICT

TO JEDBURGH

DCH

🏰 CASTLE
✈ AIRPORT

PITLOCHRY

Pitlochry

This likable tourist town, famous for its whisky and its hillwalking (both beloved by Scots), makes an enjoyable overnight stop

on the way between Inverness and Edinburgh. Just outside the craggy Highlands, Pitlochry is set amid pastoral rolling hills that offer plenty of forest hikes (brochures at TI). A salmon ladder climbs alongside the lazy river (free viewing area—salmon can run April-Oct, best in May and June, 10-minute walk from town).

Orientation to Pitlochry

Plucky little Pitlochry (pop. 2,500) lines up along its tidy, tourist-minded main road, where you'll find the train station, bus stops, TI, and bike rental. The town exists thanks to the arrival of the train, which conveniently brought Romantic Age tourists from the big cities to the south with this lovely bit of Scotland. Queen Victoria herself visited three times in the 1860s, putting Pitlochry on the tourist map. The Victorian architecture on the main street makes it clear that this was a delightful escape for city folks back in the 19th century. The River Tummel runs parallel to the main road, a few steps away. Most distilleries are a short drive out of town, but you can walk to the two best (see my self-guided hill-walk). Navigate easily by following the black directional signs to Pitlochry's handful of sights.

Tourist Information

The helpful TI provides bus and train schedules, has Internet access, and books rooms for a £4 fee. It sells maps for local hill-walks and scenic drives, including the £1 *Pitlochry Path Network* brochure, which has a handy map and is a good guide (July-early Sept Mon-Sat 9:00-18:30, Sun 9:30-17:30; April-June and early-Sept-Oct Mon-Sat 9:30-17:30, Sun 10:00-16:00; Nov-March Mon-Sat 9:30-16:30, closed Sun; exit from station and follow small road to the right with trains behind you, turn right on Atholl Road, and walk 5 minutes to TI on left, at #22; tel. 01796/472-215, www.perthshire.co.uk, pitlochry@visitscotland.com).

Helpful Hint

Bike Rental: Escape Route Bikes, located across the street and a
  block from the TI (away from town), rents a variety of bikes for
  adults and kids (£16-35/5 hours, £25-40/24 hours, price varies
  by type of bike and includes helmet and lock if you ask, Mon-
  Sat 9:00-17:30, Sun 10:00-17:00, shorter hours and sometimes
  closed Thu in winter, 3 Atholl Road, tel. 01796/473-859, www
  .escape-route.co.uk).

Self-Guided Hillwalk

Pitlochry Whisky Walk

You can spend an enjoyable afternoon hillwalking from downtown
Pitlochry to a pair of top distilleries. The entire loop trip takes two
to three hours, depending on how long you linger in the distilleries
(at least 45 minutes to an hour of walking each way). It's a good
way to see some green rolling hills, especially if you've only experienced urban Scotland. The walk is largely uphill on the way to the
Edradour Distillery; wear good shoes, bring a rain jacket just in
case, and be happy that you'll stroll easily downhill *after* you've had
your whisky samples.

At the TI, pick up the *Pitlochry Path Network* brochure. You'll
be taking the **Edradour Walk** (marked on directional signs with
the yellow hiker icons; on the map it's a series of yellow dots). Leave
the TI and head left along the busy A-924. The walk can be done
by going either direction, but I'll describe it counterclockwise.

Within 10 minutes, you'll come to **Bell's Blair Athol
Distillery.** If you're a whisky buff, stop in here (described later,
under "Sights in Pitlochry"). Otherwise, hold out for the much
more atmospheric Edradour. After passing a few B&Bs and sub-
urban homes, you'll see a sign (marked *Edradour Walk*) on the left
side of the road, leading you up and off the highway. You'll come
to a clearing, and as the road gets steeper, you'll see signs directing
you 50 yards off the main path to see the "Black Spout"—a wonderful waterfall well worth a few extra steps.

At the top of the hill, you'll arrive in another clearing, where
a narrow path leads along a field. Low rolling hills surround you in
all directions. It seems like there's not another person around for
miles, with just the thistles to keep you company. It's an easy 20
minutes to the distillery from here.

Stop into the **Edradour Distillery** (also described later).
After the tour, leave the distillery, heading right, following the
paved road (Old North Road). In about five minutes, there's a sign
that seems to point right into the field. Take the small footpath
that runs along the left side of the road. (If you see the driveway
with stone lions on both sides, you've gone a few steps too far.)

You'll walk parallel to the route you took getting to the distillery, and then you'll head back into the forest. Cross the footbridge and make a left (as the map indicates), staying on the wide road. You'll pass a B&B and hear traffic noises as you emerge out of the forest. The trail leads back to the highway, with the TI a few blocks ahead on the right.

Sights in Pitlochry

Distillery Tours
The cute **Edradour Distillery** (ED-rah-dower), the smallest in Scotland, takes pride in making its whisky with a minimum of machinery. Small white-and-red build-

ings are nestled in an impossibly green Scottish hillside. Wander through the buildings and take the £7.50 guided tour (2-3/hour in summer, 1/hour in winter, 60 minutes). They offer a 10-minute video and, of course, a free sample dram. Unlike the bigger distilleries, they allow you to take photos of the equipment. If you like the whisky, buy some here and support the Pitlochry economy—this is one of the few independently owned distilleries left in Scotland (May-Oct Mon-Sat 10:00-17:00, Sun 12:00-17:00; Nov-April Mon-Sat 10:00-16:00, Sun 12:00-16:00 except Nov-Feb, when it's closed on Sun; last tour departs one hour before closing, tel. 01796/472-095, www.edradour.com). Most come to the distillery by car (follow signs from the main road, 2.5 miles into the countryside), but you can also get there on a peaceful hiking trail that you'll have all to yourself (follow my "Pitlochry Whisky Walk," earlier).

The big, ivy-covered **Bell's Blair Athol Distillery** is more conveniently located (about a half-mile from the town center) and more corporate-feeling, offering 45-minute tours with a wee taste at the end (£6.50, Easter-Oct tours depart 2/hour daily 10:00-17:00, July-Aug until 17:30, possibly closed Sun in spring, last tour departs one hour before closing; shorter hours, fewer tours, and closed Sat-Sun off-season; tel. 01796/482-003, www.discovering-distilleries.com/blairathol).

Pitlochry Power Station
The station's visitors center, adjacent to the salmon ladder, offers a mildly entertaining exhibit about hydroelectric power in the region.

Cost and Hours: Free, salmon viewing and exhibit open April-Oct Mon-Fri 10:00-17:00, closed Sat-Sun except Bank

Holidays and in July-Aug, closed Nov-March, tel. 01796/473-152.

Getting There: Walkers can reach this easily in about 15 minutes by crossing the footbridge from the town center. Drivers will head east out of town (toward Bell's Blair Athol Distillery), then turn right on Bridge Road, cross the river, and backtrack to the power station.

Pitlochry Festival Theatre

From about May through October, this theater presents a different play every night and concerts on some Sundays (tickets cost £15-28 for Mon-Thu shows and Sat matinee, £18-33 for Fri-Sat shows; purchase tickets online, by phone, or in person; visit Just the Ticket, in town at 89 Atholl Road, or the theater—same price, box office open daily 10:00-20:00, restaurant, tel. 01796/484-626, www.pitlochryfestivaltheatre.com).

Explorers Garden

Adjacent to the theater, this six-acre woodland garden features plants and wildflowers from around the world.

Cost and Hours: £4, April-Oct daily 10:00-17:00, last entry at 16:15, tel. 01796/484-626, www.explorersgarden.com.

John Muir Exhibit

On the main street in the center of town is **The Wild Space**, established to raise awareness of the John Muir Trust and the man who inspired it. Muir (1838-1914) was born in Scotland, moved to the US when he was 10, and later helped establish the world's first national park system in the US. There's a tiny exhibit with a feel-good nature video and a small art gallery.

Cost and Hours: Free, Mon and Wed-Sat 10:00-16:00, closed Tue, off the A-9 at corner of Station and Atholl roads, www.jmt.org.

Northeast of Pitlochry

Balmoral Castle

The Queen stays at her 50,000-acre private estate, located within Cairngorms National Park, from August through early October. The grounds and the castle's ballroom are open to visitors part of the year, but they're overpriced.

Cost and Hours: £10, includes audioguide, April-July daily 10:00-17:00, closed Aug-March, last entry 30 minutes before closing, tel. 013397/42534, www.balmoralcastle.com.

Getting There: Balmoral is on the A-93, midway between Ballater and Braemar, about 50 miles northeast of Pitlochry and about 75 miles southeast of Inverness.

Nearby: For a free peek at another royal landmark, stop at **Crathie Kirk,** the small but charming parish church where the royal family worships when they are at Balmoral, and where Queen

Victoria's beloved servant John Brown is buried. The church is just across the highway from the Balmoral parking lot.

Sleeping in Pitlochry

$$ Craigroyston House is a quaint, large Victorian country house with eight Laura Ashley-style bedrooms, run by charming Gretta and Douglas Maxwell (Db-£94 July-Sept, less off-season, family room, cash only, Wi-Fi, above and behind the TI—small gate at back of parking lot—and next to the church at 2 Lower Oakfield, tel. 01796/472-053, www.craigroyston.co.uk, reservations@craig royston.co.uk).

$ Pitlochry's fine **hostel** has 53 beds in 12 rooms, including some private and family rooms. It's on Knockard Road, well-signed from the town center, about a five-minute walk above the main drag and offering nice views (£18 bunks in 3- to 6-bed rooms, Db-£60; £2 more for non-members, breakfast-£5-6, packed lunch-£5.50, closed Nov-Feb, pay guest computer, pay Wi-Fi, self-service laundry, kitchen, office open 7:00-10:00 & 16:30-23:00, tel. 01796/472-308, www.syha.org.uk, pitlochry@syha.org.uk).

Eating in Pitlochry

Plenty of options line the main drag, including several bakeries selling picnic supplies. For a heartier meal, try **Victoria's** restaurant and coffee shop, located midway between the train station and the TI (£6-10 sandwiches, £10-11 pizzas, £10-16 lunches, £13-25 dinners, daily 10:00-20:30, patio seating, free Wi-Fi, at corner of memorial garden, 45 Atholl Road, tel. 01796/472-670), or **Fern Cottage,** just behind Victoria's (pre-theater £18-22 dinner specials 17:30-18:45, Ferry Road, tel. 01796/473-840). **Port-na-Craig Inn** is a fancy option on the river, just downhill from the theater (tel. 01796/472-777).

Pitlochry Connections

The train station is open Monday to Saturday 8:00-18:30 and Sunday 10:30-18:00 (may have shorter hours in winter).

From Pitlochry by Train to: Inverness (every 1.5-2 hours, 1.5 hours), **Stirling** (every 1.5-2 hours, 1.25 hours, some transfer in Perth), **Edinburgh** (8/day direct, 2 hours), **Glasgow** (9/day, 1.75-2 hours, some transfer in Perth). Train info: tel. 08457-484-950, www.nationalrail.co.uk.

Stirling

Once the Scottish capital, the quaint city of Stirling (pop. 41,000) is a mini-Edinburgh with lots of character and a dramatic castle dripping with history and boasting sweeping views. Just outside of town are the William Wallace Monument, honoring the real-life Braveheart, and the Bannockburn Heritage Centre, marking the site of Robert the Bruce's victorious battle.

Orientation to Stirling

Stirling's old town is situated along a long, narrow, steep hill, with the castle at its apex. The old town feels like Edinburgh's Royal Mile—only steeper, shorter, and less touristy. From the castle it's a long, steep 10-block descent before you hit the thriving commercial district.

Tourist Information: The TI is near the base of the old town, just inside the gates of the touristy Old Town Jail attraction (daily 10:00-17:00, Internet access—£1/20 minutes, St. Johns Street, tel. 01786/475-019, stirling@visitscotland.com).

Getting Around: The city's three main sights (Stirling Castle, the Wallace Monument, and the Bannockburn Heritage Centre) are difficult to reach by foot from the center of town, but are easily accessible by frequent public bus (the bus station is a short walk from the train station) or by taxi (about £5 to each one).

Sights in Stirling

▲Stirling Castle

"He who holds Stirling, holds Scotland." These fateful words have proven, more often than not, to be true. Stirling Castle's strategic position—perched on a volcanic crag overlooking a bridge over the River Forth, the primary passage between the Lowlands and the Highlands—has long been the key to Scotland. This castle of the Stuart kings is one of Scotland's most historic and popular. Offering spectacular views over a gentle countryside, and an interesting exhibit inside, Stirling is worth a look.

Cost and Hours: £14, daily April-Sept 9:30-18:00, Oct-March 9:30-17:00, last entry 45 minutes before closing, Regimental Museum closes 45 minutes before castle, café.

Information: Tel. 01786/450-000, www.stirlingcastle.gov.uk.

Tours: Posted information is skimpy, so consider a tour or audioguide to help bring the site to life. You can take the included 45-minute **guided tour** (generally hourly 10:00-16:00, less off-season, depart from the well outside the Fort Major's House), or rent the £3 **audioguide**. Docents posted throughout can tell you more.

Getting There: Similar to Edinburgh's castle, Stirling Castle sits at the very tip of a steep old town. If you enter Stirling by car, follow the *Stirling Castle* signs uphill through town to the esplanade, and park at the £4 lot just outside the castle gate. In summer, there's a park-and-ride option: Leave your car at the Castleview Park-and-Ride off the A-84 and hop on the shuttle bus (£1 round-trip, runs June-Sept 7:30-18:00, 15-minute ride). Without a car, you can hike the 20-minute uphill route from the train or bus station to the castle, or take a taxi (about £5).

Background: Stirling marks the site of two epic medieval battles where famous Scotsmen defeated huge English armies despite terrible odds: In 1297, William Wallace (a.k.a. "Braveheart") fended off an invading English army at the Battle of Stirling Bridge. And in 1314, Robert the Bruce won the battle of nearby Bannockburn. Soon after, the castle became the primary residence of the Stuart monarchs, who turned it into a showpiece of Scotland (and a symbol of one-upmanship against England). But when the Crown moved to London, Stirling's prominence waned. The military, which took over the castle during the Jacobite Wars of the 18th century, bulked it up and converted it into a garrison—destroying its delicate beauty. While restored now, it feels new, with almost no historic artifacts.

◉ Self-Guided Tour: My tour covers the castle's top spots. Begin on the esplanade, just outside the castle entrance, with its grand views.

The Esplanade: Spectacularly set on a volcanic crag to oversee the place where the Lowlands meet the Highlands, Stirling Castle was the preferred home of Scottish kings and queens in the Middle Ages.

But because of its strategic setting, the castle had to weather lots of sieges. Two of the most important battles in Scottish history were fought within sight of its ramparts: Stirling Bridge (1297) and Bannockburn (1314). A statue of the hero of Bannockburn, King Robert the Bruce, stands strong on the esplanade, as if still rallying his people. The fortified grand entry showed all who approached that James IV (r. 1488-1513) was a great ruler with a powerful castle.

Stirling Castle's glory days were in the 16th century, when it provided a splendid showcase for the Stuart court. It last saw action when besieged by Jacobite forces in 1746. After the end of the Scottish threat, it became a British garrison, home base of the Argyll and Sutherland regiments. It still flies the Union Jack of Great Britain. Its esplanade, a military parade ground in the 19th century, is a tour-bus parking lot in the 21st century.

Entry and Castle Exhibition: Just inside the gate, buy your ticket (ask about tour times, and consider renting the audioguide). Pass through the inner gate, then follow the passage to the left into a delightful grassy courtyard called the Queen Anne Garden. This was the royal family's playground in the 1600s. Imagine doing a little lawn bowling with the queen here.

In the casemates (from 1710) lining the garden is the Castle Exhibition. Its "Come Face to Face with 1000 Years of History" exhibit provides an entertaining and worthwhile introduction to the castle. The video leaves you thinking that re-enactors of Jacobite struggles are even more spirited than our Civil War re-enactors.

• *Return to the Outer Close (where you'll notice the Grand Battery, with its cannons and rampart views and, underneath that, the Great Kitchens). We'll see both of those at the end of this walk. Now, turn left and hike up through the main gateway and into the center of the castle, the Inner Close.*

Inner Close: Standing at the center of Stirling Castle, you're surrounded by Scottish history. This courtyard was the core of the 12th-century castle and continued to be its center as new buildings were added.

Notice the Renaissance statues looking down on the castle courtyard from royal apartments. In 1540 King James V, inspired by French Renaissance châteaus he'd seen, had the castle covered with about 200 statues and busts to "proclaim the peace, prosperity and justice of his reign" and to validate his rule. Imagine the impression all these classical gods and goddesses had on visitors. The message: James' rule was a Golden Age for Scotland.

Each of the very different buildings in this complex was constructed by a different monarch. While all are historic, they are entirely rebuilt and none have the patina of age. Facing downhill, you'll see the Great Hall. The Chapel Royal, where Mary, Queen of Scots was crowned in 1543, is to your left. The Royal Palace with the Royal Apartments is to your right. The Stirling Heads Gallery is above that. And behind you is the Regimental Museum.

The Great Hall: Step inside the largest secular space in medieval Scotland. Dating from around 1500, this was a grand setting for the great banquets of Scotland's Renaissance kings. The impressive hammerbeam roof is a modern reconstruction, modeled on the early 16th-century roof at Edinburgh Castle.

The Chapel Royal: One of the first Protestant churches built in Scotland, the Chapel Royal was constructed in 1594 by James VI for the baptism of his first son, Prince Henry. The faint painted frieze high up survives from Charles I's coronation visit to Scotland in 1633. Clearly the holiness of the chapel ended in the 1800s when the army moved in.

The Royal Palace and Royal Apartments: Within the palace you can visit six ground-floor apartments, colorfully done up as they might have looked in the mid-16th century when James V and his queen, Mary of Guise, lived here. Costumed performers play the role of palace attendants, happy to chat with you about medieval life. Notice the 60 carved and colorfully painted oak medallions on the ceiling in the king's presence chamber. The medallions are carved with the faces of Scottish and European royalty. These are copies, painstakingly reconstructed after expert research—you'll soon see the originals up close in the Stirling Heads Gallery.

• *Outside the apartments, a staircase leads up to...*

The Stirling Heads Gallery: This is, for me, the castle's highlight—a chance to see the originals of the elaborately carved and painted portrait medallions that decorated the ceiling of the king's presence chamber.

Regimental Museum: At the top of the Inner Close, in the King's Old Building, is the excellent **Argyll and Sutherland Highlanders Museum.** Another highlight of the castle, it's barely mentioned in castle promotional material because it's run by a different organization. With lots of tartans, tassels, and swords, it shows how the spirit of Scotland was absorbed by Britain. The "In the Trenches" exhibit is a powerful look at World War I, with accounts from the battlefield. The two regiments, established in the 1790s to defend Britain in the Napoleonic age and combined in the 1880s, have served with distinction in over two centuries of British military campaigns. Their pride shows here in the building that's their headquarters, where they've been stationed since 1881.

Rampart Walk to the Kitchen: The skinny lane between church and museum leads to the secluded Douglas Gardens at the rock's highest point. From here you can walk the ramparts downhill to the Grand Battery, with its cannon rampart at the Outer Close. As you stroll the ramparts, look across the valley at the dramatic lone tower—the National Wallace Monument. The Outer Close was the service zone, with a well and the kitchen (below the cannon rampart). The great banquets of James VI didn't happen all by themselves, as you'll appreciate when you explore the fine medieval kitchen exhibit (where mannequin cooks oversee medieval recipes).

• *Your castle visit ends here, but your castle ticket includes Argyll's Lodging, a fortified noble mansion (described next).*

Argyll's Lodging

Just below the castle esplanade and across the street is a 17th-century nobleman's fortified mansion. European noblemen wanted to live near power—such as this spot below the king's palace, where the Earl of Argyll's family resided for about a century. Its hours are erratic—and you must book a tour at the castle beforehand (most likely open in peak season, June-Aug). While Stirling Castle is pretty sterile, Argyll's Landing is less so and worth a few minutes.

▲William Wallace Monument

Commemorating the Scottish hero better known to Americans as "Braveheart," this sandstone tower—built during a wave of

Scottish nationalism in the mid-19th century—marks the Abbey Craig hill on the outskirts of Stirling. This is where Wallace gathered forces for his largest-scale victory against England's King Edward I, in 1297: the Battle of Stirling Bridge. The victory was a huge boost to the Scottish cause, but England came back to beat the Scots the next year.

Cost and Hours: £8.50, audioguide-£1, daily July-Aug 10:00-18:00, April-June and Sept-Oct 10:00-17:00, Nov-March 10:30-16:00, last entry 45 minutes before closing, café and gift shop, tel. 01786/472-140, www.nationalwallacemonument.com.

Getting There: It's two miles northeast of Stirling on the A-8, signposted from the city center. You can catch a public bus from the Stirling bus station (a short walk south of the train station) to the monument's parking lot (several buses run on this route, 10/hour, 9-15 minutes). Taxis cost about £5-7. From the parking lot's Visitors Pavilion, you'll need to hike (a very steep 10 minutes) or take a shuttle bus up the hill to the monument itself.

Visiting the Monument: From the base of the monument, you can see Stirling Bridge—a stone version that replaced the original wooden one. Looking out from the same vantage point as Wallace, imagine how the famous battle played out, and consider why the location was so important in the battle (explained in more detail inside the monument).

After entering the monument, pick up the worthwhile audioguide. You'll first encounter a passionate talking Wallace replica, explaining his defiant stand against Edward I. As you listen, ogle Wallace's five-and-a-half-foot-long broadsword (and try to imagine drawing it from a scabbard on your back at a dead run). Then take a spin through a hall of other Scottish heroes. Finally, climb the 246 narrow steps inside the tower for grand views. The stairways are extremely tight and require some maneuvering—claustrophobes be warned.

▲Bannockburn Heritage Centre

Just to the south of Stirling proper is the newly rebuilt Bannock-burn Heritage Centre, commemorating what many Scots view as their nation's most significant military victory over the invading English: the Battle of Bannockburn, won by a Scottish army led by Robert the Bruce against England's King Edward II in 1314. The new and improved center is closed through March of 2014, when it reopens for the battle's 700th anniversary. Later in 2014, on September 18, Scotland will vote on a referendum for complete independence from England.

Cost and Hours: Likely £10, check online or call ahead; closed until March 2014, after that open March-Oct daily 10:00-17:30, Nov-Feb daily 10:00-17:00; café, tel. 0844/493-2139, www.nts.org.uk.

Anniversary Events: Major celebrations marking the battle's 700th anniversary will be held June 28-30, 2014. A re-enactment of the Battle of Bannockburn is planned, with 15,000 people expected to attend each of the three days (£22, requires advance purchase, heritage center not open during re-enactment except for those with special £83 King's Ticket, see www.battleofbannock burn.com for more information).

Getting There: It's two miles south of Stirling on the A-872, off the M-80/M-9. For non-drivers, it's an easy bus ride from the Stirling bus station (a short walk south from the train station; several buses run on this route, 8/hour, 9-15 minutes).

Visiting Bannockburn Heritage Centre: The rebuilt center will feature an interactive 3-D battle simulation and a short 360-degree film, along with audio narrations from fictional combatants and bystanders.

In simple terms, Robert—who was first and foremost a politician—found himself out of political options after years of failed diplomatic attempts to make peace with the strong-arming English. William Wallace's execution left a vacuum in military leadership, and eventually Robert stepped in, waging a successful guerrilla campaign that came to a head as young Edward's army marched to Stirling. Although the Scots were greatly outnumbered, their strategy and use of terrain at Bannockburn allowed them to soundly beat the English and drive Edward out of Scotland for the time being.

This victory is so legendary among the Scots that the country's unofficial national anthem, "Flower of Scotland"—written 600 years after the battle—focuses on this one event. (CDs with a version of this song performed by The Corries can be purchased at the heritage center. Buy one and learn the song, and you might soon find yourself singing along at a pub.)

Stirling Connections

From Stirling by Train to: Edinburgh (roughly 2/hour, 1 hour), **Glasgow** (3/hour, 30-45 minutes), **Pitlochry** (every 1.5-2 hours, 1.25 hours, some transfer in Perth), **Inverness** (every 1.5-2 hours, 2.75-3 hours, some transfer in Perth). Train info: tel. 08457-484-950, www.nationalrail.co.uk.

PRACTICALITIES

This section covers just the basics on traveling in Scotland (for much more information, see *Rick Steves' Great Britain*). You can find free advice on specific topics at www.ricksteves.com/tips.

Money

For currency, Scotland uses the pound sterling (£), also called a "quid": 1 pound (£1) = about $1.60. One pound is broken into 100 pence (p). To convert prices in pounds to dollars, add about 60 percent: £20 = about $32, £50 = about $80. (Check www.oanda.com for the latest exchange rates.)

Like England, Scotland issues its own pound notes. Scottish pounds are technically interchangeable across Great Britain but sometimes are not accepted by businesses in England. Banks in Scotland or England can convert your Scottish pounds into English pounds at no charge.

The standard way for travelers to get pounds is to withdraw money from ATMs (which locals call "cashpoints") using a debit card, ideally with a Visa or MasterCard logo. Before departing, call your bank or credit-card company: Confirm that your card(s) will work overseas, ask about international transaction fees, and alert them that you'll be making withdrawals in Europe. Also ask for the PIN number for your credit card in case it'll help you use Europe's "chip-and-PIN" payment machines (see below); allow time for your bank to mail your PIN to you. To keep your valuables safe, wear a money belt.

Dealing with "Chip and PIN": Much of Europe—including Great Britain—is adopting a "chip-and-PIN" system for credit cards, and some merchants rely on it exclusively. European chip-and-PIN cards are embedded with an electronic chip in addition to the magnetic stripe used on our American-style cards. This means that your credit (and debit) card might not work at payment machines, such as those at train and subway stations, toll roads, parking garages, luggage lockers, and self-serve gas pumps. Memorizing your credit card's PIN lets you use it at some chip-and-PIN machines—just enter your PIN when prompted. If a payment machine won't take your card, look for a machine that takes cash or see if there's a cashier nearby who can process your transaction. Often the easiest solution is to pay for your purchases with cash you've withdrawn from an ATM using your debit card (Europe's ATMs still accept magnetic-stripe cards).

Phoning

Smart travelers use the telephone to reserve or reconfirm rooms, reserve restaurants, get directions, research transportation connections, confirm tour times, phone home, and lots more.

To call Great Britain from the US or Canada: Dial 011-44 and then the area code (minus its initial zero) and local number. (The 011 is our international access code, and 44 is Great Britain's country code.)

To call Great Britain from a European country: Dial 00-44 followed by the area code (minus its initial zero) and local number. (The 00 is Europe's international access code.)

To call within Great Britain: If you're dialing within an area code, just dial the local number; but if you're calling outside your area code, you have to dial both the area code (which starts with a 0) and the local number.

To call from Great Britain to another country: Dial 00 followed by the country code (for example, 1 for the US or Canada), then the area code and number. If you're calling European countries whose phone numbers begin with 0, you'll usually have to omit that 0 when you dial.

Tips on Phoning: A mobile phone—whether an American one that works in Great Britain, or a European one you buy when you arrive—is handy, but can be pricey. If traveling with a smartphone, switch off data-roaming until you have free Wi-Fi. With Wi-Fi, you can use your smartphone to make free or inexpensive domestic and international calls by taking advantage of a calling app such as Skype or FaceTime.

Pay phones are relatively easy to find in Great Britain, but they're expensive. You'll pay with a major credit card (which you insert into the phone—minimum charge for a credit-card call is £1.20) or coins (have a bunch handy; minimum fee is £0.60). You can buy international phone cards, which work with a scratch-to-reveal PIN code at any phone, allowing you to call home to the US for about a dime a minute (and also work for domestic calls

From: rick@ricksteves.com
Sent: Today
To: info@hotelcentral.com
Subject: Reservation request for 19-22 July

Dear Hotel Central,

I would like to reserve a room for 2 people for 3 nights, arriving 19 July and departing 22 July. If possible, I would like a quiet room with a double bed and a bathroom inside the room.

Please let me know if you have a room available and the price.

Thank you!
Rick Steves

within Great Britain). However, since you'll pay a big surcharge to use these cards from pay phones, they're cost-effective only if used from a landline (such as one at your B&B) or a mobile phone. For much more on phoning, see www.ricksteves.com/phoning.

Making Hotel and B&B Reservations

To ensure the best value, I recommend reserving rooms in advance, particularly during peak season. Email the hotelier with the following key pieces of information: number and type of rooms; number of nights; date of arrival; date of departure; and any special requests. (For a sample form, see the sidebar.) Use the European style for writing dates: day/month/year. Hoteliers typically ask for your credit-card number as a deposit.

Know the terminology: An "en suite" room has a bathroom (toilet and shower/tub) actually inside the room; a room with a "private bathroom" can mean that the bathroom is all yours, but it's across the hall. A "standard" room could have two meanings. Big hotels sometimes call a basic en-suite room a "standard" room to differentiate it from a fancier "superior" or "deluxe" room. At small hotels and B&Bs, guests in a "standard" room have access to a bathroom that's shared with other rooms and down the hall.

Given the economic downturn, hoteliers may be willing to make a deal—try emailing several hotels to ask for their best price. In general, hotel prices can soften if you do any of the following: stay in a "standard" room, offer to pay cash, stay at least three nights, or travel off-season.

Eating

The traditional "Scottish Fry" breakfast, which is usually included at your B&B or hotel, consists of juice, tea or coffee, cereal, eggs, bacon, sausage, toast, a grilled tomato, sautéed mushrooms, and sometimes haggis, a potato scone, or black pudding. If it's too much for you, only order the items you want.

To dine affordably at classier restaurants, look for "early-bird specials" (offered about 17:30–19:00, last order by 19:00). At a sit-down place with table service, tip about 10 percent—unless the service charge is already listed on the bill.

Smart travelers use pubs (short for "public houses") to eat, drink, and make new friends. Pub grub is Scotland's best eating value. For about $15–20, you'll get a basic hot lunch or dinner. The menu is hearty and traditional: stews, soups, fish-and-chips, meat, cabbage, and potatoes, plus often a few Italian or Indian-style dishes. Meals are usually served from 12:00 to 14:00 and from 18:00 to 20:00, not throughout the day. Order drinks and meals at the bar; they might bring it to you when it's ready, or you'll pick it up at the bar. Pay as you order, and don't tip unless there's full table service.

Most pubs have lagers (cold, refreshing, American-style beer), ales (amber-colored, cellar-temperature beer), bitters (hop-flavored ale, perhaps the most typical British beer), and stouts (dark and somewhat bitter, like Guinness).

Transportation

By Train and Bus: Great Britain's 100-mph train system is one of Europe's best...and most expensive. To see if a railpass could save you money—as it often does in Britain—check www.ricksteves.com/rail. If you're buying tickets as you go, you'll get the best deals if you book in advance, leave after rush hour (after 9:30), or ride the bus. Train reservations are free and recommended for long journeys or any trip on Sundays (reserve at any train station or online). For train schedules, see www.nationalrail.co.uk; for bus routes, visit www.nationalexpress.com. Long-distance buses (called "coaches") are about a third slower than trains, but they're also much cheaper.

By Car: A car is useful for scouring the remote rural sights of the Scottish Highlands. It's cheaper to arrange most car rentals from the US. For tips on your insurance options, see www.ricksteves.com/cdw, and for route planning, consult www.viamichelin.com. Bring your driver's license. Speedy motorways (similar to our freeways) let you cover long distances in a snap. Remember that the Scottish drive on the left side of the road (and the driver sits on the right side of the car). You'll quickly master Scotland's many roundabouts: Traffic moves clockwise, cars inside the roundabout have the right-of-way, and entering traffic yields (look to your right as you merge). Note that "camera cops" strictly enforce speed limits by automatically snapping photos of speeders' license plates, then mailing them a ticket.

Local road etiquette is similar to that in the US. Ask your car-rental company about the rules of the road, or check the US State Department website (www.travel.state.gov, click on "International

Travel," then specify your country of choice and click "Traffic Safety and Road Conditions").

Helpful Hints

Emergency Help: To summon the **police** or an **ambulance**, call 999. For passport problems, call the **US Embassy** (in London, tel. 020/7499-9000, www.usembassy.org.uk) or the **Canadian High Commission** (in London, tel. 020/7258-6600, www.unitedkingdom. gc.ca).

Theft or Loss: To replace a passport, you'll need to go in person to an embassy or consulate (see above). Cancel and replace your credit and debit cards by calling these 24-hour US numbers collect: Visa: tel. 303/967-1096, MasterCard: tel. 636/722-7111, American Express: tel. 336/393-1111. In Britain, to make a collect call to the US, dial 0-800-89-0011; press zero or stay on the line for an operator. File a police report either on the spot or within a day or two; it's required if you submit an insurance claim for lost or stolen railpasses or travel gear, and can help with replacing your passport or credit and debit cards. For other concerns, get advice from your hotelier and see www.ricksteves.com/help. Precautionary measures can minimize the effects of loss—back up your digital photos and other files frequently. For more information, see www.ricksteves.com/help.

Time: Scotland uses the 24-hour clock. It's the same through 12:00 noon, then keep going: 13:00, 14:00, and so on. Scotland, like the rest of Great Britain, is five/eight hours ahead of the East/West Coasts of the US (and one hour earlier than most of continental Europe).

Holidays and Festivals: Great Britain celebrates many holidays, which can close sights and attract crowds (book hotel rooms ahead). For information on holidays and festivals, check Scotland's tourism website: www.visitscotland.com. For a simple list showing major—though not all—events, see www.ricksteves.com/festivals.

Numbers and Stumblers: What Americans call the second floor of a building is the first floor in Europe. Europeans write dates as day/month/year. For most measurements, Great Britain uses the metric system: A kilogram is 2.2 pounds, and a liter is about a quart. For driving distances, they use miles.

Resources from Rick Steves

This Snapshot guide is excerpted from my latest edition of *Rick Steves' Great Britain*, which is one of more than 30 titles in my series of guidebooks on European travel. I also produce a public television series, *Rick Steves' Europe*, and a public radio show, *Travel with Rick*

Steves. My website, www.ricksteves.com, offers free travel information, a forum for travelers' comments, guidebook updates, my travel blog, an online travel store, and information on European railpasses and our tours of Europe. If you're bringing a mobile device on your trip, you can download free information from Rick Steves Audio Europe, featuring podcasts of my radio shows, free audio tours of major sights in Europe, and travel interviews about Scotland (via www.ricksteves.com/audioeurope, iTunes, Google Play, or the Rick Steves Audio Europe free smartphone app). You can even follow me on Facebook and Twitter.

Additional Resources

Tourist Information: www.visitscotland.com
Passports and Red Tape: www.travel.state.gov
Packing List: www.ricksteves.com/packing
Travel Insurance: www.ricksteves.com/insurance
Cheap Flights: www.kayak.com
Airplane Carry-on Restrictions: www.tsa.gov/travelers
Updates for This Book: www.ricksteves.com/update

How Was Your Trip?

If you'd like to share your tips, concerns, and discoveries after using this book, please fill out the survey at www.ricksteves.com/feedback. Thanks in advance—it helps a lot.

INDEX

INDEX

Explore Europe

At ricksteves.com you can browse through thousands of articles, videos, photos and radio interviews, plus find a wealth of money-saving travel tips for planning your dream trip. And with our mobile-friendly website, you can easily access all this great travel information anywhere you go.

TV Shows

Preview the places you'll visit by watching entire half-hour episodes of Rick Steves' Europe (choose from all 100 shows) on-demand, for free.

your travel dreams into affordable reality

Radio Interviews

Enjoy ready access to Rick's vast library of radio interviews covering travel

tips and cultural insights that relate specifically to your Europe travel plans.

Travel Forums

Learn, ask, share! Our online community of savvy travelers is a great resource

for first-time travelers to Europe, as well as seasoned pros. You'll find forums on each country, plus travel tips and restaurant/hotel reviews. You can even ask one of our well-traveled staff to chime in with an opinion.

Travel News

Subscribe to our free Travel News e-newsletter, and get monthly updates from Rick on what's happening in Europe.

Audio Europe™

Pack Light and Right

Gear up for your next adventure at ricksteves.com

Light Luggage

Pack light and right with Rick Steves' affordable, custom-designed rolling carry-on bags, backpacks, day packs and shoulder bags.

Accessories

From packing cubes to moneybelts and beyond, Rick has personally selected the travel goodies that will help your trip go smoother.

Shop at ricksteves.com

Save time and energy

This guidebook is your independent-travel toolkit. But for all it delivers, it's still up to you to devote the time and energy it takes to manage the preparation and logistics that are essential for a happy trip. If that's a hassle, there's a solution.

Rick Steves Tours

A Rick Steves tour takes you to Europe's most interesting places with great

great tours, too!

with minimum stress

guides and small groups of 28 or less. We follow Rick's favorite itineraries, ride in comfy buses, stay in family-run hotels, and bring you intimately close to the Europe you've traveled so far to see. Most importantly, we take away the logistical headaches so you can focus on the fun.

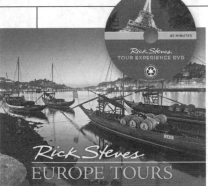

customers—along with us on 40 different itineraries, from Ireland to Italy to Istanbul. Is a Rick Steves tour the right fit for your travel dreams? Find out at ricksteves.com, where you can also get Rick's latest tour catalog and free Tour Experience DVD.

Join the fun

This year we'll take 18,000 free-spirited travelers— nearly half of them repeat

Europe is best experienced with happy travel partners. We hope you can join us.

See our itineraries at ricksteves.com

EUROPE GUIDES

Best of Europe
Eastern Europe
Europe Through the Back Door
Mediterranean Cruise Ports
Northern European Cruise Ports

COUNTRY GUIDES

Croatia & Slovenia
England
France
Germany
Great Britain
Ireland
Italy
Portugal
Scandinavia
Spain
Switzerland

CITY & REGIONAL GUIDES

Amsterdam, Bruges & Brussels
Barcelona
Budapest
Florence & Tuscany
Greece: Athens & the Peloponnese
Istanbul
London
Paris
Prague & the Czech Republic
Provence & the French Riviera
Rome
Venice
Vienna, Salzburg & Tirol

SNAPSHOT GUIDES

Basque Country: Spain & France
Berlin
Bruges & Brussels
Copenhagen & the Best of
  Denmark
Dublin
Dubrovnik
Hill Towns of Central Italy
Italy's Cinque Terre
Krakow, Warsaw & Gdansk
Lisbon
Madrid & Toledo
Milan & the Italian Lakes District
Munich, Bavaria & Salzburg
Naples & the Amalfi Coast
Northern Ireland
Norway
Scotland
Sevilla, Granada & Southern Spain
Stockholm

POCKET GUIDES

Amsterdam
Athens
Barcelona
Florence
London
Paris
Rome
Venice

NOW AVAILABLE:
eBOOKS, DVD & BLU-RAY

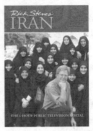

TRAVEL CULTURE

Europe 101
European Christmas
Postcards from Europe
Travel as a Political Act

eBOOKS

*Nearly all Rick Steves guides are
available as ebooks. Check with
your favorite bookseller.*

RICK STEVES' EUROPE DVDs

11 New Shows 2013–2014
Austria & the Alps
Eastern Europe
England & Wales
European Christmas
European Travel Skills & Specials
France
Germany, BeNeLux & More
Greece, Turkey & Portugal
Iran
Ireland & Scotland
Italy's Cities
Italy's Countryside
Scandinavia
Spain
Travel Extras

BLU-RAY

Celtic Charms
Eastern Europe Favorites
European Christmas
Italy Through the Back Door
Mediterranean Mosaic
Surprising Cities of Europe

PHRASE BOOKS & DICTIONARIES

French
French, Italian & German
German
Italian
Portuguese
Spanish

JOURNALS

Rick Steves Pocket Travel Journal
Rick Steves Travel Journal

PLANNING MAPS

Britain, Ireland & London
Europe
France & Paris
Germany, Austria & Switzerland
Ireland
Italy
Spain & Portugal

RickSteves.com 📘 🐦 **@RickSteves**

Rick Steves books and DVDs are available at bookstores
and through online booksellers.

Avalon Travel
a member of the Perseus Books Group
1700 Fourth Street
Berkeley, CA 94710

Text © 2014 by Rick Steves
Maps © 2014 by Rick Steves' Europe, Inc. All rights reserved.
Portions of this book originally appeared in *Rick Steves' Great Britain (20th edition)*.

Printed in Canada by Friesens.
Second printing April 2015.

ISBN 978-1-63121-079-2

For the latest on Rick's lectures, guidebooks, tours, public radio show, and public television
series, contact Rick Steves' Europe, Inc., 130 Fourth Avenue North, Edmonds, WA 98020,
425/771-8303, fax 425/771-0833, www.ricksteves.com, rick@ricksteves.com.

Rick Steves' Europe
Managing Editor: Risa Laib
Editorial & Production Manager: Jennifer Madison Davis
Editors: Glenn Eriksen, Tom Griffin, Cameron Hewitt, Deb Jensen, Suzanne Kotz, Cathy
   Lu, John Pierce, Carrie Shepherd, Gretchen Strauch
Editorial Assistant: Jessica Shaw
Editorial Intern: Zosha Milliman
Researchers: Cameron Hewitt, Cathy Lu, Lynne McAlister, Lauren Mills, Mark Seymour,
   Robyn Stencil, Gretchen Strauch
Maps & Graphics: David C. Hoerlein, Sandra Hundacker, Lauren Mills, Mary Rostad,
   Dawn Tessman Visser, Laura VanDeventer

Avalon Travel
Senior Editor and Series Manager: Madhu Prasher
Editor: Jamie Andrade
Associate Editor: Maggie Ryan
Copy Editor: Patrick Collins
Proofreader: Suzie Nasol
Indexer: Stephen Callahan
Production & Typesetting: McGuire Barber Design
Cover Design: Kimberly Glyder Design
Maps & Graphics: Kat Bennett, Mike Morgenfeld

Photo Credits
Front Cover Photo: Edinburgh's Royal Mile © 123rf.com
Additional Photography: Dominic Bonuccelli, Cutty Sark Trust: 235, Rich Earl, Barb
   Geisler, Jennifer Hauseman, Cameron Hewitt, David C. Hoerlein, Darbi Macy, Lauren
   Mills, Sarah Murdoch, Pat O'Connor, Gene Openshaw, Jennifer Schutte, Ken Hanley,
   Sarah Slauson, Rick Steves, Bruce VanDeventer, Wikimedia Commons

ABOUT THE AUTHOR

RICK STEVES

 Since 1973, Rick Steves has spent 100 days every year exploring Europe. Along with writing and researching a bestselling series of guidebooks, Rick produces a public television series *(Rick Steves' Europe),* a public radio show *(Travel with Rick Steves),* a blog (on Facebook), and an app and podcast *(Rick Steves Audio Europe);* writes a nationally syndicated newspaper column; organizes guided tours that take over 15,000 travelers to Europe annually; and offers an information-packed website (www.ricksteves.com). With the help of his hardworking staff of 90 at Rick Steves' Europe—in Edmonds, Washington, just north of Seattle—Rick's mission is to make European travel fun, affordable, and culturally enlightening for Americans.

Connect with Rick:

facebook.com/RickSteves   twitter: @RickSteves